Perspectives in Neural Computing

Springer-Verlag London Ltd.

Adrian J. Shepherd

Second-Order Methods for Neural Networks

Fast and Reliable Training Methods for Multi-Layer Perceptrons

Springer

Adrian J. Shepherd, BA, MSc, PhD
Research Fellow, Biomolecular Structure and Modelling Group,
Department of Biochemistry and Molecular Biology,
University College London,
Gower Street,
London WC1E 6BT, UK

Series Editor

J.G. Taylor, BA, BSc, MA, PhD, FInstP
Centre for Neural Networks,
Department of Mathematics, Kings College,
Strand, London WC2R 2LS, UK

British Library Cataloguing in Publication Data
Shepherd, Adrian J.
  Second-order methods for neural networks : fast and reliable training methods for
  multi-layer perceptrons. - (Perspectives in neural computing)
  1.Perceptrons 2.Neural networks (Computer science)
  I.Title
006.3
Library of Congress Cataloging-in-Publication Data
Shepherd, Adrian J., 1961-
  Second-order methods for neural networks : fast and reliable training methods for
  multi-layer perceptrons / Adrian J. Shepherd.
    p.   cm. -- (Perspectives in neural computing)
  Includes bibliographical references.

  1. Perceptrons. 2. Neural networks (Computer science) I. Title. II. Series.
Q327.S52 1997
006.3--dc20   96-35297
ISBN 978-3-540-76100-6   ISBN 978-1-4471-0953-2   (eBook)
DOI 10.1007/978-1-4471-0953-2

Typesetting: Ian Kingston Editorial Services, Nottingham

34/3830-543210 Printed on acid-free paper

Preface

About This Book

This book is about training methods – in particular, fast second-order training methods – for multi-layer perceptrons (MLPs). MLPs (also known as feed-forward neural networks) are the most widely-used class of neural network. Over the past decade MLPs have achieved increasing popularity among scientists, engineers and other professionals as tools for tackling a wide variety of information processing tasks. In common with all neural networks, MLPs are trained (rather than programmed) to carry out the chosen information processing function. Unfortunately, the 'traditional' method for training MLPs – the well-known backpropagation method – is notoriously slow and unreliable when applied to many practical tasks. The development of fast and reliable training algorithms for MLPs is one of the most important areas of research within the entire field of neural computing.

The main purpose of this book is to bring to a wider audience a range of alternative methods for training MLPs, methods which have proved orders of magnitude faster than backpropagation when applied to many training tasks. The book also addresses the well-known 'local minima' problem, and explains ways in which fast training methods can be combined with strategies for avoiding (or escaping from) local minima. All the methods described in this book have a strong theoretical foundation, drawing on such diverse mathematical fields as classical optimisation theory, homotopic theory and stochastic approximation theory. Unlike many of the proposed 'enhancements' to traditional backpropagation, these methods are not based on neural network folklore, nor do they require the user to fine-tune various parameter settings using 'rules of thumb'.

This book aims to provide the reader with:

- a thorough understanding of the principles involved in the design of efficient MLP training algorithms

- an understanding of the merits of second-order training methods, derived from classical optimisation theory, compared with conventional methods for training MLPs
- the ability to implement a range of second-order methods (including quasi-Newton methods, conjugate gradient methods and the Levenberg–Marquardt method) for training MLPs
- a valuable resource for assessing the comparative performance of different MLP training algorithms when applied to benchmark training tasks
- an understanding of how second-order training algorithms can be modified so as to increase their 'global reliability', i.e. reduce the likelihood that the network will get trapped in local minima

Who This Book is For

This book has not been written for a single audience. Rather, the aim has been to provide a bridge between the accounts of MLP training methods found in introductory texts on neural computing and the detailed up to-date research published in the neural network literature. This volume is likely to be of particular value to:

- those engaged in the development of neural network algorithms and programs
- those using MLPs for practical applications who wish to make informed choices about the training algorithms they use
- students of neural computing, in particular postgraduate students studying supervised learning with MLPs
- those with a background in numerical analysis who are interested in applying that knowledge within the neural network field

The subject matter of this book is inherently mathematical. To make the material accessible to a wide audience, very few assumptions have been made about the prior mathematical knowledge of the reader; the only prerequisite is a familiarity with vector and matrix algebra. Every effort has been made to explain concepts in clear English, rather than allow the equations to 'speak for themselves'.

The Content of the Book

What follows is a short, chapter-by-chapter summary of the material covered in this book.

Chapter 1: Multi-layer Perceptron Training A concise introduction to MLPs and MLP training, including the famous backpropagation training method. The chapter covers a number of topics that are omitted from most introductory texts on neural computing, including alternatives to the 'traditional' sum-of-squares error function; the internal dynamics of MLP training and hidden node redundancy; the characteristics of MLP training tasks and their implications for training algorithm design; and an analysis of some of the most popular modifications to the basic backpropagation algorithm.

Chapter 2: Classical Optimisation   An introduction to classical optimisation theory, explaining why second-order methods are likely to converge to the desired solution significantly faster than first-order methods (of which backpropagation is an example). The chapter also explains how second-order methods can be implemented in two contrasting ways: as line-search methods or as model-trust region (restricted step) methods. The remainder of the chapter is concerned with factors that affect the practical reliability and efficiency of second-order algorithms. The major topics covered are the effects of finite-precision computer arithmetic; the efficient storage of second-order information; and scaling and preconditioning strategies.

Chapter 3: Second-Order Methods   The first part of this chapter provides descriptions of, and algorithms for, specific line-search and model-trust region methods (including backtracking line-searches, Fletcher's method and the double dogleg algorithm). Particular emphasis is placed on algorithms which guarantee convergence to a solution by ensuring that an 'acceptable' step is taken at each iteration. These algorithms, which vary greatly in their complexity, serve as a framework for implementing specific second-order methods. The rest of the chapter gives details of a range of second-order methods, including quasi-Newton methods, conjugate gradient methods and nonlinear least-squares methods (such as the Levenberg–Marquardt method). Each method is assessed in terms of its computational and storage costs, together with its anticipated reliability and convergence characteristics.

Chapter 4: Second-Order Training Methods   This chapter explains how the fast second-order methods of Chapter 3 can be implemented for training MLPs. The chapter is in three main sections: the first section explains how to calculate exact second-derivative information using an MLP (required by a number of the methods described in Chapter 3); the second section looks at ways in which second-order methods can be tailored to the particular requirements of MLP architectures and training tasks; and the last section discusses strategies for improving the efficiency of second-order training methods when applied to large redundant training sets.

Chapter 5: An Experimental Comparison of MLP Training Methods   This chapter presents extensive test results for a wide range of MLP training algorithms when applied to a variety of benchmark training tasks. The conditions under which the tests were performed (including the values of any user-defined parameters) are documented in full. The performances of various first- and second-order training algorithms are compared in terms of both speed and, for tasks containing known local minima, 'global reliability'.

Chapter 6: Global Methods   The final chapter of the book considers strategies for improving the 'global reliability' of second-order training methods, i.e. reducing the likelihood that the network will get trapped in local minima. Global methods fall into two broad categories: stochastic methods and deterministic methods. The chapter begins by assessing the comparative suitability of different approaches to global optimisation in the context of second-order MLP training, and concludes that the development of combined stochastic/second-order training algorithms is highly problematic. The latter part of the chapter is devoted to two deterministic approaches to global optimisation: the ERA method (derived from homotopy theory), and the TRUST method (an example of a tunnelling method). These deterministic methods are shown to be particularly well-suited for use in combination with second-order MLP training algorithms.

Acknowledgements

This book would not have been written without the support of family, friends, and colleagues. Special thanks are due to Dr Denise Gorse and Professor John Taylor for their numerous helpful suggestions, and to Templer Hart for providing hardware and software support. However, my biggest debt of gratitude is to my wife, Wendy, for her diligence in checking (and re-checking) the drafts of this book, and for being an unfailing source of encouragement during the months spent chained to the word processor.

Adrian Shepherd

Contents

Nomenclature

Listed below is the general mathematical nomenclature used throughout this book. The specific notation used to denote components of the multi-layer perceptron architecture is given in Section 1.1.1 of the main text.

x	a scalar
$\|x\|$	the magnitude of scalar x
$\mathbf{v}$	a vector
v_i	the ith element of vector $\mathbf{v}$ ($1 \leq i \leq N$, where N is the number of elements in vector $\mathbf{v}$)
$\mathbf{v}_k$	the value of vector $\mathbf{v}$ at time (iteration) k
$(v_i)_k$	the value of element v_i at time (iteration) k
$\mathbf{v}^T \mathbf{w} = \displaystyle\sum_{i=1}^{N} v_i^T w_i$	the inner, dot or scalar product of two vectors
$\|\mathbf{v}\|_2 = \left(\displaystyle\sum_{i=1}^{N} v_i^2 \right)^{1/2}$	the l_2, Euclidean or least-square norm of vector $\mathbf{v}$
$\|\mathbf{v}\|$	an arbitrary norm of vector $\mathbf{v}$
$\mathbf{A}$	a matrix
A_{ij}	the element located at the intersection of row i and column j of matrix $\mathbf{A}$ ($1 \leq i \leq N$ and $1 \leq j \leq M$, where N is the number of rows and M the number of columns in matrix $\mathbf{A}$)
$\mathbf{I}$	the identity (or unit) matrix, a square matrix with all diagonal elements set to one and all other elements set to zero
$\mathbf{A}^{-1}$	the inverse of matrix $\mathbf{A}$, with $\mathbf{A} \cdot \mathbf{A}^{-1} = \mathbf{I}$
$\mathbf{A}^T$	the transpose of matrix $\mathbf{A}$ (i.e. the rows of $\mathbf{A}$ are the columns of $\mathbf{A}^T$, and vice versa); if $\mathbf{A}$ is an $N \times M$ matrix, $\mathbf{A}^T$ is an $M \times N$ matrix

$\mathbf{A}^{-T}$	the inverse of matrix $\mathbf{A}^T$, or (equivalently) the transpose of matrix $\mathbf{A}^{-1}$
$f(x)$ or f	a function of a single variable, x
$f'(x)$ or f'	the first derivative of function $f(x)$
$f''(x)$ or f''	the second derivative of function $f(x)$
$F(\mathbf{x})$ or F	a function of N variables, where $\mathbf{x}$ is an N-length vector
$g(\mathbf{x})$ or $\mathbf{g}$	the first-derivative or gradient vector, $\nabla F(\mathbf{x})$, of function $F(\mathbf{x})$
$G(\mathbf{x})$ or $\mathbf{G}$	the second-derivative or Hessian matrix, $\nabla^2 F(\mathbf{x})$, of function $F(\mathbf{x})$
$O(N)$	a given quantity is of order N
$\ln(x)$	the natural (base e) logarithm of scalar x
$\text{sign}(x)$	the sign (+ or −) of scalar x

1. Multi-Layer Perceptron Training

This chapter serves as an introduction to the main subject of this book – multi-layer perceptron (MLP) training[1]. The multi-layer perceptron is the most widely-used class of neural network. Much of the popularity of MLPs is attributable to the fact that they have been applied successfully to a wide range of information processing tasks, including pattern classification, function learning and time series prediction. Practical applications for MLPs have been found in such diverse fields as speech recognition, image compression, medical diagnosis, autonomous vehicle control and financial prediction; new applications are being discovered all the time. (For a useful survey of practical MLP applications, see Lisboa (1992).)

MLPs are trained, rather than programmed, to carry out the chosen information processing task. MLP training involves the adjustment of the network so that it is able to produce a specified output for each of a given set of input patterns. Since the desired outputs are known in advance, MLP training is an example of *supervised learning*.

Chapter 1 is in three main sections:

- Section 1.1 describes the characteristic layered architecture of MLPs and considers the physical properties and dynamics of MLP training. The section introduces much of the notation that will be used to describe specific MLP training algorithms later in the book.
- Section 1.2 investigates the essential characteristics of MLP training tasks and their implications for training algorithm design. This section views MLP training from the perspective of function optimisation, so that each combination of training task and MLP architecture defines a corresponding multi-dimensional error surface. This perspective enables many of the conditions encountered during training to be characterised in a manner that is both rigorous and useful, and is the natural approach to adopt when considering training methods derived from classical optimisation theory (Chapters 2 and 3).

---

1   As so often in the field of neural networks, there is little standard terminology. Alternative terms for MLPs are 'feed-forward neural networks' (various), 'multilayered neural networks' (MLNs) (Gori and Tesi, 1992), and 'feature-based mapping neural networks' (Hecht-Nielsen, 1990).

- Section 1.3 presents a concise survey of training methods derived from the backpropagation algorithm, the dominant training paradigm for MLPs. Several heuristic modifications to the standard backpropagation algorithm are considered, including schemes for adapting the backpropagation training rate, the addition of 'momentum' and 'stochastic' (on-line) training.

1.1 Introduction to MLPs

1.1.1 The MLP Architecture

The MLP architecture consists of units or *nodes* arranged in two or more *layers*. (The input layer, which serves only to distribute the input from each pattern, is not counted.) Some of the nodes are connected by real-valued weights, but there are no connections between nodes in the same layer. This book uses the following notation for the layers and nodes of an MLP:

- The network consists of L layers, with $l=0$ denoting the input layer and $l=L$ denoting the output layer.
- The notation for a single node is n_i^l ($1 \le i \le N^l$), N^l being the number of nodes in layer l.
- The activation of a network node depends on the strength of the input to that node with respect to a threshold value. For notational convenience, the network thresholds are treated uniformly by adding an extra node with a fixed output of 1.0 to all but the output layer. This node – called the *bias unit* – is denoted n_0^l (for $l \ne L$).
- To allow for MLPs of arbitrary connectivity, it is useful to define a set of *source nodes* S_i^l and a set of *target nodes* T_i^l for each node n_i^l. Given that node m_j^m is connected to node n_i^l, n_j^m is a source node of n_i^l (i.e. $n_j^m \in S_i^l$) if $m<l$, but a target node of n_i^l (i.e. $n_j^m \in T_i^l$) if $m>l$. Set S_i^l is null for all input nodes (i.e. $S_i^0 = \varnothing$ for $i=1,...,N^0$) and for all bias units (i.e. $S_0^l = \varnothing$ for $l=0,...,L-1$); set T_i^l is null for all output nodes (i.e. $T_i^L = \varnothing$ for $i=1,...,N^L$).
- Network weights can be represented in terms of the nodes they connect; thus weight w_{ij}^{lm} connects nodes n_j^m and n_i^l with $m<l$ (i.e. n_j^m is a source node of n_i^l and n_i^l a target node of n_j^m). However, it will often be more convenient to consider weights in terms of the weight vector $\mathbf{w}$ comprising all W weights in the network, with a single weight denoted w_i ($1 \le i \le W$).

An example of a simple two-layer MLP architecture is given in Fig. 1.1.

Although the notation used in this book allows for network architectures of arbitrary connectivity, it will often be more convenient to consider architectures of a restricted form – in particular, MLPs which are fully connected between adjacent layers, but which have no weights connecting non-adjacent layers. Henceforth, this

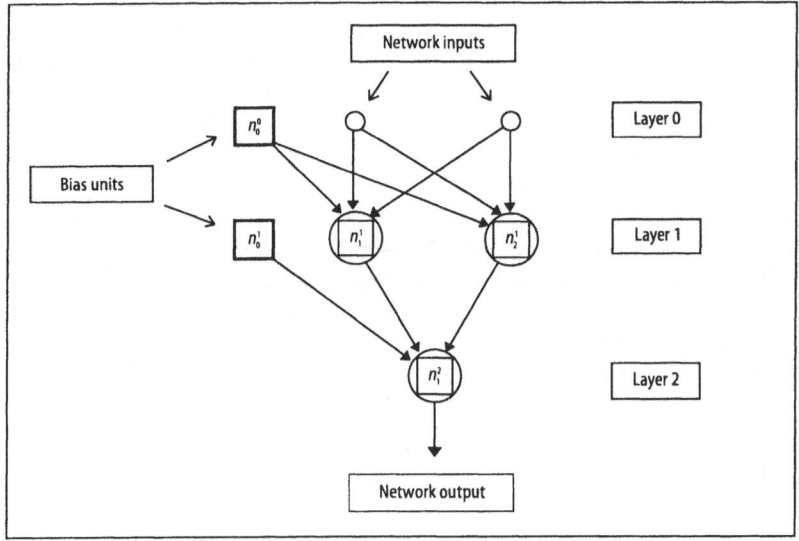

Fig. 1.1 Minimal 2–2–1 MLP architecture, suitable for learning the 2-parity (XOR) problem (see Section 5.1.1).

will be termed a 'standard' MLP architecture. The simple network in Fig. 1.1 is an example of a 'standard' MLP architecture.

The number of nodes in the input and output layers of the MLP is determined by, respectively, the pattern size and target size of the chosen training task. MLPs are typically trained using a fixed *training set* of P training pairs, with each *training pair* comprising two real-valued vectors – a pattern $\mathbf{p}_q$ $(1 \le q \le P)$ and a corresponding target (desired output) $\mathbf{t}_q$. Individual pattern and target elements are denoted $p_{i,q}$ $(1 \le i \le N^0)$ and $t_{j,q}$ $(1 \le j \le N^L)$ respectively. The output $y_{i,q}^0$ of input node i is simply $p_{i,q}$ for pattern q (except for y_0^0, the fixed output of the bias unit). For non-input node n_i^l, the output is given by the weighted sum

$$a_{i,q}^l = \sum_{n_j^m \in S_i^l} w_{ij}^{lm} y_{j,q}^m, \quad l > 0$$

$$y_{i,q}^l = f\left(a_{i,q}^l\right), \quad l > 0 \tag{1.1}$$

where $a_{i,q}^l$ is the *activation* of node n_i^l for pattern q, and the *squashing* or *activation function* $f(x)$ is both monotonic (i.e. non-decreasing) and continuously differentiable (see definition in Section 1.2.1). By far the most commonly used squashing function is the *sigmoid* or *logistic function*

$$f(x) = \frac{1}{1 + e^{-x}} \tag{1.2}$$

which compresses the output of each non-input node in the range [0,1]. The most popular alternative to the sigmoid is the *hyperbolic tangent*, $f(x) = \tanh(x)$, which gives a compressed range of [−1,1].

The layers between the input and output layers are known as *hidden layers*. The number of hidden layers and nodes has a major impact on MLP training: too few, and the network will be unable to learn the problem; too many, and the network may take excessively long to train and have poor *generalisation* capabilities – a measure of the network's ability to classify patterns which share the same general features as, but are not identical to, patterns in the training set. Upper and lower bounds on the number of hidden nodes required for an MLP to be capable of learning a given task have been established by Huang and Huang (1991), but the 'optimal' number of hidden nodes is much more difficult to determine. Numerous schemes have been developed which adapt the architecture – i.e. add or 'prune' hidden nodes – during the training process (see, for example, le Cun *et al.* (1990); Hirose *et al.* (1991); Santini (1992)).

1.1.2 MLP Training

MLP training is an iterative process which involves, at each iteration or *epoch*, the calculation of the network outputs for (one or more) patterns in the training set, and the adjustment of the network weights according to the disparity between the actual network output for a given pattern ($y_{i,q}^{L}$) (i=1,...,N^L) and the desired output for that pattern (t_q). Given a suitable network architecture and training algorithm, the network weights will be progressively adjusted to the point where the network output is acceptably close to the desired output for each pattern in the training set.

Prior to training, the weights are initialised to small random values – small to prevent *saturation* (where one or more hidden nodes is highly active or inactive for all patterns and therefore insensitive to the training process) and random to break symmetry. If, on the other hand, the initial weights are *too* small, training will tend to start very slowly. One widely used weight initialisation heuristic sets each weight randomly with a uniform distribution in the range [−r,+r], where r is given by

$$r\left(w_{ij}^{lm}\right) = \frac{2.4}{N^m + 1} \tag{1.3}$$

Setting the network weights according to (1.3) ensures that the initial standard deviations of the network activations ($a_{i,q}^{l}$) are in the same range for each node, and lie within the 'normal' operating region of the sigmoid squashing function (le Cun, 1989). That the choice of initialisation range can have a significant impact on the performance of the backpropagation training algorithm (discussed in Section 1.3) is well recognised – see for example Kolen and Pollack (1990).

The degree of success at each epoch is typically measured using an *error function* (or energy function) $E(\mathbf{w})$ – or E for short – of the form

$$E = \sum_{p=1}^{P} E_p \tag{1.4}$$

where E_p is the partial contribution of pattern p to the total network error E. The choice of error function may have as significant an impact on the performance of an MLP as the choice of training algorithm. The two most popular error functions are the *sum-of-squares* (or least squares) error function

$$E = \frac{1}{2} \sum_{p=1}^{P} \sum_{i=1}^{N^L} \left(t_{i,p} - y_{i,p}^L \right)^2 \tag{1.5}$$

and a normalised version of the sum-of-squares error function called the *mean-squared error* (MSE) function (also known as the least mean squares or LMS error function)

$$E = \frac{1}{2PN^L} \sum_{p=1}^{P} \sum_{i=1}^{N^L} \left(t_{i,p} - y_{i,p}^L \right)^2 \tag{1.6}$$

The advantage of the MSE function over the sum-of-squares error function is that, being insensitive to both the number of patterns in the training set and the number of output nodes in the network, it can be used to make meaningful comparisons between different training tasks.

One important characteristic of the MSE and sum-of-squares error functions is that a reduction in E may be associated with an increase in the number of misclassified training patterns; in fact, reducing E to its minimum achievable level with either of these error functions does not necessarily mean that the minimum number of pattern misclassifications has been achieved. This property may have undesirable consequences – for example, it increases the likelihood that the network will converge to regions of weight space where the vast majority of patterns are correctly classified, but a small number are severely misclassified. Such a distribution of correctly and incorrectly classified patterns is commonly associated with two types of feature in the MLP error surface that can be serious obstacles to successful training – local minima and multi-dimensional 'plateaus'. (The characteristics of MLP error surfaces are discussed in Section 1.2.2.)

Increasingly, researchers are turning to alternative error functions in an attempt to improve the convergence characteristics of multi-layer perceptrons. One approach is to adopt an error function that improves a network's ability to escape from bad regions of weight space. An example is the *cross-entropy* error function (Solla et al., 1988), given by

$$E = -\sum_{p=1}^{P} \sum_{i=1}^{N^L} \ln\left[\left(y_{i,p}^L \right)^{t_{i,p}} \left(1 - y_{i,p}^L \right)^{1-t_{i,p}} \right] \tag{1.7}$$

With this error function, the error gradients for poorly classified patterns are significantly higher than with the MSE and sum-of-squares error functions, making it easier for the network to progress in flat regions of weight space (i.e. when crossing a 'plateau').

A second strategy is to incorporate constraints into an error function in such a way that the network is unlikely to converge to bad regions in weight space. An example is the *exponential* error function (Møller, 1993e), given by

$$E = \frac{1}{2} \sum_{p=1}^{P} \sum_{i=1}^{N^L} e^{-\alpha\left(y_{i,p}^L - t_{i,p} + \beta\right)\left(t_{i,p} + \beta - y_{i,p}^L\right)}$$

(1.8)

where α and β are positive, user-defined scalars. The role of parameter β is to define an acceptable error level for each target element ($t_{i,p}$) in the training set. Typically β is initialised to a comparatively high value and then progressively reduced in size; Møller recommends initialising β to 0.9 and then halving its value whenever every network output ($y_{i,p}^L$) has an acceptable error level. Parameter α, on the other hand, controls the steepness of the exponentially growing error for those network outputs that have an unacceptable error level (as defined by β). When α tends to infinity, there can be no reduction in total network error E that simultaneously increases the number of pattern misclassifications with respect to the current level of β. In practice, however, the rate at which a network converges to an acceptable solution may be severely degraded if α is set to too large a value, as the range of acceptable paths to the solution is greatly restricted. Møller has found that $\alpha=1.0$ gives good results, although the optimal α is task-dependent.

MLP training is deemed to be successful when E becomes 'acceptably' small. Precisely how small is application-specific, but a close approximation to the minimum achievable E is generally undesirable since an MLP's ability to generalise decreases with *over-training* (or over-learning). The exception is function approximation tasks, for which highly accurate solutions may be desirable.

The key factor in the dynamics of MLP training is the role of the hidden nodes. A hidden node that duplicates the function of another hidden node is *redundant*, i.e. makes no useful contribution to the training process. A mathematical analysis by Annema *et al.* (1994) of the dynamics of MLP training indicates that the build-up and dissipation of hidden-node redundancy is an integral part of the training process. Before briefly summarising Annema *et al.*'s analysis, we need to define w_i^l as the weight vector comprising all the weights w_{ij}^{lm} connecting node n_i^l to its source nodes (i.e. to all $n_j^m \in S_i^l$). When an MLP is applied to a pattern classification task, the weight vector of a neuron corresponds to a hyperplane that divides the input space of that neuron into two classes; as training progresses, the weight vectors (w_i^l) converge towards specific attractors in weight space (Guo and Gelfand, 1991).

The core of the analysis by Annema *et al.*, which holds for a two-layer MLP with two hidden nodes and 'very small' initial weights, describes three distinct training phases.

- In phase one redundancy builds up in the hidden layer to the point where it is approximately reducible to a single neuron, and the entire network can be linearised, i.e. 'all neurons are activated in the approximately linear middle region' (Annema *et al.*, 1994, p. 1389). At this stage both the attractors in weight space and the weight vectors of all the neurons in the first layer are near-identical for all hidden nodes.

- In phase two the attractors remain near-identical, but the network can no longer be linearised. This phase marks the transition between the build-up of redundancy in the hidden layer and the subsequent dissipation of that redundancy. By the end of the phase the cluster of redundant hidden nodes starts to split in two.

- Phase three consists of the division of redundant hidden-layer nodes into two distinct clusters. The weight vectors associated with nodes in different clusters now converge towards different attractors in weight space.

Note that the actual attractors in weight space may vary from training run to training run (depending on the choice of initial weights) and from phase to phase. For MLPs of arbitrary size, this three-phase analysis can be applied iteratively to smaller and smaller clusters of redundant hidden nodes.

The inability of an MLP to eliminate hidden-node redundancy – that is, to proceed beyond phase two of the preceding analysis – is a frequent cause of training failure (see Section 1.2.2).

1.2   Error Surfaces and Local Minima

In order to design efficient and reliable training algorithms, it is essential to gain an understanding of the principal characteristics of MLP training tasks and their implications for different training strategies. One extremely useful way of describing a training task is in terms of function optimisation – that is, the minimisation of the MLP error function E. From this perspective, MLP training is an example of an *error-minimisation* or *optimisation* process, and each training task defines a multi-dimensional non-negative *error surface* (or energy surface), formed by plotting the value of E for all reasonable settings of the MLP weight vector $\mathbf{w}$.

This approach to MLP training has several important benefits:

- Many efficient strategies for optimising functions have been developed outside the field of neural networks. As we shall see in the remaining chapters of this book, a number of these strategies can be readily adapted for training MLPs.
- The concept of an MLP error surface aids visualisation of the training process through analogy with the 'features' of a three-dimensional landscape (e.g. valleys and plateaus).
- It leads to numerically-testable definitions for many of the conditions encountered during training.

Before examining the particular properties of MLP error surfaces, it will be useful to explain some general concepts that apply to error surfaces in general.

1.2.1   Error Surface Fundamentals

Error surfaces can be divided into different classes according to their general properties. Here we focus on the properties of a single broad class of error surface

– *smooth* error surfaces. Smooth error surfaces are exceedingly common in practice, and all the training algorithms discussed in this book are designed for this type of error surface.

The smoothness of an error surface depends on the degree to which the error function $E(\mathbf{w})$ is continuously differentiable. Function E is *continuous* if small changes in the network weights ($\mathbf{w}$) produce only small changes in E, and is *continuously differentiable* – denoted $E \in C^1$ – if the *first derivative* (∇E) of E exists and is continuous. A continuously differential function is by definition continuous, but not vice versa. (An example of a function that is continuous but not continuously differentiable is $|x|$, which is non-differentiable at $x=0$.) The first derivative or *gradient* – denoted $g(\mathbf{w})$, or $\mathbf{g}$ for short – takes the form of a W-length vector with elements

$$g_i = \frac{\partial E(\mathbf{w})}{\partial w_i}, \qquad 1 \le i \le W \qquad (1.9)$$

where the term $\partial E(\mathbf{w})/\partial w_i$ is the first partial derivative for the ith weight. A continuously differentiable function E is said to be *twice continuously differentiable* – denoted $E \in C^2$ – if the *second derivative* ($\nabla^2 E$) of E exists and is continuous. The square matrix of the W^2 second partial derivatives is the *Hessian* $G(\mathbf{w})$, or $\mathbf{G}$ for short, with elements

$$G_{ij} = \frac{\partial^2 E(\mathbf{w})}{\partial w_i \partial w_j}, \qquad 1 \le i, j \le W \qquad (1.10)$$

So long as E is twice continuously differentiable, the Hessian will be *symmetric* (i.e. $\mathbf{G} = \mathbf{G}^T$).

If an error surface is sufficiently smooth, it is possible to describe some of its most important features in ways that are both rigorous and useful. Let us begin by considering a set of error-surface features known as *stationary points*, which occur wherever the gradient $g(\mathbf{w})$ is zero. There are several different types of stationary point – maxima, minima, points of inflection (one-dimensional case) and saddle points (multi-dimensional case). These categories can be further subdivided into 'strong' and 'weak' points. The distinction between these different sorts of stationary point is easiest to grasp through an illustration of the one-dimensional case – see Figs. 1.2 and 1.3. In the multi-dimensional case, a *minimum* can be viewed as the lowest point of a 'basin' in the error surface, and a *maximum* as the highest point of an inverted 'basin'. As its name suggests, a *saddle point* – the multi-dimensional equivalent of a *point of inflection* – is exemplified by the 'seat' of a saddle-shaped ridge joining two areas of higher ground. Whereas a strong stationary point consists of a single point, weak stationary points are characterised by a line in the one-dimensional case, and may be either a line or a surface in the multi-dimensional case.

Assuming that the error function E is twice continuously differentiable, this distinction between maxima, minima and saddle points is reflected in the *eigenvalues* of the Hessian matrix $\mathbf{G}$. (Scalar λ is an eigenvalue of $\mathbf{G}$ if there is a non-zero vector $\mathbf{x}$ such that $\mathbf{Gx} = \lambda \mathbf{x}$.) Stationary point $\mathbf{w}_*$ is definitely a strong maximum if

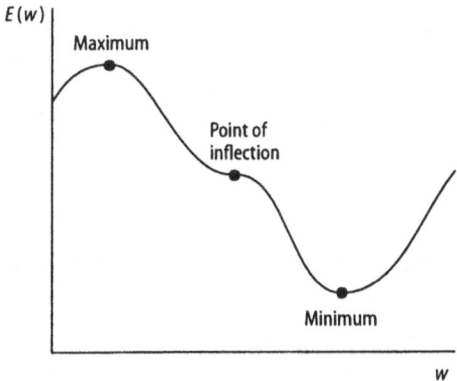

Fig. 1.2 Schematic univariate error surface with 'strong' stationary points.

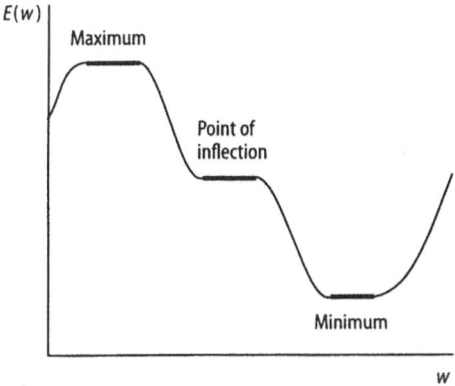

Fig. 1.3 Schematic univariate error surface with 'weak' stationary points.

$G(\mathbf{w}_*)$ is *negative definite* (i.e. all the eigenvalues of $\mathbf{G}$ are strictly negative), and definitely a strong minimum if $G(\mathbf{w}_*)$ is *positive definite* (i.e. all the eigenvalues of $\mathbf{G}$ are strictly positive). The situation is less clear-cut for weak minima and maxima. Stationary point $\mathbf{w}_*$ may be a weak maximum if $G(\mathbf{w}_*)$ is *negative semi-definite* (i.e. all the eigenvalues of $\mathbf{G}$ are non-positive), and may be a weak minimum if $G(\mathbf{w}_*)$ is *positive semi-definite* (i.e. all the eigenvalues of $\mathbf{G}$ are non-negative). With weak minima and maxima there is no guarantee; a negative or positive semi-definite Hessian is equally consistent with a weak saddle point. However, we can be certain that stationary point $\mathbf{w}_*$ is a saddle point if $G(\mathbf{w}_*)$ is *indefinite* (i.e. the eigenvalues of $\mathbf{G}$ are a mixture of positive and negative).

Since our ultimate aim is to minimise function E, minima are particularly important error-surface features. Every minimum has an associated *basin of attraction* – a region surrounding the minimum from which it is only possible to escape by passing over higher ground (or by deforming the error surface in some way). Close to the minimum, the basin will be convex or strictly convex. The definition of a convex function depends on the definition of a *convex set* – namely, a set of points which, if it contains the points **x** and **y**, also contains the line segment between points **x** and **y**. Function E defined on a convex set Ω is a *convex function* if, for every **x**, **y**$\in \Omega$ and every λ ($0 \leq \lambda \leq 1$), it holds that

$$E\left[\lambda \mathbf{x} + (1-\lambda)\mathbf{y}\right] \leq \lambda E(\mathbf{x}) + (1-\lambda)E(\mathbf{y}) \tag{1.11}$$

E is said to be *strictly convex* if, for every **x**, **y**$\in \Omega$ (**x**$\neq$**y**) and every λ ($0<\lambda<1$), it holds that

$$E\left[\lambda \mathbf{x} + (1-\lambda)\mathbf{y}\right] < \lambda E(\mathbf{x}) + (1-\lambda)E(\mathbf{y}) \tag{1.12}$$

As with stationary points, the distinction between convex, strictly convex and non-convex functions is easiest to grasp from an illustration of the one-dimensional case – see Figs. 1.4, 1.5 and 1.6. Although convex functions are rare, local convexity

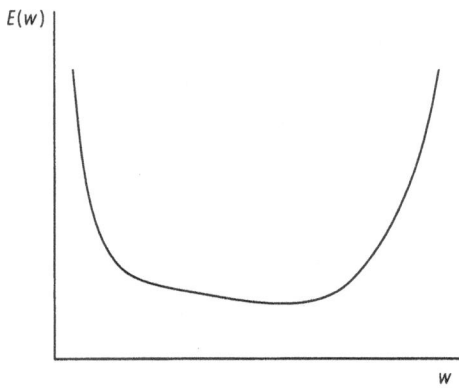

Fig. 1.4 A convex function.

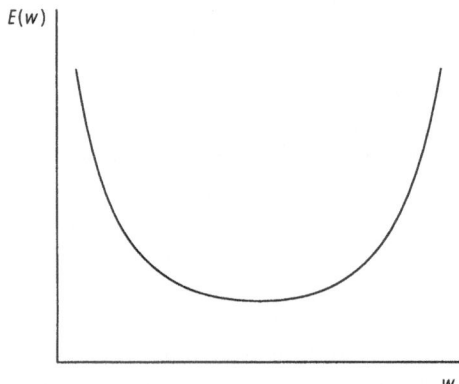

Fig. 1.5 A strictly convex function.

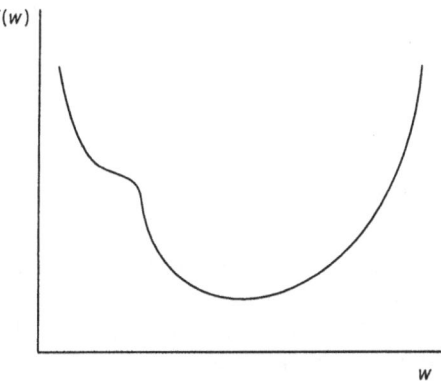

Fig. 1.6 A non-convex function.

(i.e. convexity in the neighbourhood of a minimum) is an important concept in classical optimisation. In terms of the Hessian matrix $G(\mathbf{w}_*)$ at minimum $\mathbf{w}_*$, local convexity corresponds to a positive semi-definite Hessian and strict local convexity to a positive definite Hessian.

An important distinction can be made between different types of minima on the basis of their relative heights. If minimum $\mathbf{w}_*$ is the lowest point of an error surface (i.e. $E(\mathbf{w}_*) \le E(\mathbf{w})$ for all $\mathbf{w}$), it is known as a *global minimum* (or absolute minimum); if minimum $\mathbf{w}_*$ is at a higher error level than the global minimum, it is known as a *local minimum*. In general, there is no easy way of telling whether a given minimum $\mathbf{w}_*$ is global or local, since this requires information about the entire error surface, not just the neighbourhood of $\mathbf{w}_*$. There is, however, a special case where we can guarantee that minimum $\mathbf{w}_*$ is a global minimum – that is, when $E=0$. Problems which have a global minimum at $E=0$ – known as *zero-residual* or *non-residual* problems – are the exception, rather than the rule.

Another important type of error-surface feature is the multi-dimensional 'valley'. 'Valleys', and more particularly *'narrow valleys'* or *'ravines'*, correspond to convolutions and ellipsoids of high eccentricity in the error surface. In the special case where E is quadratic with a constant positive definite Hessian, it is possible to quantify precisely the degree of eccentricity using the eigenvalues of the Hessian matrix $\mathbf{G}$. The contours of a quadratic E are W-dimensional ellipsoids surrounding a unique global minimum, with the axes of these ellipsoids pointing in the direction of the W eigenvectors of matrix $\mathbf{G}$. Note that the eigenvectors of $\mathbf{G}$ ($\mathbf{v}_i$, $i=1,...,W$) are *mutually orthogonal*, or perpendicular, i.e. $\mathbf{v}_i^T \mathbf{v}_j = 0$, $i \ne j$. The degree of eccentricity of a given ellipsoidal contour can be measured in terms of the ratio of the lengths of its axes, with the length of a given axis proportional to the inverse of the corresponding eigenvalue (Luenberger, 1984).

A final error-surface feature worthy of attention is the multi-dimensional *'plateau'*, i.e. a region where the slope is shallow in multiple dimensions simultaneously. Precisely how shallow the slope has to be for a region to qualify as a 'plateau' is not specified in a rigorous manner. However, a plateau that is sufficiently flat is indistinguishable from a weak stationary point, owing to the effects of finite-precision computer arithmetic (see Section 2.2.1).

1.2.2 MLP Error Surfaces

Having examined the properties of error surfaces in general, it is time to consider the properties of the actual error surfaces we are likely to encounter when training a multi-layer perceptron. For any viable combination of MLP architecture, test problem and error function, there is a corresponding error surface with $W+1$ dimensions for an MLP with W weights. The precise shape of the error surface is problem- and architecture-specific; since it is impractical to produce a map of an error surface that is both detailed and extensive (even for small training problems and architectures), it is no surprise that the properties of MLP error surfaces remain a subject for debate.

It is worth stressing that the common practice of inferring the presence of landscape features from training error-curve information alone is highly suspect. There is, for example, a tendency to say that an MLP has become trapped in a local minimum whenever the training curve (formed by plotting the network error E for successive training epochs) flattens out at a comparatively high level. In fact, there are a number of equally plausible causes for this behaviour that are unrelated to local minima; for example, the network is converging to a saddle point; the problem has large residuals at the solution and the network is converging to the global minimum; the network is slowly crossing a 'plateau'; the network is zigzagging down a shallow-bottomed 'narrow valley'; one or more of the network weights have become saturated; or the network is taking very small steps at each epoch. This is not simply a case of pedantry about the use of terms such as 'local minimum'; a strategy that ameliorates one cause of poor training performance is unlikely to be effective against other such causes.

What reliable evidence there is (for example, from contour plots of small sections of an error surface) suggests that most MLP error surfaces share a number of broad characteristics:

- a high degree of smoothness
- extensive 'plateaus'
- 'narrow valleys' or 'ravines'
- many weak minima, some of which may be local minima
- a degree of symmetry around the origin of the coordinate system used to plot the error surface

The latter characteristic is attributable to permutations of the weights that leave the MLP input–output function unchanged. For example, the output of the simple network in Fig. 1.1 is unaffected if the weights connecting node n_1^1 to its source nodes are swapped with the corresponding weights for node n_2^1. One consequence is that MLP error surfaces typically have multiple global minima.

The prevalence of local minima in MLP error surfaces has been the subject of serious debate for a number of years. Local minima are known to occur with specific test problems (Lisboa and Perantonis, 1991; McInerney *et al.*, 1989). On the other hand, local minima *cannot* occur if the training task is *linearly separable*[2] (Gori and Tesi, 1992), if there are as many hidden nodes as patterns in the training set (Poston *et al.*, 1991), or if the number of patterns is less than or equal to the number of pattern elements (Yu, 1992) – assuming, in each of these cases, that the chosen architecture is capable (with some set of weights) of learning the task in question. Unfortunately, none of these results gives much guidance for real-world applications, for which there is precious little hard evidence on either side of the debate. Probably the only reasonable conclusion, given our present level of knowledge, is that local minima occur with some, but far from all, realistic MLP applications.

'Plateaus', 'narrow valleys' and local minima in the MLP error surface are all potential obstacles to successful training. If an MLP encounters a region with very shallow gradients, it can take many training epochs before a significant reduction in E is made – the network is said to be stuck in a *temporary minimum* (Annema *et al.*, 1994). Training algorithms derived from the steepest descent method are prone to slow training in narrow valleys (see Section 2.1.1). And algorithms which do not allow an increase in E at any epoch are prone to becoming trapped in local minima, i.e. no amount of additional training will enable the MLP to make further downward progress. In terms of the analysis of training dynamics presented in Section 1.1.2, both local and temporary minima are closely related to the presence of redundant hidden nodes in the network. Local minima are known to have several different physical correlates in the context of MLP training; the three most frequently encountered are redundant hidden nodes, hidden node saturation and 'dead regions' of weight space where all hidden nodes are inactive (Wessels *et al.*, 1990). It is worth pointing out, however, that the presence of local minima in the MLP error surface does not necessarily mean that the network is likely to suffer from training difficulties; the local minima may be small and sparse, so that the network is unlikely to encounter one, and – recalling that we are rarely after a highly accurate solution – they may be at sufficiently low error levels that they represent satisfactory solutions to the task in question.

The characteristics of MLP error surfaces give a good indication of the kinds of strategy that are likely to engender efficient and reliable training:

- The smoothness of the error surface suggests that classical optimisation with derivatives (Chapters 2, 3 and 4) will be effective.

- Some classical methods are far less prone to slow progress in 'narrow valleys' than others (see discussion in Section 2.1).

- the effects of floating-point precision (see Section 2.2.1) are likely to be important in nearly flat regions.

---

2   A classification training task is said to be linearly separable if the input classes can be separated by a single hyperplane (of N^0-1 dimensions) in the N^0-dimensional input-space, where N^0 is the number of input nodes (equivalent to the length of the pattern vector p).

- If there are local minima, global minimisation strategies may be necessary to ensure an acceptable probability of training success.

Global minimisation is a broad term that encompasses a wide range of contrasting strategies designed to improve the chances of converging to a global, rather than a local, minimum. A number of different approaches have been proposed for reducing the likelihood of an MLP getting trapped in the attractive basin of a local minimum, including stochastic methods (Section 6.1.1); deterministic strategies, such as homotopic methods (Section 6.1.2); changing the error function (Section 1.1.2); weight initialisation schemes (see, for example, Wessels and Barnard (1992)); and schemes for dynamically changing the number of hidden nodes (see, for example, Hirose *et al.* (1991)). As these schemes apply to different aspects of the training process, it is likely that the 'optimal' strategy will combine several of these schemes in a single algorithm. It is also possible to tackle the problem of local minima from a different angle altogether. Tunnelling methods (Sections 6.1.2 and 6.3) make no attempt to prevent the network from getting trapped in local minima; rather, they enable a network to escape from a local minimum in the event that it gets trapped. Global optimisation is the subject of Chapter 6.

1.3 Backpropagation

1.3.1 An Introduction to Backpropagation

In the short introduction to MLP training presented in Section 1.1.2 it was stated that the training process involves iteratively adjusting the network weights; what was absent from that account was an appropriate scheme for updating the weights in such a way that the network converges to an acceptable solution (i.e. successfully learns the training task). The first reliable and theoretically sound algorithm for updating the MLP weights during training is known as error-backpropagation, or simply *backpropagation*. The origins of the backpropagation algorithm date back several decades, but it was not until the rediscovery of the method by Rumelhart, Hinton and Williams in the mid-1980s that it became available to a wide audience. The publication of Rumelhart *et al.* (1986) can be viewed as a decisive event in the history of multi-layer perceptrons, and one that is generally cited as the beginning of the ongoing renaissance of the entire field of neural networks. Even today, the vast majority of MLP research uses a version of the backpropagation algorithm. For this reason, backpropagation can be viewed as the benchmark against which all other training methods are judged.

In essence, the backpropagation algorithm implements, for an MLP, the *steepest descent* (or *gradient descent*) method – the most venerable, but also one of the least effective, classical optimisation strategies (see Section 2.1.1). As we shall see, there are many different versions of the basic backpropagation algorithm, and new modifications (of increasing sophistication) are regularly published in neural network journals. However, we begin by considering the 'traditional' implementation of the backpropagation algorithm (as presented in Rumelhart *et al.* (1986)) known as *batch* or *off-line backpropagation*. At each epoch k batch backpropagation calculates the gradient g_k and updates the weights according to the simple rule

$$\mathbf{w}_{k+1} = \mathbf{w}_k + \Delta \mathbf{w}_k$$

$$\Delta \mathbf{w}_k = -\eta g_k, \quad \eta > 0$$

(1.13)

where η is a constant heuristically chosen scalar, typically set in the range $(0,1)$. In the neural network literature equation (1.13) is known as the *generalised delta rule* and η as the *training rate* (or learning rate), whereas in the terminology of classical optimisation the backpropagation algorithm can be said to set the *search direction* to $-g_k$ and to move by a *step length* of η in that direction at every iteration k. (The latter terms are used throughout the subsequent chapters of this book.) The update rule given by (1.13) guarantees a reduction in total network error E at each epoch so long as the gradient is greater than zero (i.e. the network has not converged to a stationary point) and the training rate η is sufficiently small. However, for practical settings of η increases in E are possible, since η may be sufficiently large for the network to 'step over' a minimum in a given search direction.

The gradient g_k in (1.13) is calculated in two distinct phases – a forward pass and a backward pass. The *forward pass* generates the network outputs for pattern p through the calculation of each $y^l_{i,p}$, from layer $l=1$ to $l=L$, according to the weighted sum of equation (1.1). The *backward pass* calculates the partial error E_p for pattern p (see equation (1.4)), and the corresponding partial gradient g_p, with elements $\partial E_p / \partial w^l_{ij}$. These elements are calculated by applying the following rule from layers $l=L$ to $l=1$:

$$\frac{\partial E_p}{\partial w^{lm}_{ij}} = -\delta^l_{i,p} y^{l-1}_{j,p}$$

(1.14)

where the error term δ is given by

$$\delta^L_{i,p} = \left(t_{i,p} - y^L_{i,p} \right) f'\left(a^L_{i,p} \right)$$

$$\delta^m_{j,p} = f'\left(a^m_{j,p} \right) \sum_{n^l_i \in T^m_j} \delta^l_{i,p} w^{lm}_{ij}, \quad m < L$$

(1.15)

In other words, the error for pattern p is backpropagated through the network – hence the term 'backpropagation'. If squashing function f is the sigmoid of equation (1.2), then the first derivative f' in (1.15) is simply

$$f'(a) = \frac{d}{da} f(a) = f(a)\left[1 - f(a) \right] = y(1-y)$$

(1.16)

A single training epoch, which calculates the full gradient g_k by summing the P partial gradients, consists of P forward passes interleaved with P backward passes. (For a derivation of the backpropagation gradient calculation see Rumelhart *et al.* (1986).)

Batch backpropagation has proved satisfactory when applied to many training tasks, but has several important drawbacks:

- It is often slow to reach a satisfactory error level, and particularly slow when confronted with two common features of the MLP error surface – flat regions and 'narrow valleys'.
- Training performance is sensitive to the choice of training rate: too small, and the network will fail to make a sufficient reduction in network error; too large, and the network error may become stuck, owing to saturation, or oscillate wildly at a comparatively high error level.
- It is prone to getting trapped in local minima, and will also converge to saddle points.

Numerous heuristic modifications to the standard backpropagation algorithm have been proposed in an attempt to overcome these difficulties. All of these modifications have reported strengths when applied to specific problems, but tend to be ineffective in general, and often require the user to fine-tune one or more parameters on a task-by-task basis.

A detailed survey of backpropagation 'enhancements' lies outside the scope of this book; the remaining sections in this chapter examine just a few of the most significant (and popular) modifications to the backpropagation algorithm. These heuristic 'modified' backpropagation methods provide a stark contrast to the theoretically sound methods presented in the remaining chapters of the book.

1.3.2 The Bold Driver Method

One of the most obvious drawbacks with 'traditional' implementations of the backpropagation algorithm is the fixed training rate η. The 'optimal' training rate (i.e. the one that brings about the greatest reduction in network error E) is likely to vary not only from task to task, but also for different regions of a single error surface. Evidently, a strategy for adapting η as training proceeds is highly desirable.

A simple but effective strategy for adapting the backpropagation training rate, known as the *bold driver* method, involves incrementally increasing or decreasing η at each training epoch depending on whether the algorithm is making progress or not (Vogl *et al.*, 1988; Battiti, 1989). The bold driver training rate at epoch $(k+1)$ is calculated as follows:

$$\eta_{k+1} = \begin{cases} \rho\eta_k, & \text{if } E(\mathbf{w}_{k+1}) < E(\mathbf{w}_k) \\ \sigma\eta_k, & \text{if } E(\mathbf{w}_{k+1}) \geq E(\mathbf{w}_k) \end{cases} \qquad (1.17)$$

where $\rho>1$ and $0<\sigma<1$. The parameters ρ, σ and η_0 (the initial training rate) are all set heuristically by the user. It is sensible to set ρ close to one in order to prevent frequent increases in error (e.g. $\rho=1.1$), and to chose a σ that will reduce the size of η rapidly if an increase in error does occur (e.g. $\sigma=0.5$). (This approach is similar to that of the simple model-trust region strategy presented in Section 3.2.1.)

Unlike traditional, fixed training-rate backpropagation, the bold driver method can be (and invariably is) implemented as a 'strict' descent algorithm, i.e. no increase in E is allowed at any training epoch. This is achieved simply by maintaining the network weights at the same location (i.e. by setting $\mathbf{w}_{k+1} = \mathbf{w}_k$) whenever $E(\mathbf{w}_k - \eta_k \mathbf{g}_k) > E(\mathbf{w}_k)$; provided the gradient $\mathbf{g}(\mathbf{w}_k)$ is non-zero, it is guaranteed that the bold driver method will (eventually) reduce η to a small enough value to bring about a reduction in E along the negative gradient from location $\mathbf{w}_k$.

The simple strategy used by the bold driver method to adapt the backpropagation training rate proves remarkably effective in practice. The bold driver method frequently out-performs both batch backpropagation with a fixed training rate (even when η is set to its optimal fixed value), and the steepest descent algorithm, a 'classical' implementation of batch backpropagation that sets the training rate optimally at each epoch using a one-dimensional line-search procedure (see Section 2.1.1). Although the bold driver method has three user-defined parameters, compared with the single parameter of 'traditional' batch backpropagation, it is much less sensitive to the choice of parameter settings than batch backpropagation. So long as the optimal training rate η does not change rapidly as training proceeds, the bold driver method will tend to set η to a near-optimal value much of the time. Unlike the classical steepest descent method, the computational cost of adapting η is minimal.

1.3.3 Backpropagation with Momentum

Rumelhart *et al.* (1986) proposed a simple, heuristic strategy for speeding up the backpropagation training method which involves incorporating a *momentum* term in the generalised delta rule (1.13) as follows:

$$\Delta \mathbf{w}_k = -\eta \mathbf{g}_k + \alpha \Delta \mathbf{w}_{k-1} \qquad (1.18)$$

where the user-defined parameter α is set in the range $0 \le \alpha < 1$. (With momentum turned 'off', i.e. with $\alpha = 0$, the update rule given by (1.18) is equivalent to the standard backpropagation update of equation (1.13).) Experience shows that the addition of momentum can significantly speed up the backpropagation training algorithm, attributable to its impact in precisely those regions of the MLP error surface where the backpropagation algorithm performs badly – 'plateaus' and 'narrow valleys'. The momentum term accelerates convergence in flat regions by a factor that approaches $1/(1-\alpha)$ as the number of epochs (k) gets large, and reduces the number of oscillations in a narrow valley – i.e. reduces the 'narrow-valley effect' (see Section 2.1.1) – by averaging out the components of the gradient which alternate in sign (Watrous, 1987). Parameter α is typically set to 0.9, although the optimal α is task-specific.

One potential drawback with the update (1.18) is that, if α is increased, it may be necessary to make a compensatory reduction in η to maintain network stability (i.e. to prevent excessive weight changes). To counter this effect, Widrow and Lehr

(1990) propose a modified version of (1.18) which incorporates the factor $(1-\alpha)$ as follows:

$$\Delta \mathbf{w}_k = -(1-\alpha)\eta \mathbf{g}_k + \alpha \Delta \mathbf{w}_{k-1} \qquad (1.19)$$

However, this approach has its own potential drawback; if α is set to a comparatively large value, the weight update $\Delta \mathbf{w}_k$ in (1.19) will tend to be dominated by gradient information from previous epochs at the expense of information about the current gradient $\mathbf{g}_k$. The update (1.19) frequently proves less effective than (1.18) in practice.

It is interesting to compare batch backpropagation with momentum and a class of classical optimisation algorithms known as conjugate gradient methods (Section 3.3.4). The update rule for batch backpropagation with momentum can be viewed as an approximation to the conjugate gradient update, with the important difference that the former sets η and α to fixed heuristic values, whereas the latter automatically sets η and α to near-optimal values at each iteration (Møller, 1993e).

The fixed momentum term can be combined with the bold driver method for adapting the training rate η (Section 1.3.2). To preserve the strict descent properties of the bold driver method, Vogl *et al.* (1988) recommend resetting the search direction to the negative gradient $-\mathbf{g}_k$ (with the momentum term α set temporarily to zero) whenever an update brings about an increase in total network error E.

1.3.4 On-Line Backpropagation

Perhaps the single most important modified version of the standard backpropagation algorithm is known as *on-line* or *stochastic backpropagation*[3]. On-line backpropagation differs from batch backpropagation in that the weights are updated at the end of each backward pass (i.e. P times per epoch), rather than once every P backward passes (i.e. once per epoch). The weight update rule for on-line backpropagation is

$$\mathbf{w}_{k,p+1} = \mathbf{w}_{k,p} + \Delta \mathbf{w}_{k,p}$$
$$\Delta \mathbf{w}_{k,p} = -\eta \mathbf{g}_{k,p}, \quad \eta > 0 \qquad (1.20)$$

Typically, the P patterns are presented to the network in random order. If the training rate η tends to zero, on-line backpropagation can be regarded as an approximation to batch backpropagation. However, for practical settings of η the two methods diverge.

In theory, on-line backpropagation has several potential disadvantages compared with batch backpropagation:

---

3   Although 'on-line' and 'stochastic' are the two most widely used terms for this type of training, numerous alternatives are to be found in the neural network literature, including 'sequential' training (Bishop, 1995); 'local learning' (Annema *et al.*, 1994); 'immediate update' training (Kinsella, 1992); 'pattern mode' training (Gori and Tesi, 1992); and 'jump every time' (Hecht-Nielsen, 1990).

- It is not guaranteed to reduce the total network error E at each training epoch, even when η is comparatively small.
- The optimal training rate η for on-line backpropagation is poorly understood. Strategies for adapting η that are appropriate for batch backpropagation (or its classical counterpart, the steepest descent method) are not appropriate for on-line backpropagation.
- It is poor at achieving highly accurate solutions.
- It requires slightly more computational effort per epoch than batch backpropagation.
- It is much more difficult to analyse.

The most significant problem with on-line backpropagation is the choice of a suitable training rate at each iteration k. Results from *stochastic approximation theory* provide a theoretical basis for adjusting the on-line training rate η as a function of time. The usual choice of training rate schedule in the stochastic approximation literature, following Robbins and Monro (1951), is

$$\eta_k = \frac{c}{k} \tag{1.21}$$

for some constant c. Unfortunately, this simple schedule typically results in slow convergence if c is 'small', or excessive weight changes when k is small and c is set to a 'large' value (Darken and Moody, 1990). A more sophisticated on-line training rate schedule, proposed by Darken *et al.* (1992), is the *search then converge* (STC) schedule given by

$$\eta_k = \eta_0 \frac{1 + (c/\eta_0)(k/\tau)}{1 + (c/\eta_0)(k/\tau) + \tau\left(k^2/\tau^2\right)} \tag{1.22}$$

where η_k is the training rate at iteration k, parameter c is set greater than a threshold of $1/2\lambda_{min}$ (λ_{min} being the smallest eigenvalue of the Hessian of E), and parameter τ relates to the number of anticipated training epochs. The significance of the STC schedule is that, when implemented with a suitable scheme for estimating c (using, for example, the Power method, described below in Section 2.2.3), an optimal rate of asymptotic ('large time') convergence is guaranteed for on-line backpropagation. In practice, however, the convergence rate associated with the STC schedule is highly dependent on the choice of parameters η_0 and τ. Whereas it is possible to estimate c automatically, guidance for setting parameters η_0 and τ is essentially heuristic, or requires prior knowledge about the problem.

In spite of these difficulties, on-line backpropagation has several practical advantages over batch backpropagation:

- On-line backpropagation is an example of a *stochastic process* that can prevent an MLP from getting trapped in a local minimum.
- If the training set contains redundant information – as is usually the case – the more frequent weight updates of on-line backpropagation often prove more

efficient. (It may, however, be possible to remove redundant information by pre-processing the training set.)

- On-line training is essential if the full complement of training patterns is not known at the start of training.

The first two of these benefits are worth considering in greater detail.

On-Line Backpropagation as a Stochastic Process   There are two ways in which on-line backpropagation can be regarded as a stochastic process. Firstly, the total network error E may rise at one or more epochs in such a way that the network is able to escape from the basin of attraction of a local minimum. Secondly, the shape of the MLP error surface is not constant with on-line backpropagation, so that local minima are metastable states. A network that is 'trapped' at such a location will slowly decay to the global minimum at a rate of $\tilde{t}/t$ for some constant $\tilde{t}$, a rate that is much slower than the typical rate of $1/t$ by which a network reaches equilibrium inside an attractive region (Kappen and Heskes, 1992).

In its 'traditional' form, with weights updated after the presentation of every pattern, on-line backpropagation makes no attempt to regulate the amount of stochastic 'noise' added to the system at each training epoch. However, the term 'on-line' is often used in a more general sense to encompass training algorithms which update the weights after a subset n ($1 \leq n < P$) of the full training set has been presented to the network; by varying the size and membership of the subset at each training iteration it is possible to regulate the amount of stochastic noise.

On-Line Backpropagation and Redundant Training Sets   When batch backpropagation is applied to training sets containing redundant information, the network is liable to perform redundant computations when calculating the gradient by (1.14). For classification tasks, Møller (1993b) proposes a measure of training set redundancy based on standard information theory. For a training set with M classes, P discrete input patterns of length N^0 and V possible values for each pattern element, the average information content of the set is the *Conditional Population Entropy* (CPE) given by

$$\text{CPE} = -\sum_{m=1}^{M} p(c_m) \sum_{i=1}^{N^0} \sum_{v=1}^{V} p(x_{i,v}|c_m) \log p(x_{i,v}|c_m) \qquad (1.23)$$

where $p(c_m)$ is the probability that a pattern belongs to the mth class, and $p(x_{i,v}|c_m)$ is the probability that the ith element of pattern x has value v given that x belongs to class m; the smaller the value of CPE, the greater the similarity between the patterns in the training set. Møller defines the redundancy (RE) of a training set as

$$\text{RE} = \frac{\log V - (\text{CPE}/N^0)}{\log V} \qquad (1.24)$$

and gives empirical evidence for a strong correlation between the RE of a training set and the comparative performance of on-line and off-line algorithms when applied to that set. Similar approaches can be adopted to measure the redundancy of training sets with continuous input patterns and for non-classification training tasks by dividing the input and/or output ranges into discrete intervals.

It is worth noting, however, that whereas the redundancy of a training set is constant, the redundancy of the gradient calculation varies from location to location. Consequently, the RE of a given training set may be an inaccurate reflection of the degree of redundancy actually encountered during training. Training set redundancy will be considered again in Section 4.3.

1.3.5 The Delta-Bar-Delta Method

When devising new MLP training algorithms, many researchers have sought to exploit the distributed architecture of the multi-layer perceptron by assigning separate training rates and/or momentum terms to each node or weight in the network. The motivation for this approach to MLP training derives from the fact that the optimal parameter settings are likely to vary for different network weights. One important consequence of adopting such an approach is that the network is no longer performing gradient descent. This section focuses on a single 'distributed' training method – the delta-bar-delta method (Jacobs, 1988), which utilises a separate training rate for each weight in the network.

As we have seen, one of the main drawbacks with conventional backpropagation is that it is prone to slow progress in narrow valleys, attributable to oscillations in the local gradient – the so-called 'narrow-valley effect' (analysed below in Section 2.1.1). As a means of overcoming this problem, Jacobs proposes a scheme which utilises a separate adaptive training rate η_i for each network weight w_i, so that the weight update rule is given by

$$(\Delta w_i)_k = -(\eta_i)_k (g_i)_k \qquad (1.25)$$

where $(\Delta w_i)_k$ is the change in weight w_i at epoch k, and gradient element g_i is given by equation (1.9). Clearly, the key to such an approach is the strategy used to adapt the W training rates (η_i). The heuristic strategy developed by Jacobs derives from the observation that, if the derivative g_i with respect to weight w_i has the same sign at consecutive epochs, it indicates that w_i is moving steadily downhill, whereas a change in the sign of g_i is indicative of gradient oscillation. Jacobs' approach is to increase η_i if the sign of g_i is unchanged, but decrease η_i whenever the sign of g_i changes.

One way of implementing this approach – the *delta–delta*[4] method – updates each training rate η_i according to the simple rule

---

4 The name delta–delta derives from the notation δ_i used by Jacobs (1988) to denote a single element of the gradient (here denoted g_i).

$$(\Delta\eta_i)_k = \gamma(g_i)_k(g_i)_{k-1} \qquad (1.26)$$

where scalar $\gamma > 0$ is a fixed step-size parameter. Unfortunately, the delta–delta update rule is not suitable in practice because of its sensitivity to the setting of user-defined parameter γ. For this reason, Jacobs proposes a modified update rule for training rate η_i – the *delta-bar-delta* rule – defined by

$$(\Delta\eta_i)_k = \begin{cases} \gamma & \text{if } (\bar{g}_i)_k(\bar{g}_i)_{k-1} > 0 \\ -\phi(\eta_i)_k & \text{if } (\bar{g}_i)_k(\bar{g}_i)_{k-1} < 0 \end{cases} \qquad (1.27)$$

where $\bar{g}_i$ is a running average of the current and previous values of element g_i given by

$$(\bar{g}_i)_k = (1-\theta)(g_i)_k + \theta(g_i)_{k-1} \qquad (1.28)$$

with parameter θ set in the range $(0,1)$. Equation (1.27) ensures that a given training rate $(\eta_i)_k$ is incremented linearly if the corresponding 'average gradient element' $(\bar{g}_i)_k$ has the same sign as the current gradient element $(g_i)_k$, but decremented exponentially if the sign of $(g_i)_k$ is opposite to that of $(g_i)_k$. The significance of (1.27) compared with (1.26) is that the training rates are updated independently of the current size of the gradient. However, although Jacobs reports that the delta-bar-delta method can significantly improve convergence speed compared with standard backpropagation, the method has three user-defined parameters (γ, ϕ and θ), the setting of which may be crucial to the practical performance of the method. Jacobs gives no firm guidance as to how these parameters should be set in practice.

2. *Classical Optimisation*

This chapter serves as an introduction to the field of classical optimisation in general, and to second-order classical methods in particular. The aim of the chapter is to explain why second-order methods have superior convergence characteristics to first-order methods such as steepest descent (and, in the context of MLP training, the 'traditional' backpropagation algorithm). The chapter also discusses various topics of general relevance when implementing classical optimisation methods in practice. The particular characteristics and implementation requirements of specific second-order methods are the subject of Chapter 3.

2.1 Introduction to Classical Methods

Classical optimisation theory is concerned with deterministic methods for minimising functions. Here we are interested in a specific branch of classical optimisation theory, *smooth unconstrained nonlinear optimisation*[1], which is of direct relevance to the class of function typically associated with MLP training tasks (as identified in Section 1.2.2). In contrast to the essentially heuristic approaches to minimising the MLP error function discussed in Chapter 1, all the classical methods discussed in this book have a sound theoretical basis, and guarantee convergence to a minimum for a wide class of smooth functions. However, classical optimisation is concerned only with local optimisation; none of the methods presented in this chapter attempt to distinguish between global and local minima. (In Chapter 6 we shall consider some modern methods for global optimisation that are deterministic, but these lie outside the mainstream of classical optimisation theory.)

The aim of classical methods for smooth nonlinear optimisation is to find a minimum x_* of an arbitrary smooth nonlinear function $F(x_k)$, or F_k for short, with vector x comprising the N independent variables (free parameters) x_i ($i=1,...,N$). When N is greater than 1 and there are no constraints on the acceptable values of x,

---

1   Good general surveys of the field are provided by Fletcher (1987), Gill *et al.* (1981), Luenberger (1984) and Wolfe (1978).

this is known as the *multivariate unconstrained minimisation* problem. In terms of F and $\mathbf{x}$, the elements of the gradient vector $\mathbf{g}$ are given by

$$g_i = \frac{\partial F(\mathbf{x})}{\partial x_i}, \qquad 1 \leq i \leq N \tag{2.1}$$

(cf. equation (1.9)), and the elements of the Hessian matrix $\mathbf{G}$ are given by

$$G_{ij} = \frac{\partial^2 F(\mathbf{x})}{\partial x_i x_j}, \qquad 1 \leq i, j \leq N \tag{2.2}$$

(cf. equation (1.10)). It is assumed throughout that function F is twice continuously differentiable, i.e. $F \in C^2$.

That methods for solving the multivariate unconstrained minimisation problem can be used to train MLPs derives from the fact that any given combination of network architecture, error function and training set can be viewed as defining a nonlinear function $F(\mathbf{x}_k)$, with the network weights equivalent to the free parameters ($\mathbf{x} \equiv \mathbf{w}$, $N \equiv W$). In the case where the chosen MLP error function is the sum-of-squares error function (1.5), MLP training can be viewed as an example of the *nonlinear least-squares* problem – a special case of unconstrained minimisation. Classical methods which seek to exploit the special structure of nonlinear least-squares problems are discussed in Section 3.4.

All of the classical optimisation methods discussed in this book share important characteristics:

- All derive, algebraically, from the Taylor series expansion of a smooth multivariate function F in the neighbourhood of an arbitrary point $\mathbf{x}$

$$F(\mathbf{x} + \mathbf{s}) = F(\mathbf{x}) + g(\mathbf{x})^T \mathbf{s} + \tfrac{1}{2} \mathbf{s}^T G(\mathbf{x}) \mathbf{s} + \dots \tag{2.3}$$

- All are *iterative descent algorithms*, i.e. minimum $\mathbf{x}_*$ is located in a series of steps, with $F(\mathbf{x}_{k+1}) \leq F(\mathbf{x}_k)$ at each step k. The *step* taken at iteration k (equivalent to $\mathbf{x}_{k+1} - \mathbf{x}_k$) will be denoted $\mathbf{s}_k$.
- All require that *search direction* $\mathbf{p}_k$ is a *descent direction*, i.e. $\mathbf{p}_k$ must satisfy

$$\mathbf{g}_k^T \mathbf{p}_k < 0 \tag{2.4}$$

at each iteration k. In terms of search direction $\mathbf{p}_k$, step $\mathbf{s}_k$ is defined by

$$\mathbf{s}_k = \alpha_k \mathbf{p}_k \tag{2.5}$$

where α_k is a non-negative scalar called the *step length*.

Within this broad framework, a wide variety of different approaches are possible. Some of the most important considerations when designing a classical optimisation algorithm are:

- the number of terms in equation (2.3) used to model the shape of the error surface at location $\mathbf{x}_k$

- whether the derivatives used to construct the chosen model are calculated exactly or approximated
- whether the chosen model is generated anew at each iteration or built up iteratively (typically in N iterations)
- the choice of strategy for ensuring that $\mathbf{p}_k$ is a descent direction
- the accuracy with which the minimum in search direction $\mathbf{p}_k$ is located at each iteration

These choices have a direct bearing on the effectiveness of a given optimisation algorithm.

In order to compare the theoretical performance of different classical methods, it will be useful to consider their global and local convergence properties. The formal definition of convergence is as follows: a sequence of real points $\{\mathbf{x}_k\} = \{\mathbf{x}_0, \mathbf{x}_1, \mathbf{x}_2,...\}$ is said to *converge* to a solution $\mathbf{x}_*$ if

$$\lim_{k \to \infty} |\mathbf{x}_k - \mathbf{x}_*| = 0 \tag{2.6}$$

In the context of the convergence of classical algorithms, the terms 'local' and 'global' have different meanings from those introduced in Section 1.2. A method is said to be *globally convergent* if it is guaranteed to converge (eventually) to a solution $\mathbf{x}_*$ from (almost) any starting position. If F is an arbitrary smooth convex function, solution $\mathbf{x}_*$ is the unique global minimum of F, but for general nonlinear functions a method is considered to be globally convergent if it is guaranteed to converge to a stationary point of F. Thus the steepest descent method (Section 2.1.1) is deemed globally convergent even though it may converge to a saddle point rather than a minimum of F. A method's *local convergence rate*, on the other hand, is its anticipated rate of convergence close to a minimum. Although the theoretical convergence characteristics of an algorithm act as a rough guide to its performance in practice, they should be treated with caution; they require conditions that do not apply in general, and the effect of rounding error is ignored.

The global and local convergence properties of classical algorithms are not the only criteria by which their effectiveness may be judged. Other important considerations are the computational complexity of an algorithm at each iteration, its numerical stability and storage requirements, and how easy it is to implement in practice.

2.1.1   The Linear Model and Steepest Descent

Optimisation methods which derive from the *linear model*

$$F(\mathbf{x}+\mathbf{s}) \approx F(\mathbf{x}) + g(\mathbf{x})^T \mathbf{s} \tag{2.7}$$

(i.e. all but the first two terms of (2.3) are ignored) are known as *first-order methods*. The pre-eminent example is *steepest descent* or *gradient descent*, the longest- and most widely known optimisation technique of all. Steepest descent sets the search direction $\mathbf{p}_k$ to the negative gradient $-\mathbf{g}_k$ at each iteration, i.e.

$$\mathbf{x}_{k+1} = \mathbf{x}_k - \alpha_k \mathbf{g}_k \tag{2.8}$$

This is equivalent to the standard backpropagation update of equation (1.13) except that α_k is chosen to minimise $E(\mathbf{x}_k - \mathbf{g}_k)$ using a line-search strategy (see Sections 2.1.3 and 3.1), rather than set to the fixed heuristic value of the backpropagation training rate (η).

The steepest descent method is easy to implement and requires, on average, the least computational effort per iteration of any classical method. Moreover, steepest descent is guaranteed to converge to a stationary point $\mathbf{x}_*$ of F, provided that the step length α_k is chosen by a globally convergent line-search algorithm. However, these benefits are largely outweighed by the fact that the method's rate of convergence is often very slow. When the steepest descent method encounters 'narrow valleys' in the error surface, it is liable to suffer from the so-called *narrow-valley effect* (Fig. 2.1), with the path oscillating back and forth along the local gradient. Successive steepest descent directions have a tendency to interfere, i.e. a minimisation in one direction can spoil the minimisation previously achieved in other directions.

In order to assess the local convergence rate of steepest descent, it is useful to consider how the method performs when function F is quadratic with a constant and positive definite Hessian $\mathbf{G}$. In this case the optimal value for α_k can be defined explicitly as follows:

$$\alpha_k = \frac{\mathbf{g}_k^T \mathbf{g}_k}{\mathbf{g}_k^T \mathbf{G} \mathbf{g}_k} \tag{2.9}$$

Under these apparently favourable conditions, the theoretical upper bound on the convergence rate of steepest descent is given by the *convergence ratio r*,

$$r = \left(\frac{\kappa - 1}{\kappa + 1} \right)^2 \tag{2.10}$$

where κ is the *condition number* of the Hessian $\mathbf{G}$, defined by

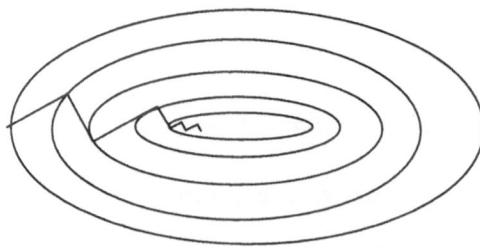

Fig. 2.1 Steepest descent and the 'narrow-valley effect'. Note that successive descent directions are perpendicular to each other and to the tangent planes of the surface contours. Unless the valley is optimally oriented, the method takes many steps to converge to the minimum, zigzagging across the valley's principal axis.

$$\kappa = \left| \frac{\lambda_{\max}}{\lambda_{\min}} \right| \tag{2.11}$$

The scalars $\lambda_{\max}$ and $\lambda_{\min}$ in (2.11) are, respectively, the largest and smallest eigenvalues of G. This amounts to an arbitrarily slow rate of linear convergence, which becomes slower as c increases. A sequence $\{x_k\}$ that converges to the minimiser x_* is said to be *linearly convergent* if there exists a constant scalar $\rho \in [0,1)$ and integer $\hat{k} \geq 0$ such that, for all $k \geq \hat{k}$,

$$|x_{k+1} - x_*| \leq \rho |x_k - x_*| \tag{2.12}$$

Since, from (2.11), only a single 'abnormal' eigenvalue is sufficient to make the condition number large, it is easy to appreciate why both steepest descent and batch backpropagation are frequently slow to converge in practice.

Both the convergence ratio r in (2.10) and the steepest descent direction $-g$ are sensitive to the scale of x. The feasibility of changing the scale of x so that κ is reduced, with a corresponding improvement in the convergence characteristics of the steepest descent and batch backpropagation algorithms, is considered in Section 2.2.3.

2.1.2 The Quadratic Model and Newton's Method

With the exception of steepest descent, all the classical methods considered in this book are *second-order methods*, based on the *quadratic model*

$$F(x+s) \approx F(x) + g(x)^T s + \tfrac{1}{2} s^T G(x) s \tag{2.13}$$

The theoretical convergence rate and practical performance of second-order methods are generally superior to those of first-order methods (provided F is sufficiently smooth). The success of the quadratic model derives from the fact that quadratic functions are a good approximation to general functions near a minimum. If successive search directions satisfy

$$p_i^T G p_j = 0, \quad i \neq j \tag{2.14}$$

that is, the directions are *mutually conjugate* with respect to the Hessian matrix G, they will (unlike successive steepest descent directions) be approximately non-interfering, with a correspondingly fast rate of convergence.

The straightforward implementation of the quadratic model, known as *Newton's method*, generates each step s_k as follows:

$$s_k = -G_k^{-1} g_k \tag{2.15}$$

If G_k is positive definite, the s_k given by (2.15), commonly denoted s_k^N, has a number of important properties (Dennis and Schnabel, 1983):

- s_k^N uniquely minimises the quadratic model at x_k and is guaranteed to be a *descent direction*.
- It defines both the direction (the *Newton direction*) and step length (the *Newton step*) to be taken at each iteration, i.e. s_k^N is equivalent to $\alpha_k p_k$ with $\alpha_k=1$.
- Unlike the steepest descent direction $-g_k$, s_k^N is unaffected by the scale of x_k.

Moreover, the availability of the Hessian matrix means that it may be possible to distinguish between saddle points and minima (see discussion in Section 1.2.1). If stationary point x_* is a saddle point with an indefinite Hessian $G(x_*)$, it is possible to 'escape' from location x_* by following a 'direction of negative curvature', i.e. a direction p that satisfies

$$p^T G(x_*)p < 0 \qquad (2.16)$$

(see Moré and Sorensen (1979)).

For quadratic functions with a positive definite Hessian, Newton's method converges in a single iteration. For non-quadratic functions, the local convergence rate is quadratic. A sequence $\{x_k\}$ that converges to the minimiser x_* is said to be *quadratically convergent* if there exists a constant scalar $\rho>0$ and integer $\hat{k} \geq 0$ such that, for all $k \geq \hat{k}$,

$$|x_{k+1} - x_*| \leq \rho|x_k - x_*|^2 \qquad (2.17)$$

Unfortunately, the unmodified Newton's method suffers from a number of drawbacks which make it unsuitable as a general optimisation method:

- It is only defined if G is positive definite and is prone to failure whenever G is ill-conditioned, so that global convergence cannot be guaranteed.
- Its computational and storage costs are comparatively high – $O(N^3)$ (to solve (2.15)) and $O(N^2)$ (to store G) respectively.
- It requires both first and second analytic derivatives to be available at every point x_k.

Newton's method can be modified so that it is globally convergent using the various strategies discussed later in this chapter for regulating the positive definiteness of the Hessian matrix and for choosing an acceptable step length at each iteration. Moreover, it is possible to reduce the high computational cost of solving (2.15) by representing the Hessian matrix in an efficient factorised form (see Section 2.2.2). However, the fundamental deterrent to using Newton's method remains – that is, the typically high cost of evaluating the Hessian matrix analytically. (In Section 4.1.1 we shall see that the cost of evaluating G exactly with an MLP is particularly severe.) For this reason, Newton's method cannot be recommended in practice.

All the remaining second-order methods considered in this book fall somewhere between steepest descent and Newton's method. Broadly speaking, all these methods aim to:

- retain the guaranteed global convergence of steepest descent
- generate search directions that are 'superior' to (i.e. interfere less than) the steepest descent direction when comparatively remote from a minimum

- approach the fast local convergence rate of Newton's method when close to a minimum

None of the methods requires the prohibitively expensive calculation of second derivatives at each iteration, although many maintain an approximation $\mathbf{H}$ of the Hessian matrix.

In view of their 'heritage', we should expect the local convergence properties of these methods (for non-quadratic functions) to lie somewhere between those of steepest descent and Newton's method. In formal terms, this amounts to linear convergence at a faster rate than steepest descent, or super-linear convergence. A sequence $\{\mathbf{x}_k\}$ that converges to the minimiser $\mathbf{x}_*$ is said to be *super-linearly convergent* if, for some sequence $\{\rho_k\}$ that converges to zero,

$$|\mathbf{x}_{k+1} - \mathbf{x}_*| \leq \rho_k |\mathbf{x}_k - \mathbf{x}_*| \tag{2.18}$$

Whether this proves acceptably fast in practice is directly related to how many iterations it takes before ρ_k becomes small.

2.1.3 Line-Search Methods vs. Model-Trust Region Methods

At each iteration, a multivariate classical algorithm generates a search direction ($\mathbf{p}_k$). This leaves, as an important sub-problem at each iteration k, the choice of a suitable step $\mathbf{s}_k$ with respect to search direction $\mathbf{p}_k$. (In practice, even the Newton step $\mathbf{s}_k^N$ is treated as a search direction, as there is no guarantee that $\mathbf{s}_k^N$ will bring about an acceptable error reduction at every iteration.) Methods for solving this sub-problem are the subject of this section.

Second-order methods can be implemented in one of two ways – as line-search methods or as model-trust region methods. Line-search and model-trust region strategies represent different approaches to the sub-problem of choosing step $\mathbf{s}_k$ given search direction $\mathbf{p}_k$. Multivariate algorithms with *line searches* share the same iterative structure, outlined in Algorithm 2.1.

Algorithm 2.1 Generic line-search algorithm
   1 Choose a random starting point $\mathbf{x}_0$
   2 At each iteration k, do the following until termination criteria are satisfied:
      2.1 Compute a search direction $\mathbf{p}_k$ that is a descent direction
      2.2 Choose a step length $\alpha_k \geq 0$ that satisfies

$$F(\mathbf{x}_k + \alpha_k \mathbf{p}_k) < F(\mathbf{x}_k) \tag{2.19}$$

      2.3 Set $\mathbf{x}_{k+1}$ to $\mathbf{x}_k + \alpha_k \mathbf{p}_k$

So long as $\mathbf{p}_k$ is a descent direction (i.e. satisfies (2.4)), the existence of a positive α_k that satisfies (2.19) is guaranteed. One-dimensional line-search algorithms that can be used to choose an appropriate α_k (step 2.2 in the preceding algorithm) are considered in Section 3.1.

Whereas for line-search methods the sub-task at each iteration is to locate the minimum along the search direction from x_k, with *model-trust region methods*[2] the aim is to find the minimum in a 'trusted' neighbourhood Ω_k around x_k. Neighbourhood Ω_k is conceived as the region surrounding x_k in which the quadratic model (derived from (2.13)) approximates function F with a fairly high degree of accuracy. Model-trust region methods aim to prevent unreliable steps by ensuring that location $x_{k+1} = x_k + s_k$ lies within Ω_k. Since we cannot expect to have detailed knowledge about the extent of region Ω_k in every direction from x_k, Ω_k is simply defined as a region with radius α_k, so that step s_k is chosen to satisfy

$$\left\| s_k \right\|_2 \le \alpha_k \tag{2.20}$$

at each iteration k, where $\left\| \cdot \right\|_2$ is the Euclidean (l_2) norm[3] and $\alpha_k > 0$. Broadly speaking, radius α_k is increased if the quadratic model of F is accurate at iteration k, but decreased if the model is inaccurate.

In practice, many model-trust region strategies control radius α_k indirectly by performing the substitution

$$\mathbf{H}_k = \mathbf{G}_k + \mu_k \mathbf{I} \tag{2.21}$$

where μ_k is a non-negative scalar and $\mathbf{I}$ the identity matrix. The significance of parameter μ_k in (2.21) is apparent from its impact on the Newton step calculated by (2.15). If $\mu_k = 0$, s_k is the same as the Newton step; as μ_k tends to infinity, s_k tends to the steepest descent direction – see Fig. 2.2. In other words, a change to the scalar μ produces an inverse change in α. (Another important feature of the substitution in (2.21), discussed in Section 2.2.2, is that parameter μ can be used to regulate the positive definiteness of the Hessian matrix.) Algorithm 2.2 provides a general framework for model-trust region methods that utilise parameter μ_k in (2.21).

Algorithm 2.2 Generic model-trust region algorithm
  1 Choose a random starting point x_0 and $\mu_0 > 0$
  2 At each iteration k, do the following until termination criteria are satisfied:
      2.1 Compute a step s_k using the Hessian $\mathbf{H}_k$, as modified by parameter μ_k in (2.21)
      2.2 Evaluate $F(x_k + s_k)$
      2.3 IF the quadratic model is sufficiently accurate,
            2.3.1 Set $\mu_{k+1} \le \mu_k$
      ELSE
            2.3.2 Set $\mu_{k+1} > \mu_k$
      2.4 IF $F(x_k + s_k) < F(x_k)$

---

2   The name comes from viewing the task as defining a *region* in which it is possible to *trust* the local quadratic *model* of function F (Dennis and Schnabel, 1983). These methods are also known as restricted step methods (Fletcher, 1987) or, simply, trust region methods.

3   Model-trust region methods using the l_2 norm are sometimes termed Levenberg–Marquardt methods. Here the latter term is reserved for the nonlinear least squares method of Section 3.4.2. Hypercube or boxstep methods, which use the l_∞ norm, have good local but poor global convergence properties (Fletcher, 1987).

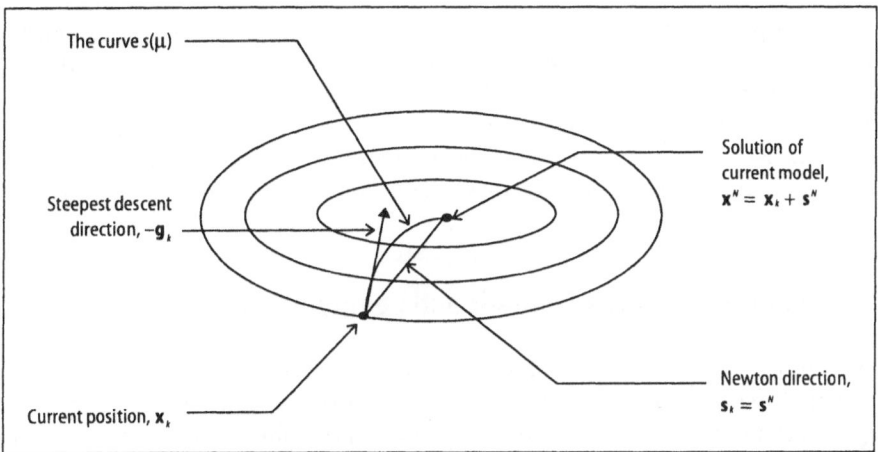

The curve $s(\mu)$

Steepest descent direction, $-\mathbf{g}_k$

Solution of current model, $\mathbf{x}^N = \mathbf{x}_k + \mathbf{s}^N$

Newton direction, $\mathbf{s}_k = \mathbf{s}^N$

Current position, $\mathbf{x}_k$

Fig. 2.2 Parameter μ and the model-trust region search direction. Curve $s(\mu)$ plots the points $\mathbf{x}_{k+1} = \mathbf{x}_k + \mathbf{s}_k$ for $0 < \mu \leq \infty$. (Adapted from Dennis and Schnabel (1983).)

     2.4.1 Set $\mathbf{x}_{k+1} = \mathbf{x}_k + \mathbf{s}_k$
ELSE
     2.4.2 Set $\mathbf{x}_{k+1} = \mathbf{x}_k$

Strategies for evaluating the accuracy of the quadratic model and for adjusting parameter μ (at step 2.3 in the preceding algorithm) are considered in Section 3.2.

Neither line searches nor model-trust region methods are clearly superior. With line searches, the optimal accuracy with which α_k approximates the minimum along $\mathbf{p}_k$ is method- and problem-dependent. With model-trust region methods, the chosen scheme for initialising and regulating α (or μ) can have a significant impact on training performance. In practice, line searches are often the first choice because they are, in general, easier to understand than model-trust region methods.

2.2 General Numerical Considerations

In their book *Practical Optimisation*, Gill, Murray and Wright issue the following sober warning (Gill *et al.*, 1981, p. 5):

> Modern numerical analysis has shown that even apparently simple computations must be implemented with great care, and that naive implementations are subject to a high probability of serious error and numerical instability.

The purpose of this section is to acquaint the reader with several factors that have a direct bearing on how the second-order algorithms presented in Chapter 3 should be implemented in order to prevent the sorts of problem to which Gill *et al.* refer. Two of these factors apply to all classical methods – namely, the effects of finite-precision computer arithmetic and the scale of the independent variables x and function F on numerical calculations. A third factor, which applies to methods that store second-order information in an explicit model of the Hessian matrix, is the form in which that matrix – known as the model Hessian – should be represented in practice. It is no exaggeration to suggest that any implementation of a classical algorithm that fails to give due regard to these factors is liable to be both inefficient and unreliable.

2.2.1   Finite-Precision Arithmetic and Computational Errors

One important and inevitable source of errors in numerical computation derives from the form in which numbers are represented on a computer. A computer represents a non-zero real number x in *floating-point format*, which has the form

$$x = \text{sign } m\beta^e \tag{2.22}$$

where m is the *mantissa*, β the *base*, and e the *exponent*. Floating-point format is analogous to standard *scientific notation*, which represents the decimal number 673.42 in the form $+6.7342 \times 10^{+2}$, where $m=6.7342$, $\beta=10$ and $e=+2$. On a computer, the base, length of mantissa (τ), and maximum and minimum values of the exponent (e_{max} and e_{min} respectively) are machine-dependent.

The representation of real numbers in floating-point format is the source of three types of computational error: *overflow errors*, caused by numbers that have a greater magnitude than that afforded by e_{max}; *underflow errors*, caused by non-zero numbers that have a lesser magnitude than that afforded by e_{min}; and *rounding* or *round-off errors*, caused by numbers that require greater *precision* than afforded by τ (i.e. with more significant digits than can be stored in the mantissa). Most computers will terminate a program that generates an overflow error, whereas it is common practice to substitute zero for a number that causes an underflow error – not always an appropriate response, as it may, for example, lead to a subsequent 'divide by zero' error. One simple scheme for reducing the likelihood of an overflow error occurring is to impose a maximum allowable step length l^{max}. Taking as an example the Newton step s_k^N of Section 2.12, it is possible to 'rescale' s_k^N according to the expression

$$\bar{s}_k = s_k^N \frac{l^{max}}{\left\| s_k^N \right\|_2} \tag{2.23}$$

whenever $\| s_k^N \|_2 > l^{max}$. A typical value for l^{max} is 10^3 (Dennis and Schnabel, 1983). This scheme has the added advantage that it helps to prevent the algorithm leaving the domain of interest.

Fortunately, none of the algorithms presented in Chapter 3 has a reputation for being prone to overflow and underflow errors when properly implemented. Rounding errors, on the other hand, are endemic in floating-point arithmetic. A machine-independent measure of the precision achievable on a given computer is the *machine precision* or *machine epsilon*, defined as the smallest positive real number

ε such that $1+\varepsilon>1$. As we shall see, certain aspects of the algorithms discussed in this chapter depend directly on the available machine precision (for example, the choice of termination criteria and the size of finite-difference interval). Assuming a machine uses 'correct' rounding – i.e. numbers are rounded up or down to the nearest representable number, rather than merely truncated – the *relative error* in representing a non-zero real number x is given by

$$\frac{\left|x - \text{fl}(x)\right|}{|x|} \leq \frac{\varepsilon}{2} \tag{2.24}$$

where $\text{fl}(x)$ is the floating-point representation of x. However, although the relative error in representing a single real number is comparatively small (or zero), certain computations risk introducing much greater relative errors, notably the subtraction of two nearly identical numbers – known as *cancellation errors* – and the addition of a sequence of numbers (particularly a sequence of numbers with decreasing absolute values). Methods that are prone to the accumulation of rounding errors are said to be *unstable*. (For a detailed consideration of the role of rounding errors in computer arithmetic see Wilkinson (1963), the seminal work in this field.)

When implemented correctly, none of the classical algorithms discussed in this book has a reputation for numerical instability. However, it is advisable that at least 10–15 base 10 digits of accuracy are available when implementing these algorithms. This amounts to *double precision* arithmetic on an IBM-compatible PC. (Algorithms that are specifically designed to be used with single precision arithmetic are to be found in Nash (1990).)

2.2.2 Positive Definiteness and the Model Hessian

In order to exploit the quadratic model given by (2.13), many second-order methods maintain an explicit model of the Hessian matrix (G), known as the *model Hessian* (commonly denoted H). Although the accuracy of the second-order information stored in the model Hessian varies from method to method (for example, Newton's method calculates the Hessian exactly at each iteration, whereas quasi-Newton methods generate an iterative approximation of G), the form in which the model Hessian is represented in practice has a direct bearing on the reliability and efficiency of all such methods.

The straightforward implementation of the model Hessian as an unmodified $N \times N$ matrix is unsatisfactory for two reasons:

- The model Hessian H_k may be indefinite. If H_k is positive definite, the search direction

$$\mathbf{p}_k = -\mathbf{H}_k^{-1}\mathbf{g}_k \tag{2.25}$$

  is guaranteed to be a descent direction, and successive search directions are exceedingly unlikely to converge to a (strong) saddle point – let alone a maximum – rather than a minimum (Dennis and Schnabel, 1983). Moreover, if H_k is positive definite, it is guaranteed to be non-singular and therefore invertible, so that (2.25) is well-posed.

- The solution of (2.25) requires the inversion of the Hessian matrix at the cost of $O(N^3)$ multiplications per iteration. In practice, therefore, there is a risk that the inversion of the model Hessian will dominate the computational costs of a given method.

In the remainder of this section we consider strategies for overcoming both of these problems.

One obvious way of reducing the computational cost of solving (2.25) is to maintain a model of the inverse Hessian $\mathbf{G}^{-1}$ rather than $\mathbf{G}$ itself; using this representation the computational cost falls to $O(N^2)$ multiplications per iteration. This approach is feasible for the quasi-Newton methods of Section 3.3.2, because any quasi-Newton update can be reformulated to produce a theoretically equivalent update incorporating the inverse model Hessian (see, for example, the inverse Hessian update formulae (3.53) and (3.54) for the DFP and BFGS quasi-Newton methods respectively).

Although the inverse Hessian approach often produces satisfactory results, there is no convenient mechanism for regulating the positive definiteness of the inverse model Hessian. A more sophisticated approach is to represent $\mathbf{H}$ by its 'modified Cholesky factors'. As we shall see, this representation requires only $O(N^2)$ operations per iteration, and involves perturbing an indefinite model Hessian in a way that guarantees positive definiteness. For these reasons, the preferred representation of the model Hessian in the classical optimisation literature is the modified Cholesky factorisation.

The standard *Cholesky factorisation* can be represented in several forms, notably

$$\mathbf{H}_k = \mathbf{L}_k \mathbf{D}_k \mathbf{L}_k^T \tag{2.26}$$

where $\mathbf{L}_k$ is a unit lower triangular matrix (i.e. all diagonals are 1) and $\mathbf{D}_k$ a diagonal matrix with positive diagonal elements, and

$$\mathbf{H}_k = \bar{\mathbf{L}}_k \bar{\mathbf{L}}_k^T = \mathbf{R}_k^T \mathbf{R}_k \tag{2.27}$$

where $\bar{\mathbf{L}}_k$ is a general lower triangular matrix and $\mathbf{R}_k$ a general upper triangular matrix. (In terms of factors $\mathbf{L}$ and $\mathbf{D}$ in (2.26), factor $\bar{\mathbf{L}}$ in (2.27) is given by $\bar{\mathbf{L}} = \mathbf{L}\mathbf{D}^{1/2}$.) Stored in any of these forms, it is no longer necessary to invert the model Hessian in order to calculate $\mathbf{p}_k$ in (2.25); instead, $\mathbf{p}_k$ can be calculated by solving the linear system

$$\mathbf{H}_k \mathbf{p}_k = -\mathbf{g}_k \tag{2.28}$$

To see how this works in practice, let us consider the more general problem of solving the linear system

$$\mathbf{A}\mathbf{x} = \mathbf{b} \tag{2.29}$$

where the non-singular $N{\times}N$ matrix $\mathbf{A}$ has the factored form

$$A = A_1 \cdot A_2 \cdot \ldots \cdot A_M \qquad (2.30)$$

Provided each A_i ($i=1,...,M$) is of a form for which the solution of (2.29) is computationally easy, the desired solution x can be computed by solving, in order,

$$A_1 b_1 = b_0$$

$$A_2 b_2 = b_1$$

$$\vdots \qquad\qquad (2.31)$$

$$A_M b_M = b_{M-1}$$

where b_0 is the original vector b in (2.29), and vector b_M is the desired solution x.

How a given $A_i \, b_i = b_{i-1}$ in (2.31) is solved depends on the form of matrix A_i. In the case where A_i is a lower triangular matrix (either L in (2.26) or $\overline{L}$ in (2.27)), the solution can be found by a process known as *forward substitution*, at an approximate cost of only $N^2/2$ multiplications and additions. To show what this entails, let us consider the solution of the linear system

$$Ly = c \qquad (2.32)$$

which becomes, when written 'in full',

$$\begin{pmatrix} L_{11} & & & & \\ L_{21} & L_{22} & & & \\ L_{31} & L_{32} & L_{33} & & \\ \vdots & \vdots & \vdots & \ddots & \\ L_{N1} & L_{N2} & L_{N3} & \cdots & L_{NN} \end{pmatrix} \begin{pmatrix} y_1 \\ y_2 \\ y_3 \\ \vdots \\ y_N \end{pmatrix} = \begin{pmatrix} c_1 \\ c_2 \\ c_3 \\ \vdots \\ c_N \end{pmatrix} \qquad (2.33)$$

It is easy to see from (2.33) that the first element of vector y is immediately available by

$$y_1 = \frac{c_1}{L_{11}} \qquad (2.34)$$

Once element y_1 is known, the other elements y_i ($i=2,...,N$) can be calculated sequentially from $i=2$ to $i=N$ by the forward substitution formula

$$y_i = \frac{c_i - \sum_{j=1}^{i-1} L_{ij} y_j}{L_{ii}} \qquad (2.35)$$

If, on the other hand, we replace matrix L in (2.32) by an upper triangular matrix (for example, matrix R in (2.27)), the solution can be found by *back substitution*, starting with element y_N with the same computational costs as forward substitution. Note that, if matrix L is singular (or nearly singular), the problem given by equation (2.32) is not numerically well posed. (One of the key advantages of the modified Cholesky factorisation, discussed later in this section, is that a non-singular triangular matrix is guaranteed.)

The algorithm for calculating the Cholesky factors is known as the *Cholesky decomposition*. In terms of the unit lower triangular matrix L and positive diagonal matrix D in (2.26), the elements of H are given by

$$H_{kk} = \sum_{i=1}^{k} D_{ii} L_{ki}^2$$

$$H_{jk} = \sum_{i=1}^{k} D_{ii} L_{ji} L_{ki}, \quad j = k+1,...,N$$

(2.36)

(The elements H_{jk} for $j<k$ are available by symmetry, i.e. $H_{jk}=H_{kj}$.) By rearranging (2.36) we get the formula

$$D_{kk} = H_{kk} - \sum_{i=1}^{k-1} D_{ii} L_{ki}^2$$

(2.37)

for calculating the diagonal elements of factor **D**, and the formula

$$L_{jk} = \frac{H_{jk} - \sum_{i=1}^{k-1} D_{ii} L_{ji} L_{ki}}{D_{kk}}, \quad j = k+1,...,N$$

(2.38)

for calculating the elements of factor **L**. The corresponding formulae for calculating the elements of the general lower triangular matrix $\bar{L}$ in (2.27) are

$$\bar{L}_{kk} = \left(H_{kk} - \sum_{i=1}^{k-1} \bar{L}_{ki}^2 \right)^{1/2}$$

(2.39)

and

$$\bar{L}_{jk} = \frac{H_{jk} - \sum_{i=1}^{k-1} \bar{L}_{ji} \bar{L}_{ki}}{\bar{L}_{kk}}, \quad j = k+1,...,N$$

(2.40)

The Cholesky decomposition requires $O(N^3)$ operations (with an additional N square roots if the factorisation is of the form given by (2.27)). However, if H_{k+1} differs from H_k in a particularly simple way – as is the case with the quasi-Newton methods of Section 3.3.2 (see, in particular, equation (3.48)) – it is possible to *update* the Cholesky factors at each iteration (rather than calculate them afresh) in $O(N^2)$ operations. (This is discussed briefly in Section 3.3.2.)

The problem with the standard Cholesky factorisation (whether in the form given by (2.26) or (2.27)) is that it requires H_k to be both symmetric and positive definite. A modified version of the standard factorisation – the *modified Cholesky factorisation* in Gill *et al.* (1981) – detects and 'corrects' an indefinite model Hessian so that (2.26) becomes

$$\overline{H}_k = L_k D_k L_k^T = H_k + E_k$$

(2.41)

where $\overline{H}_k$ is a positive-definite matrix and E_k a non-negative diagonal matrix. In other words, $\overline{H}_k$ differs from H_k – if at all – only in its diagonal elements. To ensure that the 'correction' matrix E is not much larger than necessary, the modified Cholesky factors are computed subject to two requirements: first, that all the diagonal elements of matrix D are strictly positive, i.e. for all j ($j=1,...,N$)

$$D_{jj} > \delta \tag{2.42}$$

where δ is some small positive value; and second, that the elements of factors D and L satisfy a uniform bound, i.e. for $j=1,...,N$

$$\left| L_{ij} \sqrt{D_{jj}} \right| \leq \beta, \quad i > j \tag{2.43}$$

for some positive scalar β. Parameter β in (2.43) is chosen to satisfy

$$\beta^2 = \max\left\{ \gamma, \frac{\xi}{\sqrt{N^2 - 1}}, \varepsilon \right\} \tag{2.44}$$

where ε is the machine precision, and terms γ and ξ are the maximum magnitudes of, respectively, the diagonal and off-diagonal elements of H. The modified Cholesky decomposition in the form given by equation (2.26) is summarised in Algorithm 2.3. This algorithm (which is based on the algorithm in Gill *et al.* (1981)) is renowned for its numerical stability and requires no additional storage beyond that used for H, as both the intermediate values that arise during the calculation and the Cholesky factor themselves can be stored in the relevant parts of H as they are computed. (For clarity, the intermediate values are denoted C_{ij}.)

Algorithm 2.3 The modified Cholesky decomposition
1. Compute β by (2.44)
2. Set $C_{ii}=H_{ii}$, $i=1,...,N$
3. **FROM** $j=1$ **TO** $j=N$
   - 3.1 Find the index q such that $|C_{qq}| = \max\{|C_{ii}|\}$, for $i = j,...,N$
   - 3.2 Interchange all information in rows and columns q and j of H
   - 3.3 Calculate $C_{ij} = H_{ij} - \Sigma_{k=1}^{j-1} L_{jk} C_{ik}$ for $i = j+1,...,N$
   - 3.4 IF $j<N$
     - 3.4.1 Find $\theta_j = \max\{|C_{ij}|\}$, for $i = j+1,...,N$
     - **ELSE**
     - 3.4.2 Set $\theta_j=0$
   - 3.5 Compute $D_{jj} = \max\left\{ \delta, |C_{jj}|, \theta_j^2 / \beta^2 \right\}$ and $E_{jj} = D_{jj} - C_{jj}$, where E_{jj} is the jth diagonal element of correction matrix E in (2.41)
   - 3.6 IF $j<N$
     - 3.6.1 Set $L_{jk} = C_{jk}/D_{kk}$, for $k=1,...,j-1$
     - 3.6.2 Set $C_{ii} = C_{ii} - L_{ij}C_{ij}$, for $i = j+1,...,N$

A further modification, proposed by Dennis and Schnabel (1983), uses the diagonal matrix E in (2.41) as a means of regulating the positive definiteness of the model Hessian via the model-trust region parameter $\mu_k \geq 0$ in (2.21). If the diagonal elements of E_k are zero, the model Hessian is safely positive definite, hence $\mu_k = 0$. Otherwise, μ_k is set to the minimum of two upper bounds (b_1 and b_2) on the value of μ_k necessary to make H_k positive definite. The first upper bound b_1 derives from the Gerschgorin circle theorem, which shows that a square and symmetric matrix A that is *strictly diagonally dominant* – i.e. for all i ($i=1,...,N$),

$$A_{ii} - \sum_{j=1, j \neq i}^{N} \left| A_{ij} \right| > 0 \tag{2.45}$$

– is also positive definite; b_1 is simply the smallest value of μ_k that will make H_k strictly diagonally dominant. The second upper bound b_2 is the maximum diagonal element of matrix E_k. Although the value of μ_k chosen by this scheme may be larger than the smallest possible μ_k that guarantees positive definiteness (i.e. slightly larger than the magnitude of the most negative eigenvalue of the original matrix), it is both simple and comparatively cheap to compute.

2.2.3   Scaling and Preconditioning

In Section 2.1.1 it was shown that the steepest descent method is exceedingly sensitive to the scale of the independent variables x. Second-order methods are typically far less sensitive to 'sub-optimal' scaling than steepest descent. Indeed, certain Newton-related methods (including the efficient DFP and BFGS quasi-Newton methods discussed in Section 3.3.2.) are theoretically *scale-invariant*, i.e. invariant under linear transformations of the variable space. Nevertheless, all classical methods are prone to numerical problems – ranging from a general degradation in performance and loss of stability to premature termination of the multivariate algorithm – if the scale of either the independent variables x or the function F is sufficiently poor. In practice, even 'scale-invariant' algorithms are affected by poor scaling, because finite floating-point arithmetic is scale-dependent (see Section 2.2.1), and termination, step length and other criteria rely on implicit definitions of 'large' and 'small' (Gill *et al.*, 1981). (It is worth noting that Newton-related methods are not scale-invariant – even in theory – when implemented with a model-trust region strategy, because of the role of the scale-sensitive steepest descent direction in defining the step s_k, as described in Section 2.1.3.)

Most *scaling schemes* modify the scale of the independent variables x according to the linear transformation

$$\hat{x} = Ax \tag{2.46}$$

where A is a non-singular matrix. If $\hat{F}$ is the function of the transformed variables, i.e.

$$\hat{F}(x) = F(Ax)$$

$$\hat{F}(\hat{x}) = F(A^{-1}\hat{x}) \tag{2.47}$$

the corresponding first derivatives are given by

$$\hat{g}(\mathbf{x}) = \mathbf{A}^T g(\mathbf{x})$$
$$\hat{g}(\hat{\mathbf{x}}) = \mathbf{A}^{-T} g(\mathbf{x})$$

(2.48)

and the second derivatives by

$$\hat{G}(\mathbf{x}) = \mathbf{A}^T G(\mathbf{x})\mathbf{A}$$
$$\hat{G}(\hat{\mathbf{x}}) = \mathbf{A}^{-T} G(\mathbf{x})\mathbf{A}^{-1}$$

(2.49)

The most widely used scaling schemes for multivariate optimisation represent $\mathbf{A}$ in (2.46) by a diagonal matrix ($\mathbf{D}$). The simplest approach is to initialise $\mathbf{D}$ according to a set of N user-defined *scale factors*, representing the anticipated ranges of the elements of $\mathbf{x}$. For example, if the anticipated range of element x_i is approximately $[-10^3, 10^3]$, the ith diagonal element of $\mathbf{D}$ can be set to the reciprocal $1/10^3$. Unfortunately, such a scheme depends on the availability of useful prior knowledge about the problem structure, which cannot be guaranteed for minimisation tasks in general. In the absence of any useful information, the diagonal elements of $\mathbf{D}$ are initialised to 1.0. (A possible set of 'natural' scale factors for multi-layer perceptrons is given in Rigler *et al.* (1991).)

A more sophisticated approach – known as *preconditioning* – involves transforming the Hessian matrix in such a way that matrix $\hat{G}$ has a low condition number (κ). Before examining specific preconditioning schemes, it is important to understand the significance of condition number $\kappa(G)$ with respect to the scale of $\mathbf{x}$ and F. Let us consider the solution of the linear system $Gs=-g$. If $\kappa(G)$ is 'large', small changes in G or g may produce large changes in step s; G is said to be *ill-conditioned*. If, on the other hand, $\kappa(G)$ is 'small', changes in G or g will produce similar relative changes in s, and G is said to be *well-conditioned*. The condition number of G can, in short, be viewed as a measure of the maximum sensitivity of the solution of $Gs=-g$ both to changes in the data and to the effects of finite-precision arithmetic.

If the Hessian G is positive definite and remains relatively constant in the domain of interest, the optimal preconditioning matrix $\mathbf{A}$ is given by

$$\mathbf{A} = G(\mathbf{x}_*)^{-1/2}$$

(2.50)

where $\mathbf{A}$ is an $N{\times}N$ matrix. Matrix $\mathbf{A}$ in (2.50) sets $\hat{G}(\hat{\mathbf{x}}_*)$ – the Hessian at the solution of the transformed problem – to the identity matrix $\mathbf{I}$, so that $\kappa[\hat{G}(\mathbf{x}_*)]=1$. Assuming $G(\mathbf{x}_*)$ is not known, the $\mathbf{A}$ in equation (2.50) can be approximated using $G(\mathbf{x}_0)$, or (if second derivatives are unavailable) a finite-difference approximation of $G(\mathbf{x}_0)$. However, unless G is positive definite and remains relatively constant – properties which cannot be guaranteed in general – there is a risk that such an approach will actually degrade the performance of the multivariate algorithm. Although it is possible to overcome this problem by recalculating $\mathbf{A}$ periodically (*adaptive preconditioning*), the high cost of evaluating G or computing its approximation means that this approach cannot be recommended in a neural network context. Moreover, for methods which have, as one of their main competitive advantages, $O(N)$ storage requirements (such as the 'memoryless' quasi-Newton method of Section 3.3.3 and conjugate gradient methods of Section 3.3.4), the $O(N^2)$ storage cost for **A** in (2.50) is a significant disadvantage. Similar drawbacks apply to the Cholesky factor $\overline{\mathbf{L}}$ in (2.27), which can be used (as a direct alternative to **G** in (2.50)) to set matrix **A** according to the expression $\mathbf{A} = \overline{\mathbf{L}}^{-1}$ (Fletcher, 1987).

A more practical approach is to represent the preconditioning matrix **A** by a diagonal matrix **D**, and to set the elements of **D** so as to lower the condition number of the Hessian matrix, $\kappa(\mathbf{G})$. Such an approach requires knowledge about $\kappa(\mathbf{G})$. To calculate $\kappa(\mathbf{G})$ exactly by (2.11) is prohibitive, as it requires the exact calculation of all the eigenvalues of **G**, which has $O(N^3)$ computational costs. What is needed, therefore, is a suitable estimate of $\kappa(\mathbf{G})$, for which a number of different schemes have been devised.

Let us begin by considering the case where the model Hessian **H** is represented by its modified Cholesky factors (see (2.41)), so that **H** is guaranteed to be positive definite. In this case, we already have a diagonal matrix – the Cholesky factor **D** in (2.26) with positive diagonal elements. In terms of Cholesky factor **D**, $\kappa(\mathbf{H})$ satisfies

$$\kappa(\mathbf{H}) \geq \frac{D_{\max}}{D_{\min}} \tag{2.51}$$

where $D_{\max}$ and $D_{\min}$ are the largest and smallest diagonal elements of **D**. However, the estimate of $\kappa(\mathbf{H})$ provided by (2.51) is fairly crude. (A much better, but computationally expensive, estimate of $\kappa(\mathbf{H})$ utilising the Cholesky factors of the Hessian matrix is given in Gill et al. (1981).)

When the Hessian matrix is not represented explicitly, it is possible to estimate $\kappa(\mathbf{G})$ using the *Power method*. Because the estimate of the smallest eigenvalue of **G** ($\lambda_{\min}$) by the Power method can be unstable, Møller (1993d) proposes a scheme which seeks to minimise the function

$$M(\mathbf{D}) = \left| \frac{\lambda_{\max}}{\langle \lambda \rangle} \right| \tag{2.52}$$

where $\lambda_{\max}$ is the largest eigenvalue and $\langle \lambda \rangle$ the average eigenvalue of the matrix $\hat{G}(\mathbf{x}_k) = \mathbf{D}^T G(\mathbf{x}_k)\mathbf{D}$, henceforth denoted $\hat{\mathbf{G}}_k$. Scalar $\langle \lambda \rangle$ can be calculated by

$$\langle \lambda \rangle = \tfrac{1}{N} Tr\left(\hat{\mathbf{G}}_k\right) \tag{2.53}$$

where $Tr(\hat{\mathbf{G}}_k)$ is the trace of matrix $\hat{\mathbf{G}}_k$, i.e. the algebraic sum of the elements in the leading diagonal of $\hat{\mathbf{G}}_k$.

Møller's approach is to adapt matrix **D** by gradient descent, utilising the gradient of $M(\mathbf{D})$, which is given by

$$M'(\mathbf{D}) = \text{sign}\left(\frac{\lambda_{\max}}{\langle \lambda \rangle}\right) \frac{1}{\langle \lambda \rangle^2}\left(\frac{d\lambda_{\max}}{d\mathbf{D}}\langle \lambda \rangle - \frac{d\langle \lambda \rangle}{d\mathbf{D}}\lambda_{\max}\right) \tag{2.54}$$

As Møller points out, the hard part of the adaptation is the estimation of λ_{max} (the largest eigenvalue of $\hat{\mathbf{G}}_k$) and its derivative. In terms of eigenvector $\mathbf{v}_{max}^T$ (i.e. the eigenvector corresponding to eigenvalue λ_{max}) and matrix $\hat{\mathbf{G}}_k$, λ_{max} is given by

$$\lambda_{max} = \frac{\mathbf{v}_{max}^T \hat{\mathbf{G}}_k \mathbf{v}_{max}}{\mathbf{v}_{max}^T \mathbf{v}_{max}} \tag{2.55}$$

and the derivative of λ_{max} with respect to matrix $\mathbf{D}$ is given by

$$\frac{d\lambda_{max}}{d\mathbf{D}} = \frac{\mathbf{v}_{max}^T (d\mathbf{G}_k / d\mathbf{D}) \mathbf{v}_{max}}{\mathbf{v}_{max}^T \mathbf{v}_{max}} \tag{2.56}$$

This leads to the following iterative algorithm for the *extended Power method*, devised by Møller (1993d), which can be used to calculate the diagonal elements of preconditioning matrix $\mathbf{D}$ every $K \geq 1$ iterations of the chosen multivariate algorithm.

Algorithm 2.4 The extended Power method
1 Choose a random vector $\mathbf{v}_{max}^0$, and initial values for parameters $T>0$, $M>0$ and $\mu_0>0$
2 **DO** the following **FROM** $t=1$ **TO** $t=T$:
   2.1 **DO** the following **FROM** $m=1$ **TO** $m=M$:
      2.1.1 Calculate $\mathbf{v}_{max}^m = \hat{\mathbf{G}}_k \mathbf{v}_{max}^{m-1}$
      2.1.2 Calculate

$$\lambda_{max}^m = \frac{\left(\mathbf{v}_{max}^{m-1}\right)^T \mathbf{v}_{max}^m}{\left(\mathbf{v}_{max}^{m-1}\right)^T \mathbf{v}_{max}^{m-1}}$$

      2.1.3 Set $\mathbf{v}_{max}^m = \left(1/\lambda_{max}^m\right)\mathbf{v}_{max}^m$
   2.2 Set $\lambda_{max} = \lambda_{max}^M$ and $\mathbf{v}_{max} = \mathbf{v}_{max}^M$
   2.3 Calculate derivative $d\lambda_{max}/d\mathbf{D}$ by (2.56)
   2.4 Set the diagonal elements of $\mathbf{D}$ (D_{ii}, for $i=1,...,N$) according to

$$D_{ii} = D_{ii} - \mu_{i,t} \, \text{sign}\left(\frac{\lambda_{max}}{\langle\lambda\rangle}\right) \frac{1}{\langle\lambda\rangle^2}\left(\frac{d\lambda_{max}}{dD_{ii}}\langle\lambda\rangle - \frac{d\langle\lambda\rangle}{dD_{ii}}\lambda_{max}\right) \tag{2.57}$$

where parameter $\mu_{i,t}$ is given by

$$\mu_{i,t} = \begin{cases} 1.1\mu_{i,t-1}, & \text{if } \Delta D_{ii,t}\,\Delta D_{ii,t-1} > 0 \\ 0.1\mu_{i,t-1}, & \text{otherwise} \end{cases} \tag{2.58}$$

The optimal settings for user-defined parameters K, T, M and μ_0 are problem-specific. Møller suggests that a suitable $\mathbf{D}$ can often be calculated with parameters T and M set to small values, with a configuration that yields $MT/K=1$ 'not unusual'. For example, Møller found that $K=7$, $T=14$, $M=1$ and $\mu_0=1$ gave good results when training MLPs on the XOR benchmark training task (see Section 5.1.1) using backpropagation. Møller reports that adaptive preconditioning using the extended Power method can improve the convergence rate of first-order methods by several orders of magnitude. However, the improvement for second-order methods is likely to be relatively modest.

One potential problem with the extended Power method as described above is that matrix $\mathbf{D}$ is not certain to be positive definite. To guarantee positive definiteness, Møller proposes that each diagonal element of $\mathbf{D}$ is squashed using a sigmoid function $f(\cdot)$ (see equation (1.2)), so that the trace of $\hat{\mathbf{G}}_k$ becomes

$$Tr\left(\hat{\mathbf{G}}_k\right) = \sum_{i=1}^{N} f\left(D_{ii}\right)^2 \left[G(\mathbf{x}_k)\right]_{ii} \tag{2.59}$$

(Note that it is possible to calculate both the trace of $\hat{\mathbf{G}}_k$ and the term $\hat{\mathbf{G}}_k \mathbf{v}_{\max}^{m-1}$ exactly with an MLP utilising the algorithms discussed in Chapter 4.) Møller further recommends that each D_{ii} is constrained to the heuristic range $[-6,+6]$, in order to keep the derivative of each squashed element $f(D_{ii})$ away from zero.

3. *Second-Order Optimisation Methods*

With the essential background information of Chapter 2 behind us, we are ready to turn our attention to specific second-order optimisation methods. The survey of multivariate second-order methods presented in this chapter is necessarily selective, with the focus on tried and tested methods that have a reputation for both speed and reliability. Two types of multivariate second-order method are considered – general methods (Section 3.3), and nonlinear least-squares methods (Section 3.4). The former are suitable for finding a minimum of any smooth nonlinear function $F(\mathbf{x}_k)$; the latter are suitable only when $F(\mathbf{x}_k)$ is of the special form given by (1.5).

Nearly all of the methods described in Sections 3.3 and 3.4 can be implemented as line-search methods or as model-trust region methods (see discussion in Section 2.1.3). Descriptions of, and algorithms for, specific line-search and model-trust region strategies are given in Sections 3.1 and 3.2 respectively. The algorithms in Sections 3.1 and 3.2 serve as a framework for implementing the various multivariate second-order methods discussed later in the chapter. For clarity, schemes for scaling the independent variables and for enforcing a maximum step length are omitted from these algorithms; however, these matters – together with the other implementation-related issues covered in Chapter 2 – should be taken into account when implementing the algorithms in practice.

Broadly speaking, the aim of all the multivariate second-order methods discussed in Sections 3.3 and 3.4 is to generate successive search directions that are superior to the steepest descent direction ($-\mathbf{g}$). Where the methods differ is in the strategy used to define a suitable search direction $\mathbf{p}_k$ at each iteration k, in their computational and storage costs, in their theoretical and practical rates of convergence, and in their reputation for numerical stability. None of these methods is clearly superior; indeed, there are circumstances where each one might be considered the method of choice. A comparative assessment of the various merits of each method is presented in Section 3.5. However, it is worth stressing that the most effective second-order method for tackling a specific minimisation problem can only be determined empirically.

3.1   Line-Search Strategies

For classical methods with line searches, the sub-task of locating the minimum along search direction p_k at each iteration – known as *line minimisation* – is theoretically equivalent to the task of finding the minimum of a function with a single variable – known as *one-dimensional* or *univariate minimisation*. Consequently, our discussion of line-search strategies begins (in Section 3.1.1) by contemplating the minimisation of an arbitrary smooth univariate function f with scalar minimum x_* and gradient g. In practice, however, the priorities for a line-search strategy used as part of a multivariate algorithm are somewhat different from those of univariate minimisation; in the context of multivariate optimisation, the effectiveness of a given line-search strategy is measured in terms of the overall reduction in multi-variable function F (as opposed to the sub-task of locating a minimum along search direction p_k). As we shall see, the modern preference is for inaccurate line searches (Section 3.1.2) with low computational costs, such as backtracking line searches (Section 3.1.3).

In practice, line-search algorithms may be coded using either vector-valued or scalar points. The second alternative requires some mechanism for evaluating the multi-dimensional function F in a single dimension. One simple device, described in Press *et al.* (1992), is to provide an 'artificial' uni-dimensional function $f(\alpha)$ which evaluates F at $x_k + \alpha p_k$. Since line minimisation is an iterative process, the suffix m will be used for line-search iterations to prevent confusion with the k iterations of the multivariate algorithm.

A prerequisite for all the line searches considered below is that p_k satisfies (2.4), i.e. p_k is a descent direction. Direction p_k is guaranteed to be a descent direction with the steepest descent method (provided the gradient is greater than zero), but this cannot be guaranteed in general. If the multivariate algorithm generates a p_k that is not a descent direction, the obvious solution is to reset p_k to the steepest descent direction, $-g_k$. An unfortunate by-product of *resetting* the algorithm is that potentially useful second-order information is automatically discarded. (Avoiding the necessity of resetting the algorithm is one of the major motivations for regulating the positive definiteness of the model Hessian, as described in Section 2.2.2.)

3.1.1   Line Minimisation Fundamentals

There are two broad strategies commonly used to locate a minimum x_* of univariate function f – function comparison (or interval reduction) and function approximation (commonly known as polynomial interpolation).

Given two initial values of x (x_a and x_b) which bracket x_*, *function comparison methods* iteratively reduce the interval in which x_* lies – the *interval of uncertainty* – by a fixed ratio. Linear convergence is guaranteed for *unimodal functions*. There are several non-equivalent definitions of a unimodal function in the classical optimisation literature (for example, Brent (1973) gives three different definitions). For present purposes, a function $f(x)$ is considered unimodal in the interval $[a,b]$ if, given any $x_1, x_2 \in [a,b]$ with $x_1 < x_2$, there is a unique minimum $x_* \in [a,b]$ such that $f(x_1) > f(x_2)$ if $x_2 < x_*$, and $f(x_1) < f(x_2)$ if $x_1 > x_*$. In other words, f decreases strictly monotonically between a and x_*, and increases strictly monotonically between x_* and b.

The most widely used function comparison strategy, known as *golden section search*, ensures that the interval at iteration $m+1$ is approximately 0.618 (the golden section) times the size of the interval at m. In terms of the maximum reduction of the interval for a given number of function definitions, golden section search is almost as efficient as the 'optimal' strategy, Fibonacci search. The latter is considered impractical as it requires the storage or generation of m Fibonacci numbers for m function evaluations, where m is generally not known in advance.

Function comparison methods are reliable, but make no attempt to exploit the smoothness of function f. The second approach commonly used to locate a minimum x_* of f – *polynomial interpolation* – approximates f by a simple function $\hat{f}$ and uses $\hat{f}$ to estimate the minimum of f. Typically $\hat{f}$ is a *parabolic* (quadratic) or *cubic* polynomial. *Parabolic interpolation* requires three pieces of data about function f – typically $f(x_a)$, $f(x_b)$ and $f(x_c)$. The formula for calculating the stationary point $\hat{x}_*$ of the parabola (second-order polynomial) passing through three points x_a, x_b and x_c is given by

$$\hat{x}_* = \frac{1}{2} \frac{\left(x_b^2 - x_c^2\right)f(x_a) + \left(x_c^2 - x_a^2\right)f(x_b) + \left(x_a^2 - x_b^2\right)f(x_c)}{(x_b - x_c)f(x_a) + (x_c - x_a)f(x_b) + (x_a - x_b)f(x_c)} \qquad (3.1)$$

Under suitable conditions, the local convergence rate of parabolic interpolation methods is super-linear. *Cubic interpolation*, on the other hand, requires four pieces of information about f – typically $f(x_a)$, $g(x_a)$, $f(x_b)$ and $g(x_b)$. The formula for calculating stationary point $\hat{x}_*$ of the cubic (third-order) polynomial passing through two points x_a and x_b is given by

$$\hat{x}_* = (x_b - x_a)\left[1 - \frac{g(x_b) + \gamma - \beta}{g(x_b) - g(x_a) + 2\gamma}\right] \qquad (3.2)$$

where terms β and γ are defined by

$$\beta = g(x_a) + g(x_b) - 3\frac{f(x_a) - f(x_b)}{x_a - x_b}$$

$$\gamma = \left[\beta^2 - g(x_a)g(x_b)\right]^{1/2} \qquad (3.3)$$

Under suitable conditions, the local convergence rate of cubic interpolation methods is quadratic.

There are two key problems with polynomial interpolation. Firstly, it is not specifically geared to minimisation; the stationary point $\hat{x}_*$ in (3.1) and (3.2) might as readily be a maximum as a minimum. Secondly, if $\hat{f}$ inaccurately approximates function f, polynomial interpolation is likely to be slow and unreliable. (In regions where f is comparatively non-smooth, lower order polynomials may prove more accurate than higher order polynomials.) For these reasons, global convergence is not guaranteed for polynomial interpolation in its unmodified form.

One way of modifying polynomial interpolation so that it is globally convergent is to combine it with a bracketing strategy to form a so-called *safeguarded polynomial interpolation* algorithm. Let us consider the case of safeguarded parabolic interpolation. The key feature of such an algorithm is that at each m iteration it maintains a triplet of points $x_{1,m}$, $x_{2,m}$ and $x_{3,m}$ which satisfy $x_{1,m} < x_{2,m} < x_{3,m}$ and $f(x_{1,m}) > f(x_{2,m}) < f(x_{3,m})$. Provided f is unimodal in the interval $[x_{1,1}, x_{3,1}]$ (i.e. the initial points x_1 and x_3 bracket a unique minimum), the parabolic fit to points $x_{1,m}$, $x_{2,m}$ and $x_{3,m}$ will have a minimum – rather than a maximum – in the interval $(x_{1,m}, x_{3,m})$ at each m iteration. A simple routine for establishing an initial bracketing triplet of points, which involves taking steps (of increasing size) downhill from the current location until an uphill step is located, is given in Press *et al.* (1992). (For a more extensive discussion of the global convergence properties of safeguarded polynomial interpolation algorithms, see Luenberger (1984).)

An example of a safeguarded polynomial interpolation algorithm is *Brent's method* (Brent, 1973), which is both widely used and well-regarded. Brent's method combines the strengths of interval reduction and polynomial interpolation in a single line-search algorithm with a convergence rate that approaches that of polynomial interpolation under favourable conditions, but remains close to the guaranteed rate of interval reduction in the worst case. One heuristic feature of Brent's method is that if, at a given m iteration, the interpolated step implies a movement from the best current value of x of less than half the movement of the last step but one, it switches to golden section search. Brent's method can be implemented with either parabolic or cubic interpolation. Although the latter is likely to take fewer m iterations on average, it requires the calculation of derivatives; if the cost of evaluating g and f is significantly more expensive than the cost of evaluating f alone, Brent's method with derivatives is likely to be less efficient than Brent's method without derivatives. Code for both versions of Brent's method is given in Press *et al.* (1992).

3.1.2 Inaccurate Line Searches

When a line search is used as part of a multivariate minimisation strategy, a key issue is the accuracy with which α_k is chosen to approximate the minimum along p_k. The trade-off between the effort expended to determine an α_k of a given accuracy and the corresponding benefit (in terms of the overall reduction in F) to the multivariate algorithm is problem- and algorithm-dependent. Given a sufficiently robust multivariate algorithm, current opinion clearly favours inaccurate line searches on grounds of efficiency.

The key issue when implementing an inaccurate line-search strategy is the choice of *step acceptance rule*. The common-sense requirement that step length α_k brings about a reduction in F (i.e. satisfies condition (2.19)) is insufficient to guarantee global convergence to a stationary point of F. What is needed is a rule that ensures that α_k brings about a sufficient reduction in F at each k iteration. A practical and popular condition for controlling the accuracy of α_k is

$$g\left(\mathbf{x}_k + \alpha_k \mathbf{p}_k\right)^T \mathbf{p}_k \geq \eta g\left(\mathbf{x}_k\right)^T \mathbf{p}_k \tag{3.4}$$

where scalar η is in the range $0 \leq \eta < 1$. Condition (3.4) ensures that the directional derivative $(\mathbf{g}^T\mathbf{p})$ at position $\mathbf{x}_{k+1}$ is greater than a prescribed fraction of that at position $\mathbf{x}_k$. The effect of (3.4) is to prevent steps that are too small relative to the rate of decrease of F at $\mathbf{x}_k$. If scalar η is set to a small value, an accurate line minimisation is performed, with $\eta=0$ giving an 'exact' line search. (For exact line searches, the limiting factor is the floating-point precision available; owing to rounding error, it is a waste of effort to evaluate $f(\mathbf{x}_m)$ if point $\mathbf{x}_m$ is closer than the square root of the machine precision to a previously evaluated point.) A variation on condition (3.4), advocated by Gill *et al.* (1981), is given by

$$\left| g\left(\mathbf{x}_k + \alpha_k \mathbf{p}_k\right)^T \mathbf{p}_k \right| \leq -\eta g\left(\mathbf{x}_k\right)^T \mathbf{p}_k \tag{3.5}$$

Condition (3.5) ensures that the *magnitude* of the directional derivative at position $\mathbf{x}_{k+1}$ is less than a prescribed fraction of that at position $\mathbf{x}_k$.

Since condition (3.4) takes no account of the actual reduction in F, it is usual to supplement it with the condition

$$F\left(\mathbf{x}_k\right) - F\left(\mathbf{x}_k + \alpha_k \mathbf{p}_k\right) \geq -\mu \alpha_k g\left(\mathbf{x}_k\right)^T \mathbf{p}_k \tag{3.6}$$

where μ is in the range $0 < \mu \leq 0.5$. Condition (3.6) ensures that the average rate of decrease of function F from $\mathbf{x}_k$ to $\mathbf{x}_{k+1}$ is sufficient with respect to the initial rate of decrease. Condition (3.6) prevents steps that are too long, i.e. steps which reduce F too slowly relative to the length of those steps.

Setting $q > \mu$ guarantees that equation (3.4) (or (3.5)) and equation (3.6) can be satisfied simultaneously; if μ is set to a small value (such as $\mu=10^{-4}$), a step α that satisfies (3.4) will almost certainly satisfy (3.6). Algorithms which satisfy both (3.4) and (3.6) at each iteration are globally convergent (under the mild assumptions that F is bounded below and the angle between $\mathbf{p}_k$ and $\mathbf{g}_k$ is bounded away from 90°) (Dennis and Schnabel, 1983). Moreover, since the Newton step $\mathbf{s}_k^N$ will satisfy both conditions simultaneously when $\mathbf{x}_k$ is close to $\mathbf{x}_*$ (assuming $\mathbf{G}$ is positive definite), (3.4) and (3.6) are compatible with fast rates of local convergence.

To test condition (3.4) or (3.5) entails the evaluation of the gradient $\mathbf{g}$ at each m iteration; conditions (3.4) and (3.5) are, therefore, inappropriate for line minimisation without derivatives. An alternative condition, proposed in Gill *et al.* (1981), replaces the left-hand side of (3.5) by a finite-difference approximation, i.e.

$$\frac{\left| F\left(\mathbf{x}_k + \alpha_k \mathbf{p}_k\right) - F\left(\mathbf{x}_k + v \mathbf{p}_k\right) \right|}{\alpha_k - v} \leq -\eta g\left(\mathbf{x}_k\right)^T \mathbf{p}_k \tag{3.7}$$

where v is a scalar satisfying $0 \leq v < \alpha$. With v set to zero, no additional function evaluations are required to test condition (3.7) at each m iteration.

3.1.3   Backtracking Line Searches

Using the strategies explored in the earlier part of Section 3.3 it is possible to devise an inaccurate safeguarded polynomial interpolation algorithm that is both globally convergent and reasonably efficient. However, such algorithms have two potential drawbacks: they entail a minimum of three function evaluations per k iteration (to establish the bracketing triplet described in Section 3.1.1) and they are not specifically geared to testing the suitability of the Newton step s^N (equivalent to αp for $\alpha=1$). The significance of the latter observation is that, for multivariate methods that derive from Newton's method, the Newton step is a 'natural' step to take at each iteration. Provided the Hessian matrix is positive definite, there is a good chance that s^N will produce an acceptable decrease in F; near the solution, allowing the full Newton step is a key to fast convergence (Dennis and Schnabel, 1983).

Backtracking line searches suffer from neither of the potential drawbacks associated with inaccurate safeguarded polynomial interpolation. At iteration $m=1$, backtracking line searches test the suitability of the Newton step s^N. Provided the chosen step acceptance rule requires only a small reduction in F, there is a good chance that step s^N will be acceptable. In the best case, therefore, backtracking line searches require only a single function evaluation per k iteration. If $F(x_k+s_\kappa^N)$ is not acceptable, backtracking algorithms iteratively 'backtrack' – that is, reduce step length α – until an acceptable F is found.

An example of a backtracking algorithm is that developed by Dennis and Schnabel (1983). The *Dennis–Schnabel backtracking algorithm* uses parabolic interpolation at iteration $m=2$ and cubic interpolation thereafter. The latter is performed without expensive derivative calculations by storing $F(x_k)$, $g(x_k)$ and the two most recent test values for $F(x_k + \alpha_{k,m}p_k)$. To prevent reductions in α that are too large or too small, the choice of α at a given m iteration is subject to upper and lower bounds as follows:

$$\alpha_{k,m+1} \geq l\alpha_{k,m}$$

$$\alpha_{k,m+1} \leq u\alpha_{k,m}, \qquad 0 < l < u < 1 \tag{3.8}$$

Dennis and Schnabel recommend a lower bound of $l=0.1$ and an upper bound of $u=0.5$.

Dennis and Schnabel present two versions of their backtracking line-search algorithm – a 'standard' version and a 'quasi-Newton' (or 'secant') version – which differ in the choice of step acceptance rule. With the 'standard' version, the condition given by (3.4) is deemed redundant because of the bounds placed on the choice of α by (3.8). However, when using their backtracking algorithm with quasi-Newton methods, Dennis and Schnabel recommend that (3.4) is satisfied explicitly at each iteration. (For an explanation of why this may be desirable, see Section 3.3.2.) Both versions of the Dennis–Schnabel backtracking algorithm implement condition (3.6) with parameter μ set to a small value (10^{-4}), so that a small reduction in F is sufficient for the acceptance of a given α. Clearly, the 'quasi-Newton' version of the algorithm is computationally more expensive, as it requires derivative calculations (unless condition (3.4) or (3.5) is replaced by (3.7)).

The following algorithm is for the 'standard' Dennis–Schnabel backtracking line-search algorithm. The algorithm is designed to be used at step 2.2 of the generic multivariate algorithm with line search (Algorithm 2.1) in Section 2.1.3. It is assumed that function $F(\mathbf{x}_k)$ and gradient $g(\mathbf{x}_k)$ have already been evaluated, and that search direction $\mathbf{p}_k$ is a descent direction.

Algorithm 3.1 The Dennis–Schnabel backtracking line-search algorithm
 1 Calculate slope $\sigma_k = \mathbf{g}_k^T \mathbf{p}_k$
 2 Set minimum allowable value of parameter α_k to

$$\alpha_{min} = \frac{\varepsilon^{2/3}}{\max_{1 \le i \le N} \left\{ |(p_i)_k| / \max\{|(x_i)_k|,1.0\} \right\}} \tag{3.9}$$

where ε is the machine precision (see Section 2.2.1), and $(p_i)_k$ and $(x_i)_k$ are the ith elements of $\mathbf{p}_k$ and $\mathbf{x}_k$ respectively
 3 Set $\alpha_{k,1}=1.0$ and *finished*=false
 4 At each m iteration from $m=1$, **DO** the following **UNTIL** *finished*=true:
   4.1 Set $\mathbf{x}_{k,m} = \mathbf{x}_{k,0} + \alpha_{k,m}\mathbf{p}_k$
   4.2 Evaluate $F_{k,m}=F(\mathbf{x}_{k,m})$
   4.3 **IF** condition (3.6) is satisfied **OR** $\alpha_m < \alpha_{min}$:
     4.3.1 Set *finished*=true
   ELSE
     4.3.2 **IF** $\alpha_{k,m} = 1.0$:
       4.3.2.1 Set $\bar{\alpha}$ using quadratic interpolation:

$$\bar{\alpha} = \frac{-\sigma_k}{2\left(F_{k,m} - F_{k,0} - \sigma_k\right)} \tag{3.10}$$

   ELSE
     4.3.2.2 Calculate scalars b and c:

$$b = \frac{\left[\left(d/\alpha_{k,m}^2\right) - \left(e/\alpha_{k,m-1}^2\right)\right]}{\alpha_{k,m} - \alpha_{k,m-1}}$$

$$c = \frac{\left[\left(-\alpha_{k,m-1}d/\alpha_{k,m}^2\right) + \left(\alpha_{k,m}e/\alpha_{k,m-1}^2\right)\right]}{\alpha_{k,m} - \alpha_{k,m-1}} \tag{3.11}$$

$$d = F_{k,m} - F_{k,0} - \alpha_{k,m}\sigma_k$$

$$e = F_{k,m-1} - F_{k,0} - \alpha_{k,m-1}\sigma_k$$

   4.3.2.3 **IF** $b=0.0$:
     4.3.2.3.1 Set $\bar{\alpha}$ using quadratic interpolation:

$$\bar{\alpha} = -\sigma / 2c \tag{3.12}$$

ELSE
   4.3.2.3.2 Set $\bar{\alpha}$ using cubic interpolation:

$$\bar{\alpha} = \frac{-c + \sqrt{c^2 - 3b\sigma_k}}{3b} \tag{3.13}$$

  4.3.2.4 IF $\bar{\alpha} > \lambda_m/2$:
    4.3.2.4.1 Set $\bar{\alpha} = \lambda_m/2$
  4.3.3 IF $\bar{\alpha} \leq \alpha_{k,m}/10$:
    4.3.3.1 Set $\alpha_{k,m+1} = \alpha_{k,m}/10$
ELSE
    4.3.3.2 Set $\alpha_{k,m+1} = \bar{\alpha}$

The 'quasi-Newton' version of the Dennis–Schnabel backtracking algorithm, which exploits the gradient information used to test condition (3.4) at every m iteration, is considerably more complicated. Algorithms for both versions of the Dennis–Schnabel backtracking algorithm can be found in the appendix to Dennis and Schnabel (1983); code for the 'standard' version is given in Press $et\ al.$ (1992).

There is no theoretical basis for using backtracking line searches with non-Newton-related multivariate methods (such as the conjugate gradient methods of Section 3.3.4), as the Newton step is not defined for such methods. It is therefore no surprise that conjugate gradient methods often converge slowly when implemented with backtracking line searches. However, in experiments conducted by the author, it has been found that a hybrid Brent/backtracking strategy is typically more effective than Brent's method alone with non-Newton related methods. The novel hybrid Brent/backtracking line search presented in Shepherd (1995) uses the efficient backtracking strategy under 'average' conditions, but switches to Brent's method under unfavourable conditions – that is, whenever the number of backtracking m iterations exceeds a user-defined limit (e.g. $m=3$), or the multivariate algorithm generates a search direction that is not a descent direction (i.e. $\mathbf{p}_k$ that fails to satisfy (2.4)). A few k iterations of Brent's method are often sufficient to find a position in a more favourable region of weight space, so that backtracking can be resumed without further interruption.

3.2 Model-Trust Region Strategies

When implementing second-order multivariate optimisation algorithms, the model-trust region approach has become an increasingly popular alternative to the long-established line-search approach. Within the broad framework for model-trust region strategies laid out in Section 2.1.3, a number of different approaches are possible. (Readers are advised to familiarise themselves with Algorithm 2.2 in Section 2.1.3 before proceeding.) The various model-trust region algorithms described in this section differ in several important aspects of their implementation, notably:

- whether radius parameter α in (2.20) is controlled directly, or indirectly via parameter μ in (2.21)
- the choice of criteria for assessing whether or not parameter α requires adjustment at a given iteration
- the choice of scheme for adjusting parameter α

For strategies that control α indirectly via parameter μ, an important consideration is the choice of μ_0. There is no 'natural' choice for μ_0. The usual advice is to set μ_0 to a 'small' value, but there is little agreement about just how small; Press *et al.* (1992) set $\mu_0=0.001$, Nash (1990) uses $\mu_0=0.0001$ and Møller (1993a) recommends $0 < \mu_0 \le 10^{-6}$.

3.2.1 A Simple Model-Trust Region Algorithm

We begin by considering an exceedingly simple model-trust region strategy, based on the Levenberg–Marquardt algorithms in Nash (1990) and Press *et al.* (1992). This strategy makes no serious attempt to assess the accuracy of the quadratic model at each iteration k. Rather, a given μ_k is deemed satisfactory or unsatisfactory purely on the basis of whether or not step s_k produces a reduction in F. If $F(x_k + s_k) < F(x_k)$, then μ_k is divided by a fixed *reduction constant* $\rho > 1$; if, on the other hand, $F(x_k+s_k) \ge F(x_k)$, then μ_k is multiplied by a fixed *growth constant* $\sigma > 1$. The algorithm is comparatively insensitive to the setting of the user-defined parameters ρ and σ, although it is advisable to set $\sigma > \rho$ so that recovery from a μ_k that fails to produce a reduction in F is comparatively rapid. (Typical settings for ρ and σ are $\rho=2$ and $\sigma=4$, or $\rho=4$ and $\sigma=10$, although the choice is essentially arbitrary.) The full strategy is given by the following algorithm.

Algorithm 3.2 A simple model-trust region strategy
  1 Choose a $\mu_0 > 0$ and random starting point x_0
  2 At each iteration k, do the following until termination criteria are satisfied:
    2.1 Compute a step s_k using the Hessian H_k, as modified by parameter μ_k in (2.21)
    2.2 Evaluate $F(x_k + s_k)$
    2.3 IF $F(x_k + s_k) < F(x_k)$:
      2.3.1 Set $x_{k+1} = x_k + s_k$
      2.3.2 Set $\mu_{k+1} = \mu_k/\rho$
    ELSE
      2.2.3 Set $x_{k+1} = x_k$
      2.2.4 Set $\mu_{k+1} = \sigma\mu_k$

This simple strategy often proves satisfactory in practice, and has minimal computational costs (beyond the inevitable cost of computing s_k at step 2.1). However, it is likely to be relatively inefficient; with reduction and growth constants set to typical values, the condition $F(\mathbf{x}_k + \mathbf{s}_k) \geq F(\mathbf{x}_k)$ is likely to occur on a fairly frequent basis, with the result that no progress will be made at a significant percentage of the total number of iterations. Another characteristic of this approach is that μ_k is either raised or lowered at every iteration. As a consequence, the value of parameter μ_k is prone to oscillate up and down in regions where the appropriate value of μ remains relatively constant. This behaviour is particularly severe if the reduction and growth constants are set to the same, relatively large, values (as advocated in Press *et al.* (1992)).

3.2.2 Fletcher's Method

A better strategy – sometimes called *Fletcher's method* (Wolfe, 1978) – is to choose a μ_k that ensures that 'sufficient' agreement is maintained between the actual and predicted quadratic error change at each iteration (ΔF_k and ΔQ_k respectively). This is conveniently measured in terms of the ratio r, given by

$$r_k = \frac{\Delta F_k}{\Delta Q_k} \tag{3.14}$$

where ΔF_k is simply

$$\Delta F_k = F\left(\mathbf{x}_k\right) - F\left(\mathbf{x}_k + \mathbf{s}_k\right) \tag{3.15}$$

The closer r_k is to 1, the better the approximation. The predicted error change ΔQ_k can be calculated according to the expression

$$\Delta Q_k = F\left(\mathbf{x}_k\right) - Q(\mathbf{s}_k) \tag{3.16}$$

where the current quadratic model $Q(\mathbf{s}_k)$ is given by

$$Q(\mathbf{s}_k) = F\left(\mathbf{x}_k\right) + \mathbf{g}_k^T \mathbf{s}_k + \tfrac{1}{2} \mathbf{s}_k^T \mathbf{H}_k \mathbf{s}_k \tag{3.17}$$

(cf. equation (2.13)), with $\mathbf{H}_k = \mathbf{G}_k + \mu \mathbf{I}$. This reduces to

$$\Delta Q = -\left(\mathbf{g}_k^T \mathbf{s}_k + \tfrac{1}{2} \mathbf{s}_k^T \mathbf{H}_k \mathbf{s}_k\right) \tag{3.18}$$

The benefit of this approach compared with the simple model-trust region strategy of Section 3.2.1 is that, by monitoring the accuracy of the quadratic model and adjusting μ_k accordingly, the situation where $F(\mathbf{x}_k + \mathbf{s}_k) \geq F(\mathbf{x}_k)$ – with its associated wasteful resetting of $\mathbf{x}_{k+1}$ to $\mathbf{x}_k$ – may be prevented. In addition, it is possible to maintain μ_k at a constant level in regions where this is appropriate.

Fletcher's method uses the same reduction and growth constants, ρ and σ, as the simple model-trust region strategy described in Section 3.2.1, and two additional parameters – the upper and lower limits for an 'acceptable' ratio r. If r_k is greater than upper ratio limit r^U, μ_k is divided by reduction constant ρ; if r_k is less than the lower ratio limit r^L, μ_k is multiplied by growth constant σ. If, on the other hand, $r^L < r_k < r^U$, μ_k is not changed.

This leads to the following algorithm, based on the Levenberg–Marquardt algorithm in Fletcher (1987):

Algorithm 3.3 Fletcher's model-trust region strategy
  1 Choose a random starting point x_0 and $\mu_0 > 0$
  2 At each iteration k, do the following until termination criteria are satisfied:
      2.1 Compute a step s_k using the Hessian H_k, as modified by parameter μ_k in (2.21)
      2.2 Evaluate $F(x_k + s_k)$ and calculate r_k by (3.14)
      2.3 IF $r_k < r^L$:
            2.3.1 Set $\mu_{k+1} = \sigma \mu_k$
        ELSE IF $r_k > r^U$:
            2.3.2 Set $\mu_{k+1} = \mu_k / \rho$
        ELSE
            2.3.3 Set $\mu_{k+1} = \mu_k$
      2.4 IF $r_k \leq 0$:
            2.4.1 Set $x_{k+1} = x_k$
        ELSE
            2.4.2 Set $x_{k+1} = x_k + s_k$

This algorithm is relatively insensitive to changes in the various constants. The lower and upper ratio limits r^L and r^L are invariably chosen so that $0 < r^L < r^U < 1$, and are generally set to the following values: $r^L = 0.25$ and $r^U = 0.75$. Typical settings for ρ and σ are the same as those for the simple model-trust region strategy of Section 3.2.1. Under mild assumptions, Fletcher's method can be shown to be globally convergent. (For a detailed proof of global convergence, see Fletcher (1987).)

3.2.3 Modern Model-Trust Region Algorithms

With both the simple model-trust region method (Section 3.2.1) and Fletcher's method (Section 3.2.2), step s_k is chosen by an indirect and somewhat arbitrary mechanism involving the adaption of parameter μ in (2.21) according to the value of fixed user-defined constants. More recent model-trust region methods seek to satisfy condition (2.20) explicitly. To be specific, step s_k is chosen such that

$$\|s_k\| \approx \alpha_k \tag{3.19}$$

whenever the length of the Newton step s_k^N is greater than α_k; otherwise s_k^N is accepted without modification.

In Section 2.1.3 it was shown that the length and direction of step s with respect to parameter μ ($0 \leq \mu < \infty$) forms the curve $s(\mu)$, as plotted in Fig. 2.2. To find an s_k that satisfies (3.19), the *dogleg algorithm* of Powell (1970) approximates curve $s(\mu)$ by a piecewise linear function connecting the so-called Cauchy point to the Newton point. The *Cauchy point*, denoted x_k^C, is the location $x_k^C = x_k + s_k^C$, where s_k^C – the *Cauchy step* – minimises the quadratic model in the steepest descent direction ($-g_k$);

the *Newton point,* denoted $\mathbf{x}_k^N$, is the location $\mathbf{x}_k^N = \mathbf{x}_k + \mathbf{s}_k^N$, where $\mathbf{s}_k^N$ is the familiar Newton step given by (2.15), i.e. the step that minimises the quadratic model in the Newton direction. The Cauchy point $\mathbf{x}_k^C$ can be calculated as follows:

$$\mathbf{x}_k^C = \mathbf{x}_k - \lambda \mathbf{g}_k$$

$$\lambda = \frac{\|\mathbf{g}_k\|_2^2}{\mathbf{g}_k^T \mathbf{G}_k \mathbf{g}_k} \tag{3.20}$$

Provided the Hessian $\mathbf{G}_k$ is positive definite, it is guaranteed that $\|\mathbf{s}_k^C\|_2 \leq \|\mathbf{s}_k^N\|_2$, with $\|\mathbf{s}_k^C\|_2 < \|\mathbf{s}_k^N\|_2$ in all but special and rare cases (Dennis and Schnabel, 1983). If the Cauchy point $\mathbf{x}_k^C$ does not lie within the trust region defined by radius α_k, i.e.

$$\alpha_k \leq \lambda \|\mathbf{g}_k\|_2 \tag{3.21}$$

the dogleg algorithm takes the step

$$\mathbf{s}_k = -\frac{\alpha_k}{\|\mathbf{g}_k\|_2} \mathbf{g}_k \tag{3.22}$$

at iteration k. Otherwise, we are left with the situation where the Cauchy point lies inside the trust region and the Newton point outside. In this case, the appropriate step lies on the line connecting $\mathbf{x}^C$ and $\mathbf{x}^N$, which we can define as

$$\mathbf{s}(\varphi) = \mathbf{s}^C + \varphi\left(\mathbf{s}^N - \mathbf{s}^C\right), \quad 0 < \varphi < 1 \tag{3.23}$$

In terms of equation (3.23), the dogleg step at iteration k is given by the φ for which $\|\mathbf{s}_k\| = \alpha_k$. The appropriate φ can be calculated by finding the positive root of the quadratic equation

$$\left\|\mathbf{s}_k^C + \varphi\left(\mathbf{s}_k^N - \mathbf{s}_k^C\right)\right\|_2^2 = \alpha_k^2 \tag{3.24}$$

A modified version of the dogleg algorithm, known as the *double dogleg algorithm* (Dennis and Mei, 1979), replaces the Newton step $\mathbf{s}^N$ in (3.23) and (3.24) with a step $\mathbf{s}^{\hat{N}}$ in the Newton direction satisfying $\|\mathbf{s}_k^C\|_2 < \|\mathbf{s}_k^{\hat{N}}\|_2 < \|\mathbf{s}_k^N\|_2$. This has the effect of shifting the direction of the chosen step – the so-called 'double dogleg step' – towards the Newton direction, which appears to improve the convergence characteristics of the algorithm. Dennis and Mei (1979) suggest the following heuristic formula for calculating $\mathbf{s}^{\hat{N}}$:

$$\mathbf{s}_k^{\hat{N}} = \eta_k \mathbf{s}_k^N$$

$$\eta_k = 0.8 \frac{\|\mathbf{g}_k\|_2^4}{\left(\mathbf{g}_k^T \mathbf{G}_k \mathbf{g}_k\right)\left(\mathbf{g}_k^T \mathbf{s}_k^N\right)} + 0.2 \tag{3.25}$$

An algorithm for the double dogleg model trust-region method (Algorithm 3.4) is given at the end of this section.

An alternative approach to finding an s_k that satisfies (3.19) involves finding an approximate solution μ_k to the scalar equation

$$\Phi(\mu) = \left\|s(\mu)\right\| - \alpha_k = 0 \qquad (3.26)$$

An example of a model-trust region algorithm that chooses s_k by approximately solving (3.8) is the *locally constrained optimal ('hook') step algorithm* in Dennis and Schnabel (1983). Although the s_k chosen by this approach may be slightly superior to the s_k chosen by the double dogleg algorithm, the computational costs are significantly higher – $O(N^3)$ for the locally constrained optimal ('hook') step algorithm compared with $O(N^2)$ for the double dogleg algorithm.

Whichever strategy is used to choose a step s_k, there is no guarantee that the chosen s_k will bring about an acceptable reduction in F; what is needed is some criteria for deciding whether to set $x_{k+1} = x_k + s_k$ having evaluated $F(x_k + s_k)$. The approach recommended by Dennis and Schnabel (1983) combines an evaluation of the accuracy of the quadratic model (along similar lines to Fletcher's method, described in Section 3.2.2) with the criteria used to guarantee the global convergence of inaccurate line-search algorithms (see Section 3.1.2). By this approach, the current step s_k is rejected if it fails to satisfy

$$F(x_k) - F(x_k + s_k) \geq -\nu g_k^T s_k \qquad (3.27)$$

(cf. equation (3.6)), where the user-defined scalar ν is in the range $0 < \nu \leq 0.5$ (Dennis and Schnabel recommend $\nu = 10^{-4}$). Under these circumstances, the trust region radius α_k is reduced by a factor between $\frac{1}{10}$ and $\frac{1}{2}$ chosen by the same quadratic backtracking strategy used by the line-search algorithm described in Section 3.1.3. On the other hand, even when step s_k satisfies (3.27), it may be desirable to increase α_k, rather than automatically accept s_k, if it is likely that a larger step will bring about a further decrease in F. There are two circumstances where Dennis and Schnabel recommend doubling the size of α_k rather than automatically accepting step s_k. The first is when there is sufficient relative agreement between the actual error change ΔF_k (given by (3.15)) and the predicted error change ΔQ_k (given by (3.16)), that is if

$$\left|\Delta Q_k - \Delta F_k\right| \leq \rho\left|\Delta F_k\right| \qquad (3.28)$$

where user-defined scalar ρ is set in the range $0 < \rho < 1$ (Dennis and Schnabel recommend $\rho = 0.1$). The second is when the error reduction is sufficiently large, that is if

$$\Delta F_k \geq -g_k^T s_k \qquad (3.29)$$

Finally, there is the question of how α_k should be updated at the end of iteration k after an acceptable s_k has been found. Here the approach is essentially the same as Fletcher's method, except that Dennis and Schnabel use different constants (given below).

The following algorithm is for a single k iteration of the double dogleg model trust-region method (based on the double dogleg algorithm in Dennis and Schnabel (1983)). It assumes that the Newton step s_k^N has already been calculated using a suitable Newton-related multivariate optimisation method.

Algorithm 3.4 The double dogleg model-trust region strategy

1 Calculate the Newton length $l^N = \|\mathbf{s}_k^N\|_2$
2 Set *finished*=false
3 At each m iteration from $m=1$, **DO** the following **UNTIL** *finished*=true:
    3.1 **IF** $l^N \leq \alpha_{k,m}$:
       3.1.1 Set $\mathbf{s}_k = \mathbf{s}_k^N$, $\alpha_{k,m} = l^N$ and *Newton-step*=true
    ELSE
       3.1.2 Set *Newton-step*=false
       3.1.3 **IF** $m=1$:
          3.1.3.1 Calculate Cauchy point $\mathbf{x}_k^C$ by (3.20) and hence $\mathbf{s}_k^C$
          3.1.3.2 Calculate Cauchy length, $l^C = \|\mathbf{s}_k^C\|_2$
          3.1.3.3 Calculate scalar η_k and point $\mathbf{s}_k^{\hat{N}}$ by (3.25)
          3.1.3.4 Calculate vector $\mathbf{d} = \mathbf{s}_k^N - \mathbf{s}_k^C$
       3.1.4 **IF** $\eta_k \, l^N \leq \alpha_{k,m}$:
          3.1.4.1 Set $\mathbf{s}_{k,m} = (\alpha_{k,m}/\,l^N)\mathbf{s}_k^N$
       ELSE IF $l^C \geq \alpha_{k,m}$:
          3.1.4.2 Set $\mathbf{s}_{k,m} = (\alpha_{k,m}/l^C)\mathbf{s}_k^C$
       ELSE
          3.1.4.3 Set $\mathbf{s}_{k,m} = \mathbf{s}_k^C + \lambda\mathbf{d}$, where scalar λ is given by

$$\lambda = \frac{-\mathbf{d}^T\mathbf{s}_k^C + \sqrt{\left(\mathbf{d}^T\mathbf{s}_k^C\right)^2 - \mathbf{d}^T\mathbf{d}\left[\left(l^C\right)^2 - \left(\alpha_{k,m}\right)^2\right]}}{\mathbf{d}^T\mathbf{d}} \tag{3.30}$$

    3.2 Calculate step length $l^S = \|\mathbf{s}_{k,m}\|_2$
    3.3 Set $\mathbf{x}_{k,m} = \mathbf{x}_{k,0} + \mathbf{s}_{k,m}$
    3.4 Evaluate $F_{k,m} = F(\mathbf{x}_{k,m})$, and hence the current value of ΔF_k
    3.5 Calculate $\sigma_{k,m} = \mathbf{g}_{k,0}\mathbf{s}_{k,m}$
    3.6 **IF** $F_{k,m} \geq F_{k,m-1}$ **OR** condition (3.27) is not satisfied:
       3.6.1 Set $\mathbf{x}_{k,m} = \mathbf{x}_{k,m-1}$ and $F_{k,m} = F_{k,m-1}$
       3.6.2 Set $\alpha_{k,m+1} = \alpha_{k,m}/2$
    ELSE IF $F_{k,m} - F_{k,0} \geq \nu\sigma_k$:
       3.6.3 Calculate relative step length l^R by

$$l^R = \max_{1 \leq i \leq N}\left\{\frac{\left|(s_i)_{k,m}\right|}{\max\left\{\left|(x_i)_{k,m}\right|,1.0\right\}}\right\} \tag{3.31}$$

    where $(s_i)_{k,m}$ and $(x_i)_{k,m}$ are the ith elements of $\mathbf{s}_{k,m}$ and $\mathbf{x}_{k,m}$ respectively
       3.6.4 **IF** $l^R < \varepsilon^{2/3}$ (where ε is the machine precision, defined in Section 2.2.1):
          3.6.4.1 Set $\mathbf{x}_{k+1} = \mathbf{x}_{k,0}$ and *finished*=true
       ELSE
          3.6.4.2 Set $\overline{\alpha}$ using quadratic interpolation (cf. equation (3.10)):

$$\bar{\alpha} = \frac{-\sigma_k l^S}{2\left(F_{k,m} - F_{k,0} - \sigma_k\right)} \qquad (3.32)$$

    3.6.4.3 IF $\bar{\alpha} < 0.1\alpha_{k,m}$:
        3.6.4.3.1 Set $\alpha_{k,m+1}=0.1\alpha_{k,m}$
    ELSE IF $\bar{\alpha} > 0.5\alpha_{k,m}$:
        3.6.4.3.2 Set $\alpha_{k,m+1}=0.5\alpha_{k,m}$
    ELSE
        3.6.4.3.3 Set $\alpha_{k,m+1}=\bar{\alpha}$
ELSE
    3.6.5 Calculate predicted function value ΔQ by (3.18)
    3.6.6 IF either condition (3.28) **OR** (3.29) is satisfied, **AND** *Newton-step*=false:
        3.6.6.1 Set $\alpha_{k,m+1}=2\alpha_{k,m}$
    ELSE
        3.6.6.2 Set *finished*=true
        3.6.6.3 Calculate ratio r_k by (3.14)
        3.6.6.4 IF $r_k \le r^L$:
            3.6.6.4.1 Set $\alpha_{k+1}= \alpha_{k,m}/2$
        ELSE IF $r_k \ge r^U$:
            3.6.6.4.2 Set $\alpha_{k+1}=2\alpha_{k,m}$

Dennis and Schnabel recommend lower and upper ratio limits of r^L=0.1 and r^U=0.75 respectively, and a default setting for α_0 – the initial radius – of $\alpha_0 = \|g_0\|_2$. Algorithms for the locally constrained optimal ('hook') step and double dogleg step strategies are given in Dennis and Schnabel (1983). For a useful survey of modern model-trust region methods, see Moré (1983).

3.2.4 Møller's 'Scaled' Model-Trust Region Strategy

The preceding model-trust region algorithms assume that the chosen multivariate strategy maintains a model of the Hessian matrix. This makes them inherently unsuitable for multivariate strategies that do not store an explicit model of the Hessian, such as the conjugate gradient methods of Section 3.3.4. This section describes an algorithm devised by Møller (1993a) which incorporates aspects of the model-trust region approach in a scheme for adapting the step-length parameter α_k, but which does not require the explicit representation of the model Hessian. The algorithm was designed specifically for training MLPs using conjugate gradient methods (hence Møller's name for the algorithm: the 'scaled conjugate gradient algorithm'); however, Møller's approach has much wider application, and stands on its own merits as a useful contribution to the field of nonlinear optimisation.

    Møller's method derives from the observation that, if function F is strictly quadratic with a positive definite and constant Hessian, the optimal α_k at each iteration is

$$\alpha_k = \frac{-g_k^T p_k}{p_k^T G p_k} \qquad (3.33)$$

Møller's idea is to modify equation (3.33) so that it can be used to estimate the optimal α_k for non-quadratic functions – when a given G_k may be indefinite – as follows:

$$\alpha_k = \frac{-g_k^T p_k}{p_k^T G_k p_k + \mu_k p_k^T p_k} \qquad (3.34)$$

where μ_k is the familiar model-trust region scalar. The significance of using scalar μ in (3.34) rather than (2.21) is that it is possible to approximate the term $G_k p_k$ in (3.34) without storing G explicitly using the finite-difference formula

$$G_k p_k \approx \frac{g(x_k + \sigma_k p_k) - g(x_k)}{\sigma_k}$$

$$\sigma_k = \frac{\omega}{p_k^T p_k} \qquad (3.35)$$

for $0 < \omega \ll 1$. Empirical tests suggest that the algorithm is relatively insensitive to the value of ω provided it is set to a small value ($\omega \leq 10^{-4}$). An alternative approach to setting parameter ω, presented in Møller (1993e), derives from the observation that the ideal σ_k is $\sigma_k = \alpha_k$. If ω is adapted according to the rule

$$\omega_{k+1} = \sigma_k \left(\frac{\alpha_k}{\sigma_k} \right)^\tau, \qquad 0 \leq \tau \leq 1 \qquad (3.36)$$

with τ set to a non-zero value, the values of σ_k and α_k will tend to equalise. (Setting τ to zero is equivalent to using the initial value ω_0 at every epoch.) However, Møller has found that the exact calculation of the term $G_k p_k$ in (3.34) yields the fastest average convergence rate. (An algorithm for the exact calculation of the product of the Hessian times a vector with an MLP, which has the same order of computational costs as the finite-difference approach given by (3.35) and $O(N)$ storage costs, is described in Section 4.1.2.)

A key feature of Møller's algorithm is the scheme used to adapt parameter μ_k. Let us first consider the role of μ_k in regulating the positive definiteness of the Hessian matrix. If the scalar δ_k given by

$$\delta_k = p_k^T G_k p_k + \mu_k p_k^T p_k \qquad (3.37)$$

is non-positive, the current value of μ_k is insufficient to make the Hessian positive definite, i.e. μ_k should be increased. Møller's approach is to raise μ_k according to the formula

$$\bar{\mu}_k = 2 \left(\mu_k - \frac{\delta_k}{p_k^T p_k} \right) \qquad (3.38)$$

whenever $\delta_k \leq 0$. A second role of parameter μ_k is that of maintaining sufficient agreement between the actual and predicted quadratic error change at each iteration. In this context, Møller's approach is very similar to Fletcher's (Section 3.2.2), i.e. μ_k is raised or lowered according to the value of ratio r_k given by (3.14). As the modified Hessian $H = G + \mu I$ is not available, r_k is calculated by

$$r_k = \frac{2\delta_k \left[F(\mathbf{x}_k) - F(\mathbf{x}_k + \alpha_k \mathbf{p}_k) \right]}{\left(\mathbf{g}_k^T \mathbf{p}_k \right)^2} \qquad (3.39)$$

where δ_k is given by equation (3.37). As with Fletcher's algorithm, μ_k is divided by a fixed reduction constant ρ (Møller recommends $\rho = 4$) whenever r_k is greater than upper ratio limit $r^U = 0.75$, and is increased whenever r_k is less than lower ratio limit $r^L = 0.25$. However, rather than multiply μ_k by a fixed growth constant, Møller increases μ_k according to the expression

$$\mu_{k+1} = \mu_k + \frac{\delta_k (1 - r_k)}{\mathbf{p}_k^T \mathbf{p}_k} \qquad (3.40)$$

The following algorithm for Møller's method is based on the algorithm given in Møller (1993a).

Algorithm 3.5 Møller's 'scaled' model-trust region strategy
1 Choose a random starting point $\mathbf{x}_0$ and scalars $\omega > 0$ and $\mu_0 > 0$
2 Set $\bar{\mu}_k = 0$ and *success*=true
3 Select an initial search direction $\mathbf{p}_0$ (typically $-\mathbf{g}_0$)
4 At each iteration k, do the following until termination criteria are satisfied:
    4.1 IF *success*=true:
        4.1.1 Calculate σ_k and an approximation of term $G_k \mathbf{p}_k$ by (3.35), OR calculate term $G_k \mathbf{p}_k$ exactly (see Section 4.1.2)
        4.1.2 Set $\delta_k = \mathbf{p}_k^T G_k \mathbf{p}_k$
    4.2 Set $\delta_k = \delta_k + (\mu_k - \bar{\mu}_k) \mathbf{p}_k^T \mathbf{p}_k$
    4.3 IF $\delta_k \leq 0$:
        4.3.1 Calculate $\bar{\mu}_k$ by (3.38)
        4.3.2 Set $\delta_k = -\delta_k + \mu_k \mathbf{p}_k^T \mathbf{p}_k$
        4.3.3 Set $\mu_k = \bar{\mu}_k$
    4.4 Calculate α_k by (3.34)
    4.5 Evaluate $F(\mathbf{x}_k + \alpha_k \mathbf{p}_k)$ and calculate r_k by (3.39)
    4.6 IF $r_k \geq 0$:
        4.6.1 Set $\mathbf{x}_{k+1} = \mathbf{x}_k + \alpha_k \mathbf{p}_k$, $\bar{\mu}_{k+1} = 0$ and *success*=true
        4.6.2 Calculate $\mathbf{p}_{k+1}$, as prescribed by the chosen multivariate algorithm
        4.6.3 IF $r_k \geq r^U$:
            4.6.3.1 Set $\mu_{k+1} = \mu_k / 4$
    ELSE
        4.6.4 Set $\bar{\mu}_{k+1} = \mu_k$ and *success*=false
    4.7 IF $r_k < r^L$:
        4.7.1 Calculate μ_{k+1} by (3.40)

3.3 Multivariate Methods for General Nonlinear Optimisation

The line-search and model-trust region strategies of Sections 3.1 and 3.2 have shown us ways of calculating a suitable step at each iteration k, given a search direction p_k. Calculating an effective p_k at each iteration is the job of the multivariate method. This section provides a concise survey of multivariate methods for general unconstrained nonlinear optimisation. In contrast to steepest descent (a first-order method) and Newton's method (a second-order second-derivative method), all the algorithms considered here are second-order first-derivative methods.

The survey begins with two Newton-related methods – the finite-difference Newton's method (Section 3.3.1) and quasi-Newton methods (Section 3.3.2). Both approaches maintain an approximation of the Hessian matrix, so that the strategies for the regulation and efficient storage of the model Hessian (Section 2.2.2) are highly relevant. Both methods can be readily combined with the line-search strategies of Section 3.1 and model-trust region strategies of Sections 3.2.1 to 3.2.3. The key to these methods is the scheme for generating an approximation of the Hessian G, with search direction p_k generated by equation (2.25).

The remaining methods discussed in this section – the 'memoryless' quasi-Newton method (Section 3.3.3) and conjugate gradient methods (Section 3.3.4) – have only $O(N)$ storage requirements. Both methods can be used in conjunction with the line-search strategies of Section 3.1 and with Møller's model-trust region strategy (Section 3.3.4). These methods generate successive search directions without explicit reference to the Hessian matrix.

3.3.1 Finite-Difference Newton's Method

As its name suggests, the *finite-difference Newton's method* (or discrete Newton's method) is identical to the standard Newton's method except that the analytic Hessian matrix G_k is replaced by a finite-difference approximation $\overline{G}_k$. The finite-difference Newton's method is, therefore, a natural alternative to Newton's method in circumstances where analytic second-derivatives are impossible or expensive to compute. Unfortunately, although the method has excellent convergence characteristics, it cannot be recommended (except for small-scale problems) because of the high computational costs at each iteration. The method is included here because it provides an opportunity to explain how to calculate a finite-difference approximation of the Hessian in practice, allowing for the effects of finite-precision arithmetic.

The key to the finite-difference Newton's method is the strategy used to calculate the finite-difference approximation of the Hessian G_k. The usual approach is to calculate a *forward-difference approximation* of G_k at a cost of $N+1$ gradient evaluations. The forward-difference formula is given by

$$\left(\mathbf{a}_k\right)_j = \frac{g\left(\mathbf{x}_k + h\mathbf{e}_j\right) - g\left(\mathbf{x}_k\right)}{h}, \qquad j = 1,\ldots,N \tag{3.41}$$

where $(\mathbf{a}_k)_j$ is an approximation of the jth column vector of $\mathbf{G}_k$, scalar h is the *finite-difference interval* and $\mathbf{e}_j$ is the *unit vector* or *finite-difference vector* – that is, the jth row of the identity matrix $\mathbf{I}$ with elements e_i $(i=1,\ldots,N)$ given by

$$e_i = 0, \qquad i \neq j$$
$$e_i = 1, \qquad i = j \tag{3.42}$$

If we define $\mathbf{A}_k$ as the matrix comprising the N vectors $(\mathbf{a}_k)_j$ (i.e. $\mathbf{A}_k \approx \mathbf{G}_k$), then the Hessian approximation $\overline{\mathbf{G}}_k$ is calculated according to the expression

$$\overline{\mathbf{G}}_k = \frac{\mathbf{A}_k + \mathbf{A}_k^T}{2} \tag{3.43}$$

to ensure symmetry.

Provided the finite-difference interval h is sufficiently small, the anticipated error of the approximation $\overline{\mathbf{G}}_k$ with respect to the exact Hessian $\mathbf{G}_k$ is $\|\overline{\mathbf{G}}_k - \mathbf{G}_k\| = O(h)$, where $\|\cdot\|$ is a norm for which $\|e_j\|=1$. However, the effect of finite-precision arithmetic mean that h must not be too small, owing to the risk of cancellation errors (see Section 2.2.1). In practice, it is better to use N separate finite-difference intervals h_j $(j=1,\ldots,N)$, and to set a given h_j in a way that relates to the value of the jth element of $\mathbf{x}$. One reasonable approach, advocated by Dennis and Schnabel (1983), sets h_j according to the expression

$$h_j = \sqrt{\eta}\max\left\{\left|x_j\right|, x_j^E\right\}\text{sign}(x_j) \qquad \eta \geq \varepsilon \tag{3.44}$$

where η is an estimate of the relative error in computing $g(\mathbf{x}_k)$, x_j^E is a user-defined estimate of the 'typical' size of the jth element of $\mathbf{x}$, and ε is the machine precision.

If the finite-difference interval is chosen properly, the finite-difference Newton's method retains the quadratic local convergence rate, but also the unreliable global convergence properties, of Newton's method. Practical implementations of the finite-difference Newton's method incorporate a strategy for regulating the positive definiteness of matrix $\overline{\mathbf{G}}_k$ and for choosing a suitable step length at each iteration (either a line-search or a model-trust region method). However, although a properly implemented finite-difference Newton's algorithm may be both reliable and efficient when applied to small-scale problems, the $O(N)$ gradient calculations required to calculate matrix $\overline{\mathbf{G}}_k$ at each iteration are a major disincentive to using the method for moderate- to larger-scale problems.

3.3.2 Quasi-Newton Methods

Quasi-Newton methods[1] (or secant methods) differ from Newton's method and the finite-difference Newton's method in that an approximation of the Hessian matrix (or its inverse) is built up iteratively, rather than calculated afresh at each k iteration. There are three important consequences of this iterative approach:

- It takes about N iterations to build up a reasonable approximation of **G**.
- The computational cost of updating the model Hessian **H** at each iteration is much less than that required to evaluate (or approximate) **G** afresh at each iteration.
- It is possible to ensure that $\mathbf{H}_{k+1}$ differs from $\mathbf{H}_k$ in a comparatively simple way.

In generating the model Hessian $\mathbf{H}_{k+1}$ from $\mathbf{H}_k$ using the derivative information collected during iteration k, all quasi-Newton methods satisfy the so-called *quasi-Newton condition*

$$\mathbf{H}_{k+1}\mathbf{s}_k = \mathbf{y}_k \tag{3.45}$$

where $\mathbf{y}_k$ is the gradient change at iteration k, i.e.

$$\mathbf{y}_k = \Delta\mathbf{g}_k = \mathbf{g}_{k+1} - \mathbf{g}_k \tag{3.46}$$

and $\mathbf{s}_k$ is the change in position $\mathbf{x}$ at iteration k, i.e.

$$\mathbf{s}_k = \Delta\mathbf{x}_k = \mathbf{x}_{k+1} - \mathbf{x}_k \tag{3.47}$$

Where quasi-Newton methods differ is in the choice of updating formula that satisfies (3.45).

Quasi-Newton methods are categorised in terms of the simple equation

$$\mathbf{H}_{k+1} = \mathbf{H}_k + \mathbf{C}_k \tag{3.48}$$

where $\mathbf{C}_k$ is a *correction* or *update matrix*. The best-known methods use a rank-two matrix for $\mathbf{C}_k$: the *Davidon–Fletcher–Powell* (DFP) update

$$\mathbf{H}_{k+1} = \mathbf{H}_k + \left(1 + \frac{\mathbf{s}_k^T\mathbf{H}_k\mathbf{s}_k}{\mathbf{y}_k^T\mathbf{s}_k}\right)\frac{\mathbf{y}_k\mathbf{y}_k^T}{\mathbf{y}_k^T\mathbf{s}_k} - \frac{\mathbf{y}_k\mathbf{s}_k^T\mathbf{H}_k + \mathbf{H}_k\mathbf{s}_k\mathbf{y}_k^T}{\mathbf{y}_k^T\mathbf{s}_k} \tag{3.49}$$

and the *Broyden–Fletcher–Goldfarb–Shanno* (BFGS) update (the complement of the DFP update) given by

$$\mathbf{H}_{k+1} = \mathbf{H}_k + \frac{\mathbf{y}_k\mathbf{y}_k^T}{\mathbf{y}_k^T\mathbf{s}_k} - \frac{\mathbf{H}_k\mathbf{s}_k\mathbf{s}_k^T\mathbf{H}_k}{\mathbf{s}_k^T\mathbf{H}_k\mathbf{s}_k} \tag{3.50}$$

The DFP and BFGS updates share several important properties:

- Update matrix $\mathbf{C}_k$ in (3.48) is guaranteed to be symmetric; if $\mathbf{H}_k$ is symmetric, then $\mathbf{H}_{k+1}$ is guaranteed to be symmetric.

---

1   There is some confusion in the numerical analysis literature about the use of the term 'quasi-Newton methods'. Dennis and Schnabel (1983) use the term to mean any globally convergent Newton-type method. The methods described as 'quasi-Newton methods' in this book and elsewhere (see, for example, Fletcher (1987) and Gill *et al.* (1981)) are termed 'secant methods' in Dennis and Schnabel (1983). Quasi-Newton methods are also commonly termed 'variable metric methods'.

- Given a positive definite H_k, the updated matrix H_{k+1} is guaranteed to be positive definite if and only if

$$s_k^T y_k > 0 \qquad (3.51)$$

  This property is known as *hereditary positive definiteness*.
- Both are scale-invariant (see discussion in Section 2.2.3).
- Under fairly stringent conditions (including the strict convexity of F) both the DFP and BFGS methods are globally convergent with a super-linear rate of local convergence. In practice, both methods are globally convergent for a much wider class of function. (Various convergence results for quasi-Newton methods, including relevant proofs, are discussed in Dennis and Schnabel (1983) and Gill *et al.* (1981).)

The first two of these shared characteristics (i.e. the symmetry and, whenever possible, the positive definiteness of H_k) explain the names given to the DFP and BFGS updates by Dennis and Schnabel (1983) – the 'inverse positive definite secant update' and the 'positive definite secant update' respectively.

The form of equation (3.51) explains Dennis and Schnabel's recommendation that condition (3.4) is satisfied explicitly at each iteration with quasi-Newton methods, ensuring a sufficient reduction in the directional derivative $g^T s$ (see the discussion in Section 3.1.3 regarding the implementation of the Dennis–Schnabel backtracking strategy); equation (3.51) is equivalent to

$$g_k^T s_{k+1} > g_k^T s_k \qquad (3.52)$$

which must be satisfied if (3.4) is satisfied. In other words, condition (3.4) helps to guarantee the hereditary positive definiteness of both the DFP and BFGS quasi-Newton methods.

Although the theoretical properties of the DFP and BFGS quasi-Newton methods are very similar, there is considerable empirical evidence that the BFGS update is superior to the DFP update in practice. It has often been observed, for example, that the BFGS update is better than the DFP update when used in conjunction with inaccurate line searches (Dixon, 1972; Fletcher, 1987). Indeed, there is a broad consensus that the BFGS update is almost certainly the most effective of all quasi-Newton updates (Dennis and Schnabel, 1983; Fletcher, 1987; Gill *et al.*, 1981).

The Cholesky factorisation described in Section 2.2.2 is a particularly efficient way of representing the DFP or BFGS model Hessian H, because of the simple form of update matrix C_k in equation (3.48); in this case, the Cholesky factors can be updated with only $O(N^2)$ computational costs, compared with the $O(N^3)$ costs associated with either inverting H or computing the Cholesky factors afresh at each iteration. Schemes for updating the quasi-Newton Cholesky factors are described in Dennis and Schnabel (1983) and Gill *et al.* (1981). A simpler alternative is to reformulate the DFP and BFGS Hessian update formulae in terms of the inverse Hessian, so that search direction p_k can be computed trivially with $O(N^2)$ computational costs. In terms of the inverse Hessian, equation (3.49) becomes

$$\mathbf{H}_{k+1}^{-1} = \mathbf{H}_k^{-1} + \frac{\mathbf{s}_k \mathbf{s}_k^T}{\mathbf{s}_k^T \mathbf{y}_k} - \frac{\mathbf{H}_k^{-1} \mathbf{y}_k \mathbf{y}_k^T \mathbf{H}_k^{-1}}{\mathbf{y}_k^T \mathbf{H}_k^{-1} \mathbf{y}_k} \tag{3.53}$$

and (3.50) becomes

$$\mathbf{H}_{k+1}^{-1} = \mathbf{H}_k^{-1} + \left(1 + \frac{\mathbf{y}_k^T \mathbf{H}_k^{-1} \mathbf{y}_k}{\mathbf{s}_k^T \mathbf{y}_k}\right) \frac{\mathbf{s}_k \mathbf{s}_k^T}{\mathbf{s}_k^T \mathbf{y}_k} - \frac{\mathbf{s}_k \mathbf{y}_k^T \mathbf{H}_k^{-1} + \mathbf{H}_k^{-1} \mathbf{y}_k \mathbf{s}_k^T}{\mathbf{s}_k^T \mathbf{y}_k} \tag{3.54}$$

However, the modified Cholesky factorisation of Algorithm 2.3 is the preferred representation of the quasi-Newton model Hessian in the classical optimisation literature for the reasons given in Section 2.2.2.

Finally, an important consideration for any quasi-Newton method is the initialisation of the model Hessian $\mathbf{H}_0$. The standard choice is to set $\mathbf{H}_0$ to the identity matrix $\mathbf{I}$, so that the initial search direction $\mathbf{p}_0$ is the steepest descent direction, but it is equally possible to set $\mathbf{H}_0$ to the exact Hessian $G(\mathbf{x}_0)$, to a finite-difference approximation of $G(\mathbf{x}_0)$ or (if function F is of the special form given by (1.5)) to one of the nonlinear least-squares approximations of $\mathbf{G}$ discussed in Section 3.4. Dennis and Schnabel (1983) give empirical results which suggest that the most effective initialisation in practice is a scaled version of the identity matrix,

$$\mathbf{H}_0 = \max\left\{\left|F(\mathbf{x}_0)\right|, t\right\} \cdot \mathbf{D}^2 \tag{3.55}$$

where matrix $\mathbf{D}$ is the diagonal scaling matrix described in Section 2.2.3, and scalar t is a user-defined estimate of the typical value of function F.

3.3.3 The 'Memoryless' Quasi-Newton Method

With large-scale problems, the $O(N^2)$ memory cost of storing the quasi-Newton model Hessian matrix may be prohibitive. This has led to the development of a *'memoryless' quasi-Newton method* in which the inverse BFGS formula of (3.50) is applied to the identity matrix $\mathbf{I}$ rather than the model Hessian $\mathbf{H}_k$, reducing the storage costs to $O(N)$. (This method is sometimes called the *one-step BFGS method*.) The memoryless quasi-Newton method generates successive search directions $\mathbf{p}_k$ according to the expression

$$\mathbf{p}_{k+1} = -\mathbf{g}_{k+1} - \frac{\mathbf{s}_k^T \mathbf{g}_{k+1}}{\mathbf{s}_k^T \mathbf{y}_k}\left(1 + \frac{\mathbf{y}_k^T \mathbf{y}_k}{\mathbf{s}_k^T \mathbf{y}_k}\right)\mathbf{s}_k + \frac{\mathbf{y}_k \mathbf{s}_k^T \mathbf{g}_{k+1} + \mathbf{s}_k \mathbf{y}_k^T \mathbf{g}_{k+1}}{\mathbf{s}_k^T \mathbf{y}_k} \tag{3.56}$$

with the initial search direction $\mathbf{p}_0$ set to the steepest descent direction $-\mathbf{g}_0$.

The 'memoryless' BFGS method is equivalent to the Polak–Ribiere conjugate gradient method – discussed in detail in the next section – when exact line searches are used, and is reputedly superior to that method when used with inaccurate line searches (Luenberger, 1984). As with conjugate gradient methods, it is advisable to reset $\mathbf{p}_k$ to the steepest descent direction every N (or $N+1$) iterations.

3.3.4 Conjugate Gradient Methods

Conjugate gradient methods – introduced by Hestenes and Stiefel (1952) – are a class of second-order methods which, unlike Newton-type methods, do not entail the storage of the model Hessian. For this reason, conjugate gradient methods are particularly well suited to large-scale problems, for which the $O(N^2)$ storage costs associated with Newton-type methods may be prohibitive.

Conjugate gradient methods exploit the fact that a sequence of mutually conjugate search directions (that is, a sequence $\{p_i\}$, $i=0,...,k$, satisfying equation (2.14)) can be generated iteratively – without direct reference to the Hessian matrix – according to the expression

$$p_{k+1} = -g_{k+1} + \beta_k p_k \qquad (3.57)$$

with the initial search direction set to the steepest descent direction ($p_0=-g_0$). Where conjugate gradient methods differ is in the formula – the so-called *conjugate gradient formula* – used to calculate scalar β_k in equation (3.57). In terms of the Hessian G, β_k is defined by

$$\beta_k = -\frac{g_{k+1}^T G_k p_k}{p_k^T G_k p_k} \qquad (3.58)$$

With conjugate gradient methods, where the aim is to avoid evaluating the Hessian matrix, (3.58) is reformulated using first derivative information. The three most popular conjugate gradient formulae for β_k are the *Hestenes–Stiefel* formula

$$\beta_k = \frac{\left(g_{k+1} - g_k\right)^T g_{k+1}}{\left(g_{k+1} - g_k\right)^T p_k} \qquad (3.59)$$

the *Fletcher–Reeves* formula

$$\beta_k = \frac{g_{k+1}^T g_{k+1}}{g_k^T g_k} \qquad (3.60)$$

and the *Polak–Ribiere* formula

$$\beta_k = \frac{\left(g_{k+1} - g_k\right)^T g_{k+1}}{g_k^T g_k} \qquad (3.61)$$

All three formulae for scalar β_k are equivalent when applied to quadratic functions using exact line searches; under such circumstances, all three conjugate gradient methods will converge to the minimum of the quadratic in N or fewer iterations (ignoring the effects of rounding errors). However, when applied to nonlinear functions, the performance of the Hestenes–Stiefel, Fletcher–Reeves and Polak–Ribiere conjugate gradient methods diverges. Although the 'optimal' conjugate gradient method for a given task can only be established empirically, it is widely accepted that the Polak–Ribiere formula is, in general, the most effective conjugate gradient formula. One reason why the Polak–Ribiere formula appears to be so successful in practice is that it tends to automatically reset p_k to the steepest descent direction whenever the algorithm fails to make much progress. Why the automatic resetting of the Polak–Ribiere conjugate gradient method may be advantageous will become apparent in the light of the next topic for discussion, namely *conjugate gradient restarts*.

When applied to non-quadratic functions, conjugate gradients methods generally take more than N iterations to converge to a minimum. Although it is possible to use the chosen conjugate gradient formula to generate search direction p_k at every iteration k – often with acceptable results when the chosen formula is the Polak–Ribiere formula (see, for example, Wolfe (1978)) – it is usually more efficient to reset or restart the conjugate gradient algorithm roughly every N iterations. (It may, in any case, be necessary to restart a conjugate gradient algorithm if it generates a search direction that is not a descent direction, i.e. a p_k that fails to satisfy (2.4).)

A variety of conjugate gradient restart schemes have been devised, differing in the choice of restart direction and the interval between restarts. The simplest and most popular option is to reset p_k to the steepest descent direction $-g_k$ every N (or $N+1$) iterations. The conjugate gradient method with steepest descent restarts every N iterations is sometimes known as the *traditional conjugate gradient method*. One reason why the steepest descent restart is important is that a conjugate gradient method which resets p_k periodically to $-g_k$ is guaranteed to be globally convergent. On the other hand, an obvious drawback with resetting p_k to the steepest descent direction is that potentially useful derivative information generated during previous iterations is discarded. An example of a conjugate gradient restart scheme that aims to retain some of the prior derivative information while guaranteeing that p_k is a descent direction is the *Powell restart* (Powell, 1977).

To assess the local convergence rate of conjugate gradient methods, it is useful to consider how they perform when function F is quadratic with a constant and positive definite Hessian. As with the steepest descent method (Section 2.1.1), the convergence rate of conjugate gradient methods depends on the distribution of the eigenvalues of the Hessian matrix G. The convergence ratio r for conjugate gradient methods is

$$r = \left(\frac{\sqrt{\kappa} - 1}{\sqrt{\kappa} + 1} \right)^2 \tag{3.62}$$

where κ is the condition number of G (cf. equation (2.10) for the steepest descent method). This amounts to linear convergence, but at a significantly faster rate than steepest descent. In fact, it can be shown that, in theory, the traditional conjugate gradient method is super-linearly convergent for a wide class of functions. However, these results assume both exact line searches and exact arithmetic; conjugate gradient methods usually prove linearly convergent in practice, though at a much faster rate than steepest descent (Gill *et al.*, 1981). (For a more detailed consideration of the convergence properties of conjugate gradient methods in terms of the distribution of the eigenvalues of the Hessian matrix, see Luenberger (1984).)

3.4 Special Methods for Nonlinear Least Squares

In this section we look at a special case of unconstrained minimisation known as the *nonlinear least squares* problem, which commonly occurs when fitting model functions to experimental data. A typical data fitting problem involves fitting a function $\Phi(a,\mathbf{x})$ to a set of M data points (a_i, b_i) $(i=1,...,M)$; to solve the problem it is necessary to adjust vector $\mathbf{x}$, comprising the N free parameters x_j $(j=1,...,N)$, so that function $\Phi(a,\mathbf{x})$ 'best fits' the M data points. Typically $M>N$, i.e. the corresponding system of equations is *over-determined*.

With nonlinear least squares problems, the objective function used to measure the accuracy with which function $\Phi(a,\mathbf{x})$ fits the data is given by

$$F(\mathbf{x}_k) = \tfrac{1}{2} r(\mathbf{x}_k)^T r(\mathbf{x}_k) \tag{3.63}$$

where $r(\mathbf{x}_k)$ – or $\mathbf{r}_k$ for short – is the *residual vector* with elements

$$r_i = \Phi(a_i,\mathbf{x}) - b_i, \qquad 1 \le i \le M \tag{3.64}$$

From the perspective of MLP training, we can define the elements of the residual vector as

$$r_{i,p} = y_{i,p}^L - t_{i,p}, \qquad 1 \le i \le N^L, 1 \le p \le P \tag{3.65}$$

where $t_{i,p}$ is the ith element of target $\mathbf{t}_p$, and $y_{i,p}^L$ is the output of output-layer node n_i^L for pattern p (i.e. the network's current estimation of the value of $t_{i,p}$). The number of patterns times the number of output-layer nodes (PN^L) is equivalent to the number of data values (M). In terms of (3.65), function F in (3.63) is, in effect, equivalent to the sum-of-squares error function given by (1.5).

Functions of the form (3.63) can, of course, be tackled by any of the general unconstrained minimisation methods considered earlier in the chapter; the main reason why nonlinear least-squares problems are treated as a special case of unconstrained minimisation is that the gradient and Hessian of (3.63) have a special structure with respect to residual vector $\mathbf{r}$, and the $M \times N$ *Jacobian matrix* J with elements

$$J_{ij} = \frac{\partial r_i}{\partial x_j} \tag{3.66}$$

In terms of $\mathbf{r}$ and J at iteration k, the gradient is given by

$$\mathbf{g}_k = J_k^T \mathbf{r}_k \tag{3.67}$$

and the Hessian by

$$\mathbf{G}_k = J_k^T J_k + S_k$$
$$S_k = \sum_{i=1}^{M} r_{i,k} . \nabla^2 r_{i,k} \tag{3.68}$$

where $\nabla^2 r_i$ is the second derivative (Hessian) matrix of the ith element of residual vector $\mathbf{r}$.

Unfortunately, (3.68) is unsuitable as the basis of a general nonlinear least-squares algorithm because the second-order term S is typically unavailable. One option is to ignore S altogether on the assumption that the first-order term of (3.68) dominates the second-order term near the solution – a reasonable assumption so long as the residuals at the solution are small or zero. Nonlinear least-squares algorithms which approximate G according to

$$G_k \approx J_k^T J_k \tag{3.69}$$

are considered below.

In order to improve the performance of nonlinear least-squares methods when applied to problems with moderate to large residuals at the solution, a number of alternative Hessian approximations to that given by (3.69) have been proposed in the optimisation literature. One of the most popular approaches is to approximate the second-order term S_k in (3.68) by a quasi-Newton (secant) approximation A, so that the Hessian approximation becomes

$$G_k \approx J_k^T J_k + A_k \tag{3.70}$$

Using the Broyden–Fletcher–Goldfarb–Shanno (BFGS) update given by (3.50), A can be updated iteratively according to the formula

$$A_{k+1} = A_k + \frac{y_k y_k^T}{y_k^T s_k} - \frac{B_k s_k s_k^T B_k}{s_k^T B_k s_k} \tag{3.71}$$

$$B_k = J_{k+1}^T J_{k+1} + A_k$$

If A_{k+1} satisfies (3.71), matrix $J_{k+1}^T J_{k+1} + A_{k+1}$ is guaranteed to be positive definite provided B_k is positive definite (Gill *et al.*, 1981). Methods derived from (3.70) are superior to those derived from (3.69) for medium- and large-residual problems.

The significance of (3.69) and (3.70) is that, given only r_k and J_k, it is possible to approximate the Hessian matrix G_k immediately at each iteration, whereas with general unconstrained minimisation strategies (such as the quasi-Newton methods of Section 3.3.2) it may take N iterations to calculate a satisfactory approximation of the ($N \times N$) Hessian. For this reason, least squares methods are generally preferred to general unconstrained minimisation methods for functions of the form given by (3.63) on grounds of convergence speed.

3.4.1 The Gauss–Newton Method

The *Gauss-Newton method*, which implements (3.69) without modification, has the update

$$\mathbf{s}_k = -\left[\mathbf{J}_k^T \mathbf{J}_k\right]^{-1} \mathbf{J}_k^T \mathbf{r}_k \tag{3.72}$$

(cf. equation (2.15)). The convergence properties of the Gauss–Newton method depend on the size of S in (3.68), a measure of the nonlinearity and residual size associated with a given problem. If S_k is small relative to $\mathbf{J}_k^T \mathbf{J}_k$, the method is locally quadratically convergent. However, an increase in either the relative residual size or nonlinearity of the problem increases the relative size of S, with a corresponding decrease in convergence speed; if S is too large the method may fail altogether, even in the neighbourhood of a minimum (Dennis and Schnabel, 1983; Fletcher, 1987). Moreover, the method is ill-defined whenever J does not have full column rank, a condition that is guaranteed to occur if $M<N$. (Since $M<N$ is equivalent to $PN^L<W$ for an MLP, this makes the Gauss–Newton method inherently unsuitable for the famous XOR benchmark training task, described in Section 5.1.1; otherwise, this condition rarely arises.)

This 'unmodified' Gauss–Newton method of (3.72) can be improved by combining it with a line-search algorithm so that x_k is updated by

$$\mathbf{x}_{k+1} = \mathbf{x}_k - \alpha_k \left[\mathbf{J}_k^T \mathbf{J}_k\right]^{-1} \mathbf{J}_k^T \mathbf{r}_k \tag{3.73}$$

where α_k is the familiar step-length parameter. This method – the *damped Gauss–Newton method* (or Hartley method (Wolfe, 1978)) – is more reliable than the unmodified version of (3.72), but otherwise suffers from similar drawbacks.

3.4.2 The Levenberg–Marquardt Method

The preferred modification of the Gauss–Newton method, based on the model-trust region approach of Section 3.2, is the *Levenberg–Marquardt method* (or Marquardt method). The Levenberg–Marquardt update is given by

$$\mathbf{x}_{k+1} = \mathbf{x}_k - \left[\mathbf{J}_k^T \mathbf{J}_k + \mu_k \mathbf{I}\right]^{-1} \mathbf{J}_k^T \mathbf{r}_k \tag{3.74}$$

The Levenberg–Marquardt method has several advantages over the damped Gauss–Newton method: it is well defined when J does not have full column rank; several versions of the Levenberg–Marquardt algorithm have been proved to be globally convergent (see, for example, Osborne (1976)); and, when the step length is too long, the Levenberg–Marquardt update (which tends to the steepest descent direction) is often superior. The theoretical local convergence characteristics of the Gauss–Newton, damped Gauss–Newton and Levenberg–Marquardt methods are broadly similar: quadratic convergence for zero-residual problems; fast linear convergence for problems that are not too nonlinear and have fairly small residuals; and slow linear convergence for problems that are sufficiently nonlinear or have comparatively large residuals (Dennis and Schnabel, 1983).

3.5 Comparison of Methods

There are a number of criteria that may be used to assess the comparative strengths and weaknesses of different classical optimisation methods. Probably the most popular criteria are:

- *Convergence speed* The convergence speed of a given method is commonly assessed in terms of its theoretical local convergence rate, and empirically by counting either the number of k iterations, or the number of function and gradient evaluations that the method expends in practice. The computational complexity of a method at each k iteration may also be taken into account.

- *Robustness* A broad measure of the likelihood that a particular method will suffer numerical problems. For example, certain methods are more sensitive than others to the scale of the independent variable, to the effects of rounding error and to the use of inaccurate line searches.

- *Storage costs* As we have seen, classical methods for multivariate optimisation can be conveniently divided into two types – those with $O(N)$ storage costs, and those with $O(N^2)$ storage costs.

- *Ease of implementation* For programmers, the amount of time it takes to turn a particular classical algorithm into code is likely to be a significant factor.

With respect to both robustness and theoretical rates of local convergence, conventional wisdom ranks the classical multivariate optimisation methods in the following order (see, for example, Gill *et al.* (1981)):

- Newton's method (Section 2.1.2) with appropriate global convergence modifications and – for zero-residual problems only – the Levenberg–Marquardt method (Section 3.4.2)

- the finite-difference Newton's method (Section 3.3.1) with appropriate global convergence modifications

- quasi-Newton methods (Section 3.3.2)

- conjugate gradient methods (Section 3.3.4) and the 'memoryless' quasi-Newton method (Section 3.3.3)

- steepest descent (Section 2.1.1)

The preceding ordering is fairly intuitive, as it reflects the extent to which the various methods exploit the problem structure and store useful curvature information. However, this ordering is misleading, as it takes no account of the computational cost at each iteration, or of the way in which a given method is implemented. Moreover, whereas steepest descent is consistently rated as the poorest method by a wide margin, the distinction between the others is less clear-cut. In practice, the most effective second-order method for a given problem can only be determined by experimentation.

On balance, an efficient implementation of the BFGS quasi-Newton method probably deserves the highest recommendation. It has lower computational costs at each iteration than Newton's method, the finite-difference Newton's method or nonlinear least-squares method; it is not sensitive to the presence of residuals at the solution, in contrast to the Levenberg–Marquardt method; and it is more robust and has a higher (theoretical) rate of local convergence than conjugate gradient methods, or the 'memoryless' quasi-Newton method.

Unfortunately, the $O(N^2)$ storage costs and $O(N^2)$ computational costs associated with quasi-Newton methods mean that they may be impractical, or relatively inefficient, for large-scale problems. Under these circumstances, there is little to choose between the Polak–Ribiere conjugate gradient method and the 'memoryless' BFGS quasi-Newton method. (An alternative option, explored in Section 4.2.1, is to replace the $O(N^2)$ Hessian matrix by an $O(N)$ diagonal or near-diagonal approximation.)

The choice of line-search or model-trust region strategy is to some extent determined by the choice of multivariate algorithm. With methods that store an explicit representation of the Hessian matrix, an inaccurate backtracking line search (Section 3.1.3), or suitable model-trust region strategy (Sections 3.2.1–3.2.3) is likely to be more efficient than safeguarded polynomial interpolation (Section 3.1.1). However, experience has shown that conjugate gradient methods can be less effective with inaccurate line searches; in this case, Møller's 'scaled' model-trust region strategy (Section 3.2.4) is an attractive alternative to the 'traditional' safeguarded polynomial interpolation approach. With nonlinear least-squares problems, the Levenberg–Marquardt method (Section 3.4.2), which takes the model-trust region approach, is nearly always preferred to the damped Gauss–Newton method (Section 3.4.1), which uses a line-search strategy.

Finally, with respect to ease of implementation, the ordering of the multivariate algorithms is roughly reversed from that given above for robustness and rate of convergence. When implementing classical methods for training MLPs, the most important distinction is between first- and second-derivative methods; the former are relatively trivial to implement, as all that is required is the familiar gradient calculation that lies at the heart of the standard backpropagation algorithm (Section 1.3.1), whereas special algorithms are required for the exact calculation of the Hessian matrix (Newton's method) and the Jacobian matrix (nonlinear least-squares methods) with an MLP – see Section 4.1.

Although the 'traditional' line-search approach is easier to understand than the model-trust region approach, the simple model-trust region strategy described in Section 3.2.1 and Fletcher's method of Section 3.2.2 are, in fact, easier to implement than any of the line-search algorithms discussed in Section 3.1. For most programmers, it is unlikely that the substantial increase in time and effort required to implement a modern model-trust region strategy (Section 3.2.3) can be justified in view of the 'simple, but effective' Fletcher's method.

4. Second-Order Training Methods for MLPs

The idea of using second-order methods to train multi-layer perceptrons is far from a new one. The earliest publications on this subject to reach a wide audience were probably those of Parker (1987) and Watrous (1987); now, a decade later, the catalogue of published MLP research concerned with second-order training methods is substantial[1]. The aim of this chapter is to explain the major ways in which neural net researchers have sought to adapt the various second-order classical techniques of Chapters 2 and 3 to the particular requirements of MLP training.

Most of the classical methods discussed in this book are first-derivative methods. These methods can be implemented as training methods for MLPs in a particularly straightforward manner – indeed, without any significant modification; all that is required is the calculation of the gradient at each iteration using the standard backpropagation equations (1.1) and (1.14). (For the remaining second-derivative methods an equivalent set of equations for calculating second-derivative information with an MLP is presented in Section 4.1.) Second-order methods implemented without modification have proved highly effective when applied to many MLP training tasks, and form the basis for the benchmark test results presented in Chapter 5.

Unfortunately, there are several important circumstances where the 'straightforward' implementation of a classical method is likely to prove impractical or inefficient:

- The MLP architecture contains a large number of weights. In this case, it is clearly desirable to find ways of reducing the computational and/or storage costs of classical methods – in particular the $O(W^2)$ storage costs and $O(W^2)$ (or $O(W^3)$) computational costs of Newton-related methods[2].

---

1   For those interested in the chronology of second-order MLP training algorithm development, some of the earliest neural implementations of the various second-order methods discussed in Chapters 2 and 3 are as follows: Parker (1987) (Newton's method); Watrous (1987) (quasi-Newton methods); Kramer and Sangiovanni-Vincentelli (1988) (conjugate gradient methods); Kollias and Anastassiou (1989) (the Levenberg–Marquardt method); and Battiti and Masulli (1990) (the 'memoryless' quasi-Newton method).

2   Note that this chapter reverts to the MLP-style notation of Chapter 1; W (the number of network weights) is equivalent to N (the number of free parameters) in Chapters 2 and 3.

- The MLP training set contains redundant information. In this case, it is desirable to train the network using a subset of the full training set at each iteration – that is, in on-line mode – for the reasons given in Section 1.3.4.
- The MLP error surface contains local minima.

A wide range of strategies, of varying sophistication, have been developed which seek to improve the performance of second-order training methods under these circumstances. In this chapter we shall consider strategies for reducing the computational and storage costs of second-order training algorithms (Section 4.2) and on-line strategies that are appropriate for classical training methods (Section 4.3); a consideration of global second-order training is deferred until Chapter 6.

4.1   The Calculation of Second Derivatives

Most of the second-order methods discussed earlier in this book are first-derivative methods, and can therefore be implemented using the standard backpropagation gradient calculation given by equations (1.1) and (1.14). However, the availability of exact second-derivative information is either essential or desirable when implementing certain of the classical algorithms described in Chapters 2 and 3. For example, Newton's method (Section 2.1.2) requires the exact Hessian matrix **G** at every iteration, whereas Møller's 'scaled' model-trust region strategy (Section 3.2.4) benefits from the exact calculation of the Hessian times a vector (**Gp**). Furthermore, the nonlinear least-squares algorithms discussed in Section 3.6 all require the evaluation of the Jacobian matrix **J** in order to approximate the Hessian **G**.

The purpose of this section is to explain how to evaluate the Hessian matrix (Section 4.1.1), the Hessian times a vector (Section 4.1.2) and the Jacobian matrix (Section 4.1.3) using an MLP. In each case, the calculation of **G**, **Gp** or **J** involves propagating information forwards (from layer $l=1$ to layer $l=L$) and backwards (from $l=L$ to $l=1$) through the network in a similar manner to the standard backpropagation gradient calculation. Where the algorithms for calculating **G**, **Gp** and **J** differ is in the type of information passed forwards and backwards through the net, and in the number of forward and backward propagations required. (Note that the emphasis here is on the practical implementation of algorithms for calculating second-derivative information with MLPs; readers interested in the derivation of each algorithm should consult the references cited below, or the useful summary in Bishop (1995).)

4.1.1   Exact Evaluation of the Hessian Matrix

In terms of the MLP weights and error function, the W^2 elements of the Hessian matrix **G** are of the form $\partial^2 E / \partial w_{rs}^{tv} \partial w_{ij}^{lm}$. Assuming that error function E is a sum of terms (i.e. of the form given by equation (1.4)), the second derivative with respect to weights w_{rs}^{tv} and w_{ij}^{lm}, where layer $t \leq l$, is obtained by summing the partial second derivatives for each pattern, i.e.

$$\frac{\partial^2 E}{\partial w_{rs}^{tv} \partial w_{ij}^{lm}} = \sum_{p=1}^{P} \frac{\partial^2 E_p}{\partial w_{rs}^{tv} \partial w_{ij}^{lm}} \tag{4.1}$$

those second derivatives where $t>l$ can be obtained from the symmetry of the Hessian matrix without further calculation.

An algorithm for calculating each partial second derivative $\partial^2 E_p / \partial w_{rs}^{tv} \partial w_{ij}^{lm}$ using an MLP – devised by Bishop (1992) – can be summarised as follows:

$$\frac{\partial^2 E_p}{\partial w_{rs}^{tv} \partial w_{ij}^{lm}} = y_{s,p}^{v} \left[\delta_{i,p}^{l} f'\left(a_{j,p}^{m}\right) \sigma_{jr,p}^{mt} + y_{j,p}^{m} \beta_{ri,p}^{tl} \right] \tag{4.2}$$

where $a_{j,p}^{m}$ is the activation and $y_{j,p}^{m}$ the output of node n_j^m with respect to pattern p, and f is the chosen squashing function. (Recall that, in the case where f is the sigmoid given by (1.2), the first derivative $f'(a_{j,p}^{m})$ is simply $y_{j,p}^{m}(1 - y_{j,p}^{m})$.) The error term $\delta_{i,p}^{l}$ in (4.2) is the same as for backpropagation (equation (1.15)), i.e.

$$\delta_{i,p}^{L} = \left(t_{i,p} - y_{i,p}^{L}\right) f'\left(a_{i,p}^{L}\right) \tag{4.3}$$

$$\delta_{j,p}^{m} = f'\left(a_{j,p}^{m}\right) \sum_{n_i^l \in T_j^m} w_{ij}^{lm} \delta_{i,p}^{l}, \quad m < L \tag{4.4}$$

The remaining, undefined terms in (4.2) are as follows:

$$\sigma_{jr,p}^{mt} = \frac{\partial a_{j,p}^{m}}{\partial a_{r,p}^{t}} \tag{4.5}$$

and

$$\beta_{ri,p}^{tl} = \frac{\partial \delta_{r,p}^{t}}{\partial a_{i,p}^{l}} \tag{4.6}$$

The term $\sigma_{jr,p}^{mt}$ can be calculated by forward propagation using the formula

$$\sigma_{jj,p}^{mm} = 1$$

$$\sigma_{jk,p}^{mm} = 0, \quad j \neq k$$

$$\sigma_{jr,p}^{mt} = 0, \quad m < t \tag{4.7}$$

$$\sigma_{jr,p}^{mt} = \sum_{n_u^v \in S_j^m} f'\left(a_{u,p}^{v}\right) w_{ju}^{mv} \sigma_{ur,p}^{vt}, \quad m > t$$

and the term $\beta^{tl}_{ri,p}$ by backward propagation using the formula

$$\beta^{Lm}_{ij,p} = \sigma^{Lm}_{ij,p}\left[f''\left(a^{L}_{i,p}\right)\frac{\partial E_p}{\partial y^{L}_{i,p}} + f'\left(a^{L}_{i,p}\right)^2\frac{\partial^2 E_p}{\left(\partial y^{L}_{i,p}\right)^2}\right] \tag{4.8}$$

$$\beta^{tl}_{ri,p} = f''\left(a^{t}_{r,p}\right)\sigma^{tl}_{ri,p}\sum_{n^{c}_{b}\in T^{t}_{r}}w^{ct}_{br}\delta^{c}_{b,p} + f'\left(a^{t}_{r,p}\right)\sum_{n^{c}_{b}\in T^{t}_{r}}w^{ct}_{br}\beta^{cl}_{bi,p}, \quad t < L \tag{4.9}$$

If squashing function f is the sigmoid of equation (1.2), then the second derivative f'' in equations (4.8) and (4.9) is simply

$$f''(a) = f(a)\left[1 - f(a)\right]\left[1 - 2f(a)\right] = y(1-y)(1-2y) \tag{4.10}$$

Note that, in practice, the first summation in (4.9) will already have been calculated by equation (4.4).

To calculate the full Hessian matrix G using the above algorithm requires $O(W^2)$ operations per pattern and $O(W^2)$ storage.

4.1.2 Exact Evaluation of the Hessian Times a Vector

With certain classical algorithms, what needs to be evaluated is not the Hessian itself, but the Hessian times a vector. For example, Møller's 'scaled' model-trust region strategy of Section 3.2.4 requires the calculation of the Hessian times the search direction $(G_k p_k)$ at each iteration. We have already seen that it is possible to approximate $G_k p_k$ using a finite-difference formula (equation (3.35)). In this section we examine an efficient algorithm, given in Møller (1993c), that enables an MLP to calculate $G_k p_k$ exactly with the same order of computational and storage costs as the finite-difference approach.

Let us consider the calculation of the vector $\mathbf{b}=\mathbf{Gd}$ with elements

$$b_i = \sum_{j=1}^{W}G_{ij}d_j \tag{4.11}$$

where $\mathbf{d}$ is an arbitrary W-length vector and $\mathbf{G}$ the Hessian matrix. In order to explain Møller's algorithm for calculating $\mathbf{b}$, it is necessary to view the elements of $\mathbf{b}$ and $\mathbf{d}$ as having the same arrangement with respect to the MLP architecture as the network weights, so that individual elements of $\mathbf{b}$ and $\mathbf{d}$ are denoted b^{lm}_{ij} and d^{lm}_{ij} respectively. Møller's algorithm calculates vector $\mathbf{b}$ by the summation

$$\mathbf{b} = \sum_{p=1}^{P}G_p(\mathbf{w})\mathbf{d} \tag{4.12}$$

where $G_p(\mathbf{w})$ is the partial Hessian of the partial error E_p in equation (1.4). The contribution to element b^{lm}_{ij} for pattern p can be calculated according to the formula

$$b_{ij,p}^{lm} = \delta_{i,p}^{l} f'\left(a_{j,p}^{m}\right)\varphi_{j,p}^{m} + \left(\mu_{i,p}^{l} + \beta_{i,p}^{l}\right)y_{j,p}^{m} \qquad (4.13)$$

where $\delta_{i,p}^{l}$ is the standard backpropagation error term used in the exact Hessian calculation of Section 4.1.1 (see equations (4.3) and (4.4)). The term $\varphi_{j,p}^{m}$ in (4.13) can be calculated by forward propagation according to the formula

$$\varphi_{j,p}^{0} = 0$$

$$\varphi_{j,p}^{m} = \sum_{n_i^r \in S_j^m} \left[d_{js}^{mr} y_{s,p}^{r} + w_{js}^{mr} f'\left(a_{s,p}^{r}\right)\varphi_{s,p}^{r} \right], \qquad m > 0 \qquad (4.14)$$

and terms $\mu_{i,p}^{l}$ and $\beta_{i,p}^{l}$ by backward propagation according to the formulae

$$\mu_{i,p}^{L} = \varphi_{i,p}^{L} \left[f''\left(a_{i,p}^{L}\right)\frac{\partial E_p}{\partial y_{i,p}^{L}} + f'\left(a_{i,p}^{L}\right)^2 \frac{\partial^2 E_p}{\left(\partial y_{i,p}^{L}\right)^2} \right]$$

$$(4.15)$$

$$\mu_{i,p}^{l} = f'\left(a_{i,p}^{l}\right) \sum_{n_c^h \in T_i^l} w_{ci}^{hl} \mu_{c,p}^{h}, \qquad l < L$$

$$\beta_{i,p}^{L} = 0$$

$$\beta_{i,p}^{l} = \sum_{n_c^h \in T_i^l} \left\langle f'\left(a_{i,p}^{l}\right)w_{ci}^{hl}\beta_{c,p}^{h} + \delta_{c,p}^{h}\left[d_{ci}^{hl} f'\left(a_{i,p}^{l}\right) + w_{ci}^{hl} f''\left(a_{i,p}^{l}\right)\varphi_{i,p}^{l}\right] \right\rangle \qquad (4.16)$$

The preceding algorithm has $O(PW)$ computational costs and $O(W)$ storage costs. To understand how Møller's algorithm relates to Bishop's algorithm for calculating the exact Hessian (Section 4.1.1), it is interesting to note that, if the calculation $\mathbf{b}=\mathbf{Gd}$ is performed W times with $\mathbf{d}$ ($\mathbf{d}_1,...,\mathbf{d}_W$) set successively to each of the W unit vectors (see equation (3.42)), the resultant W vectors ($\mathbf{b}_1,...,\mathbf{b}_W$) are the columns of $\mathbf{G}$. In other words, Møller's algorithm can be used to calculate the exact Hessian with the same order of computational costs as Bishop's algorithm, although the former is less efficient because of redundant calculations (Bishop, 1995).

4.1.3 Exact Evaluation of the Jacobian Matrix

All of the nonlinear least-squares methods discussed in Section 3.4 require the evaluation of the Jacobian matrix $\mathbf{J}_k$ at each iteration k (see equations (3.67) and (3.68)). In terms of the MLP architecture and training set, the Jacobian matrix has $PN^L \times W$ elements of the form $\partial r_{b,p} / \partial w_{ij}^{lm}$, where P is the number of patterns in the training set and N^L is the number of output nodes (equivalent to the number of elements in each target vector $\mathbf{t}_p$). Each element $\partial r_{b,p} / \partial w_{ij}^{lm}$ of matrix $\mathbf{J}$ can be calculated exactly according to the simple expression

$$\frac{\partial r_{b,p}}{\partial w_{ij}^{lm}} = \delta_{i,b,p}^{l} y_{j,p}^{m} \tag{4.17}$$

The term $\delta_{i,b,p}^{l}$ in (4.17) can be calculated by backward propagation according to the formula

$$\delta_{i,b,p}^{L} = f'\left(a_{i,p}^{L}\right), \quad i = b$$

$$\delta_{i,b,p}^{L} = 0, \qquad i \neq b \tag{4.18}$$

$$\delta_{j,b,p}^{m} = f'\left(a_{j,p}^{m}\right) \sum_{n_{i}^{l} \in T_{j}^{m}} w_{ij}^{lm} \delta_{i,b,p}^{l}, \quad m < L$$

Using the algorithm encapsulated by equations (4.17) and (4.18), it is possible to calculate the Jacobian matrix exactly with P standard forward propagations (to calculate each activation $a_{j,p}^{m}$ and output $y_{j,p}^{m}$ by equation (1.1)) and PN^{L} backward propagations based on equation (4.18). For MLPs with a single output node, the number of forward and backward propagations required is the same as for back-propagation.

4.2   Reducing Storage and Computational Costs

This section explores strategies for reducing the computation and/or storage costs of classical MLP training methods. Two broad approaches are considered. The first approach, discussed in Section 4.2.1, involves using diagonal (or near-diagonal) approximations of the Hessian matrix in place of the regular $W \times W$ Hessian representation. This approach is designed to reduce the high cost of storing and maintaining the full Hessian matrix with Newton-type methods. The second approach involves reducing the number of function and/or gradient evaluations performed at each epoch (k iteration). Several different strategies for reducing the number of evaluation per epoch are discussed in Section 4.2.2.

Before proceeding, however, it is worth sounding a note of caution. There is often a price to pay for reducing a method's storage costs and/or computational costs at each epoch. Most of the strategies for reducing a method's costs presented below entail a loss of potentially useful derivative information. In such cases, a reduction in the storage and/or computational cost of a given training method is liable to be accompanied by a degradation in the method's performance, with a corresponding increase in the total number of training epochs required to reach a satisfactory solution. In general, the optimal strategy in terms of total training time is task-specific and can only be determined empirically.

4.2.1 Diagonal Approximations of the Hessian Matrix

Most of the second-order methods discussed in this book are Newton-related methods, requiring the explicit representation of the Hessian matrix (or its inverse). The storage costs associated with such methods are $O(W^2)$ and the computational costs at each iteration at least $O(W^2)$. (In cases where the model Hessian has to be inverted or the Cholesky decomposition performed at each iteration, the computational costs rise to $O(W^3)$.) Although the $O(W^2)$ storage requirements of Newton-related methods have become less prohibitive as the number of megabytes of memory available on a typical computer has increased, the desirability of reducing the storage and computational costs of such methods is self-evident.

The approach we consider here involves neglecting all or most of the off-diagonal elements of the Hessian matrix $\mathbf{G}$, so that $\mathbf{G}$ is approximated by a diagonal, or near-diagonal, matrix. All such schemes have $O(W)$ storage costs. Let us begin by considering schemes for approximating the Hessian matrix with a diagonal form. Assuming that the error function E consists of a sum of terms as defined by equation (1.4), the diagonal elements of the Hessian matrix – i.e. the W elements $\partial^2 E / (\partial w_{ij}^{lm})^2$ – can be calculated exactly by a straightforward adaptation of the general Hessian evaluation formula given by equation (4.2). This scheme forms the basis of the 'diagonalised' Newton method in Ricotti *et al.* (1988), and can also be used to calculate the trace of the Hessian matrix, as required by Algorithm 2.4 for the extended Power method (Section 2.2.3).

Although the cost of evaluating the diagonal element of the Hessian is cheaper than the cost of evaluating the Hessian in full, it is not yet an $O(W)$ operation. In order to reduce the computational costs to only $O(W)$, it is possible to neglect the second-order terms (by dropping the second-order component $f''(a_{i,p}^l)(\partial E_p / \partial y_{i,p}^l)$ of the term $\beta_{ri,p}^{tl}$ in equations (4.8) and (4.9)). This leads to the scheme given in le Cun (1989), which approximates each diagonal element $\partial^2 E_p / (\partial w_{ij}^{lm})^2$ as follows:

$$\frac{\partial^2 E_p}{\left(\partial w_{ij}^{lm}\right)^2} = \frac{\partial^2 E_p}{\left(\partial a_{i,p}^l\right)^2} \left(y_{j,p}^m\right)^2 \tag{4.19}$$

$$\frac{\partial^2 E_p}{\left(\partial a_{i,p}^l\right)^2} \approx f'\left(a_{i,p}^l\right)^2 \sum_{n_c^h \in T_i^l} \left(w_{ci}^{hl}\right)^2 \frac{\partial^2 E_p}{\left(\partial a_{c,p}^h\right)^2} \tag{4.20}$$

This approach is similar to that of the Gauss–Newton and Levenberg–Marquardt nonlinear least-squares methods (Sections 3.4.1 and 3.4.2 respectively), which neglect the second-order terms when approximating the Hessian by $\mathbf{J}^T \mathbf{J}$ (see equations (3.68) and (3.69)).

A simpler $O(W)$ strategy is to approximate each diagonal element of the Hessian $\partial^2 E / \partial w_i^2$ by the one-sided difference formula

$$\left(\frac{\partial^2 E}{\partial w_i^2}\right)_k \approx \frac{g\left(w_{i,k}\right) - g\left(w_{i,k-1}\right)}{w_{i,k} - w_{i,k-1}} \tag{4.21}$$

where w_i,k is the value of the ith weight at epoch k. Equation (4.21) lies at the heart of the *quickprop method* (Fahlman, 1989). This approach can be viewed as a crude diagonal version of the finite-difference Newton's method described in Section 3.3.1.

These diagonal Newton-type methods have obvious attractions. On the one hand, their computational and storage costs are much less than those of full-scale Newton-type methods. On the other hand, they are easier to adapt for on-line training than conventional classical methods with $O(W)$ storage costs (such as the conjugate gradient methods of Section 3.3.4 and 'memoryless' quasi-Newton method of Section 3.3.3) because the diagonal Hessian approximation is calculated afresh at each epoch. (We return to this topic in Section 4.3.)

However, experience suggests that methods based on diagonal approximations of the Hessian frequently achieve only modest improvements in convergence speed compared with backpropagation (see, for example, the verdict in le Cun (1989)). Indeed, there are good reasons for thinking that diagonal approximations are unlikely to be effective in general. As Bishop (1995, p. 271) observes, 'in practice, the weights in a typical neural network are strongly coupled, leading to a Hessian matrix which is often far from diagonal'.

A possible way of overcoming this difficulty is to retain some of the off-diagonal elements of the Hessian, so that G is approximated by a near-diagonal (e.g. tridiagonal) matrix. Such an approach forms part of the 'adaptive least squares' algorithm in Kollias and Anastassiou (1989). However, it appears that no systematic assessment of the effectiveness of near-diagonal Hessian approximations has yet been undertaken.

4.2.2 Reduced Function and Gradient Evaluations

One characteristic feature of MLP training is the way in which the error function E and gradient $\mathbf{g}$ are calculated jointly, one pattern at a time, so that the calculation of the partial error E_p for pattern p is followed immediately by the calculation of the partial gradient $\mathbf{g}_p$ for that pattern. This contravenes a widespread assumption in the classical optimisation literature – namely that the function and the gradient can be evaluated separately, i.e. given that $E(\mathbf{x}_k)$ has already been evaluated, the subsequent calculation of $g(\mathbf{x}_k)$ does not require the re-evaluation of $E(\mathbf{x}_k)$.

The advantage of being able to evaluate E and $\mathbf{g}$ separately is that it is possible to perform fewer function and/or gradient evaluations than in the case where E and $\mathbf{g}$ must be evaluated simultaneously, without loss of information. The ability to evaluate E and $\mathbf{g}$ separately makes it possible to avoid evaluating E at the same point twice; for example, when a non-derivative line-search strategy has evaluated $E(\mathbf{x}_k + \alpha_k\mathbf{p}_k)$, the multivariate algorithm need only evaluate $g(\mathbf{x}_{k+1})$, not $E(\mathbf{x}_{k+1})$. It is also possible to avoid unnecessary gradient evaluations; for example, with certain model-trust region strategies it is possible to evaluate $E(\mathbf{x}_k + \mathbf{s}_k)$, and only if $\mathbf{s}_k$ is an acceptable step calculate $g(\mathbf{x}_k + \mathbf{s}_k)$.

When developing classical MLP training algorithms, the only way to exploit these opportunities for avoiding unnecessary function and gradient evaluations is to store, for each pattern in the training set, the output of every non-input node in the network, i.e. every $y_{i,p}^l$ for $l>0$. With the intermediate output values of the network nodes stored in this manner, it is possible to calculate the gradient in P consecutive backward passes; it is no longer necessary to interleave the forward passes and backward passes, as is the case with the usual backpropagation gradient calculation (see Section 1.3.1). This approach has NP storage costs for a network with N (non-input) nodes and a training set with P patterns.

For an MLP implemented in the normal manner (i.e. without the storage of the NP $y_{i,p}^l$ s), the necessity of evaluating the error function and gradient simultaneously has important implications for the choice of line-search strategy. Consider, for example, the efficient non-derivative backtracking strategy of Section 3.1.3. If the mean number of function evaluations per k iteration is less than two – which is likely to be the case under moderately favourable conditions, provided 'error-reduction' parameter μ in equation (3.6) is set to a small value (as recommended) – it is typically more efficient to evaluate the gradient at the same time (i.e. at each m iteration of the line-search algorithm), even if that gradient information is not used by the line-search strategy itself. For instance, at those k iterations when $\alpha_k{=}1$ is an acceptable step, the non-derivative backtracking method will evaluate $E(\mathbf{w}_k + \alpha_k\mathbf{p}_k)$, then $E(\mathbf{w}_{k+1})$ and $g(\mathbf{w}_{k+1})$, whereas the derivative version need only evaluate $E(\mathbf{w}_k + \alpha_k\mathbf{p}_k)$ and $g(\mathbf{w}_k + \alpha_k\mathbf{p}_k)$. For this reason, derivative line searches are likely to be more efficient than non-derivative line searches in the context of MLP training, provided the required approximation of the minimum in search direction $\mathbf{p}_k$ at each k iteration is sufficiently inaccurate (see discussion in Section 3.1.2).

The efficient model-trust region strategies of Section 3.2 and backtracking line searches of Section 3.1.3 have, until recently, received comparatively little attention from those designing MLP training algorithms. Many neural network researchers continue to use safeguarded polynomial interpolation line searches, such as Brent's method (Section 3.1.1), in spite of their comparatively high computational costs at each training epoch. A number of neural net researchers have proposed simple heuristic strategies for reducing the average number of function evaluations per epoch required by safeguarded polynomial line-search algorithms. (Invariably, non-derivative safeguarded polynomial line searches are preferred to derivative ones.) For example, Kinsella (1992) places an upper limit on the number of m iterations of Brent's method allowed at any given training epoch (k iteration); Kinsella recommends an upper limit of $m{=}5$. A second option is to perform a line search periodically, rather than at every epoch. (This latter approach forms the basis of a simple on-line training strategy discussed in Section 4.3.)

Rather than dwell on the subject of heuristic step-length strategies, the important point to make here is that such approaches are largely redundant given the low computational costs at each iteration of the backtracking line-search and model-trust region strategies discussed in Chapter 3. When training a network in batch mode using a second-order training strategy, it rarely (if ever) makes sense to adopt a simple heuristic strategy for setting the step length in preference to an efficient classical strategy. Classical methods for choosing an appropriate step length at each epoch are theoretically sound, robust in practice and relatively insensitive to the choice of parameter settings; heuristic step-length strategies tend to be ineffective in general and sensitive to the setting of one or more user-defined parameters.

There is, however, one important circumstance when heuristic step-length strategies may have an important role to play – that is, when the network is trained in on-line mode. This topic is addressed in the next section.

4.3   Second-Order On-Line Training

4.3.1   An Introduction to Second-Order On-Line Training Strategies

An underlying assumption in classical optimisation theory is that the error surface remains constant throughout the optimisation process. When MLPs are trained in on-line mode the error surface is not constant, as the set of training patterns presented to the network is liable to change from one iteration to the next. As a consequence, the only 'natural' way to implement a classical training algorithm is off-line (i.e. in batch mode).

Nevertheless, if classical training methods are to be applied to training sets containing redundant information, the ability to use these methods in on-line mode is highly desirable (see on-line versus off-line discussion in Section 1.3.4). Like traditional batch backpropagation, classical training methods implemented in batch mode are liable to perform many redundant derivative calculations when applied to redundant training sets. Indeed, on-line backpropagation can out-perform second-order training methods implemented in batch mode if the training set contains sufficient redundant information.

Implementing a second-order method for on-line training is not the straightforward task that it is for backpropagation with a fixed step-length. Broadly speaking, it is possible to take two contrasting approaches to second-order on-line training:

- The first approach is to implement a 'full-blooded' on-line training strategy, similar to on-line backpropagation. As with on-line backpropagation, a key issue for such a strategy is the choice of on-line training rate (step length). Owing to the effects of stochastic noise, this approach to second-order on-line training is not suitable for second-order methods that update the search direction using stored derivative information from previous iterations (such as the quasi-Newton methods, conjugate gradient methods and 'memoryless' quasi-Newton method described in Chapter 3).

- The second approach is to implement a 'noise-free' on-line training strategy, i.e. one that isolates the chosen second-order algorithm from the usual stochastic effects of on-line training. This approach has two key advantages over the 'full-blooded' approach to second-order on-line training: it can be used in conjunction with second-order methods that depend on stored derivative information from previous iterations; and the step length can be chosen optimally at each iteration using a classical line-search or model-trust region strategy. However, 'noise-free' on-line training strategies are much more difficult to implement.

In the remainder of this introduction to second-order on-line training we shall briefly consider two contrasting on-line strategies that are both simple and 'noisy'. These strategies are appropriate for only a limited class of classical methods. 'Noise-free' on-line training strategies, which can be used in conjunction with any of the classical methods described in Chapters 2 and 3, are the subject of Section 4.3.2.

In Section 4.2.1 we considered various schemes for calculating a diagonal approximation to the Hessian matrix. Le Cun (1989) uses the diagonal approximation given by equations (4.19) and (4.20) as the basis for an on-line training strategy that utilises a separate training-rate (step-length) parameter α_i $(1 \le i \le W)$ for each weight in the network. Le Cun's approach is to set the W training-rate parameters using a formula that incorporates a running estimate of the Hessian's diagonal elements. To explain le Cun's strategy, we revert to vector notation, so that $(w_i)_k$ denotes the value of the ith weight at epoch k. Le Cun's weight update rule is given by

$$(w_i)_{k+1} = (w_i)_k + (\alpha_i)_k \left(\frac{\partial E}{\partial w_i} \right)_k \tag{4.22}$$

with the training rate α_i set according to the formula

$$\alpha_i = \frac{\lambda}{\mu + H_{ii}} \tag{4.23}$$

where scalar H_{ii} is the estimated value of the ith diagonal element of the Hessian matrix. The scalars λ and μ in equation (4.23) are heuristic constants. Le Cun's formula for updating H_{ii} in (4.23) is given by

$$(H_{ii})_k = (1-\gamma)(H_{ii})_{k-1} + \gamma \left(\frac{\partial^2 E}{\partial w_i^2} \right)_k \tag{4.24}$$

where the constant $\gamma\,(0 < \gamma \le 1)$ determines the degree to which the diagonal element H_{ii} at iteration k is determined by the current, as opposed to the previous, value(s) of $\partial^2 E / \partial w_i^2$.

Although le Cun's on-line scheme has attractive properties (notably its simplicity), it has two major drawback. First, the diagonal approximation of the Hessian matrix can be ineffective, for the reasons given in Section 4.2.1. Second, no guidance is given in le Cun (1989) about how the parameters λ, μ and γ should be set in practice.

Finally, an even simpler approach to setting the on-line step length α is proposed in Barnard (1992). Barnard's scheme, which is designed to be used with the classical steepest descent method, calculates α periodically – rather than at every epoch – by performing a classical line search on the entire training set; α is then scaled using the norm of the local gradient. At other epochs (i.e. between successive line searches), the network is trained using a subset of patterns, with α fixed at the value calculated during the last line-search epoch.

The key to the effectiveness of Barnard's strategy is the number of training epochs that elapse between successive line searches. Too few, and the network will still perform a significant number of redundant gradient calculations; too many, and step length α will have an inappropriate value most of the time. Clearly, the optimal interval between successive line searches will vary from task to task; indeed, there is no guarantee that the optimal interval will not change considerably during a single training run. Barnard's approach is to perform a line search whenever a proposed step does not decrease the network error, or when the number of epochs that have elapsed since the last line search exceeds a fixed heuristic limit (Barnard recommends a limit of 20 epochs).

4.3.2 'Noise-Free' On-Line Training Schemes

Whenever on-line training has been discussed in this book, it has been assumed that the subset of training patterns, and hence the MLP error surface, varies substantially from one epoch to the next. Indeed, this is precisely what occurs with 'traditional' on-line training strategies. However, it is possible to take a completely different approach to on-line training. If the subset of patterns presented to the network is chosen in an appropriate way, it is possible to prevent large changes in the shape of the MLP error surface at each training epoch. The significance of this approach from the perspective of second-order training is that, provided the on-line strategy ensures that the MLP error surface is sufficiently unchanged from one epoch to the next, second-order classical methods can be applied in on-line mode without modification – that is, as if they are being used in batch mode. An on-line strategy that fulfils this role will be termed a 'noise-free' on-line training strategy.

The obvious way to prevent changes in the shape of the MLP error surface is to present the same subset of patterns to the network at successive epochs. One simple, naïve strategy would be to train the network on a small, randomly chosen subset of patterns until it converges, and then progressively increase the subset size by adding new patterns from the full training set. Unfortunately, this sort of scheme is liable to be ineffective in practice because a decrease in error with respect to the subset of patterns does not guarantee a decrease for the whole training set; as a consequence, solving the sub-problem (defined by the subset of patterns) may have a detrimental effect on the network's ability to solve the full problem (defined by the full training set).

A more rigorous approach is to select a subset of patterns for which the corresponding error surface is an approximation to the error surface for the entire training set. To achieve this it is necessary to normalise the error for each subset – so that, for example, the sum-of-squares error function given by equation (1.5) becomes

$$E^B = \frac{1}{2B} \sum_{p=1}^{B} \sum_{i=1}^{N^L} \left(t_{i,p} - y_{i,p}^L \right)^2 \qquad (4.25)$$

where E^B is the normalised error for a subset containing B patterns. With this approach, the difficult part is how to select an appropriate subset at each training epoch, i.e. one that is highly 'representative' of the entire training set, so that a reduction in E^B is very likely to produce a corresponding reduction in the total network error. The choice of subset size B is crucial in this regard. If B is too small, it is unlikely that a chosen subset will satisfy the preceding criterion; if B is too large, only a small number of redundant calculations will be avoided. The optimal subset size is problem-specific, and is likely to vary as training proceeds.

An example of a scheme which combines a strategy for adapting the subset size with a mechanism for ensuring that the chosen subset has a high probability of producing a reduction in the total error E is the *update validation* scheme devised by Møller (1993b). Møller's scheme involves two subsets of patterns: an *update block* used to update the network weights and a *sample block* used to validate each update; at each iteration, the update block contains patterns selected uniformly from the sample block of the preceding iteration. The sample block, which is chosen using standard sampling techniques, is used to estimate an *update probability* P_k – that is, the probability that an update based on that block will decrease the total network error. The weights at iteration k are then updated with that (estimated) probability. Provided the mean errors for different subsets of patterns have a normal distribution around the mean error for the total training set, P_k can be estimated by

$$\hat{P}_k = \frac{1}{\sqrt{2\pi}} \int_{-\infty}^{M} e^{-\frac{1}{2}t^2} \, dt$$

$$M = \frac{E_{k1}^S - E_{k2}^S}{\sigma_k}$$

(4.26)

where E_{k1}^S and E_{k2}^S are the mean errors of the sample block before and after the update at iteration k, and σ_k is the standard error of the sample block. The sample block size B_k^S is chosen such that the error of the block is very close to the error of the complete training set with a high degree of probability, i.e.

$$P\left(\frac{\left| E_k^S - E_k \right|}{E_k} \geq r \right) = \alpha$$

(4.27)

where α is an (unspecified) 'small probability' and r the relative error. (To prevent a sample block having too great a size, Møller suggests an upper bound on B^S of 5% of the total number of patterns in the training set.) The update block size B^U is optimised using a binary search algorithm (subject to $B_k^U \leq B_{k-1}^S$), with the suitability of a given B^U measured in terms of the gain function $\Phi_k(B^U)$ given by

$$\Phi_k\left(B^U \right) = \frac{B_{k-1}^S \left(E_{(k-1)1}^S - E_{(k-1)2}^S \right) + B^U \left(E_{k1}^U - E_{k2}^U \right)}{\left(B_{k-1}^S + B^U \right) B^U E_{k1}^U}$$

(4.28)

Full details of Møller's scheme are given in the appendices of Møller (1993b).

Rather than select the subset patterns by random sampling, a number of re-searchers have proposed schemes for actively selecting subset patterns, an approach known as *active data selection*. The challenge for such schemes is how to maximise the information content of the subset without greatly adding to the computational costs. An example of a scheme that takes a Bayesian approach to active data selection is given in MacKay (1992).

4.4 Conclusion

In this chapter we have seen that there are a many ways in which second-order methods can be tailored to the particular requirements of MLP training. However, there is as yet no 'definitive' way of implementing a second-order training method. Indeed, many of the heuristic strategies for lowering storage costs (Section 4.2) or for reducing the number of redundant gradient evaluations (Section 4.3) risk 'throwing the baby (i.e. the benefits of a quadratic model) out with the bath-water'.

Probably the most principled approach to date is Møller's update validation scheme (Section 4.3.2) designed to improve the efficiency of second-order training methods when applied to large redundant training sets. When implemented with a suitable $O(W)$ storage second-order algorithm (such as Møller's own 'scaled' con-jugate gradient algorithm), both goals – i.e. low storage costs and few redundant gradient evaluations – are achieved simultaneously. However, one objection to this approach (voiced by Battiti (1992)) is that it may often be possible to achieve an equivalent saving in redundant computations by *pre-processing* the training set. (For an excellent introduction to pre-processing and feature extraction, see Bishop (1995).)

5. *An Experimental Comparison of MLP Training Methods*

This chapter is dedicated to presenting a detailed analysis of the performance of first- and second-order training algorithms when applied to a range of benchmark training tasks. The chapter is in three main sections: Section 5.1 gives details of the chosen benchmark tasks; Section 5.2 provides a detailed description of the architectures, training algorithms and parameter settings used in the tests; and Section 5.3 presents an analysis of the test results in terms of training speed and 'global reliability'. The training data are reproduced in tabulated form in the Appendix.

Throughout the remainder of the book, the term 'global' is used in the original sense introduced in Section 1.2.1 – that is, to distinguish between local and global minima (cf. the term 'global convergence' used in Chapters 2 and 3).

5.1 Benchmark Training Tasks

The choice of appropriate benchmark test problems is a difficult but crucial aspect of MLP research. Desirable properties of a benchmark training task include: widespread usage (enabling comparisons with earlier research); small size (so that a large number of training runs can be performed within a reasonable length of time); and similarity to 'real-world' MLP problems (giving a degree of confidence that a successful training method can be extended to practical applications). Unfortunately, there are no MLP training problems which meet all of these criteria, mainly because there is an approximate trade-off between the size of a problem and its applicability to the 'real world'. Given finite computational resources and time, this leaves a difficult choice.

One option is to perform a small number of training runs with a medium- to large-scale problem. This approach has produced some impressive results, for example:

- Pattichis *et al.* (1991) report that the Polak–Ribiere conjugate gradient algorithm required a much smaller MLP architecture than backpropagation with momentum to successfully solve an electromyography (EMG) diagnosis task with 740 patterns. Average training times were reduced from 3 hours for backpropagation to 1 minute for the conjugate gradient algorithm (using a DEC Microvax III workstation). (The number of training runs performed is not documented.)

- Kollias and Anastassiou (1989) found that two modified Levenberg–Marquardt algorithms were both faster and more accurate than batch backpropagation with momentum when applied to a digital image halftoning task with 16 000 samples. Only a single training run was performed with each algorithm.

- The results in Møller (1993b) show that an on-line 'scaled' conjugate gradient algorithm (combining Møller's 'scaled' model-trust region strategy of Section 3.2.4 with the update validation on-line training scheme described in Section 4.3.2) was consistently faster than on-line backpropagation when applied to the highly redundant 1000 word NETtalk problem with 5438 patterns. Ten training runs were performed with each algorithm.

Unfortunately, only the last of these results inspires real confidence. This is because, under otherwise identical training conditions, the performance of a training algorithm – in terms of both the length of training time and the final error level – can vary dramatically with different sets of starting weights (even when initialised within the same range); consequently, our confidence that a set of results represents the 'typical' performance of an algorithm (when applied to a given problem) is proportional to the number of training runs undertaken.

A second option – and the one adopted for this book – is to perform a large number of training runs with small, but non-trivial, test problems. Although this approach has obvious disadvantages in terms of the lack of similarity to 'real-world' applications, it has two clear advantages. First, many important trends in the comparative performance of different training methods only emerge if sufficient training runs are performed. Second, a detailed analysis of the MLP error surface and network behaviour is currently only feasible with small-scale training tasks. The benchmark training tasks used in this book are described in the remainder of Section 5.1.

5.1.1 *N*-Parity

N-parity is the name given to a set of binary problems that are widely used in benchmark training tests for MLPs. The *N*-parity training set consists of 2^N training pairs, with each training pair comprising an *N*-length input vector and a single binary target value. The 2^N input vectors represent all possible combinations of *N* binary numbers. If a given input vector contains an odd number of 1s, the corresponding target value is 1; otherwise the target value is 0. As an example, the 3-parity training set is given in Table 5.1. The minimal 'standard' MLP architecture capable of learning *N*-parity is *N*–*N*–1.

The 2-parity problem is the famous *exclusive-OR* or *XOR* problem, the most widely used and extensively analysed of all MLP benchmark training tasks. XOR has

Table 5.1 The eight training pairs
of the 3-parity training set

Input Pattern	Target Output
000	0
001	1
010	1
011	0
100	1
101	0
110	0
111	1

played a prominent role in the history of neural computing. It was used by Minsky and Papert (1969), in their famous book *Perceptrons*, to expose the limitations of single-layer perceptrons when applied to linearly inseparable training tasks, and also by Rumelhart *et al.* (1986) to demonstrate the (relative) effectiveness of multi-layer perceptrons trained by backpropagation.

When learning the XOR problem with any 'standard' $2-m-1$ architecture ($m \geq 2$) and using the mean-squared error function of equation (1.6), local minima are known to occur at two distinct error levels, $E \approx 0.08333$ and $E = 0.0625$. That these are true local minima has been demonstrated by a numerical analysis of the XOR problem by Lisboa and Perantonis (1991). Although it has often been assumed that local minima occur at a third error level of $E = 0.125$, a recent analysis of the XOR error surface for an MLP with two hidden nodes indicates that local minima *cannot* occur at $E = 0.125$ (Hamey, 1995); in other words, the $E = 0.125$ stationary points are saddle points, not local minima. The XOR global minima are at $E = 0$, i.e. there are no residuals at the solution. The configuration of pattern classifications and mis-classifications for each XOR stationary point is as follows:

- $E = 0.125$ saddle points: 4 patterns 50% correct
- $E \approx 0.0833$ local minima: 1 pattern 100% correct, 1 pattern 66.7% correct and 2 patterns 33.3% correct
- $E = 0.0625$ local minima: 2 patterns 100% correct and 2 patterns 50% correct
- $E = 0$ global minima: 4 patterns 100% correct

Sample MLP output values for each of these stationary points are given in Fig. 5.1. It is worth noting that if the usual sigmoid squashing function given by equation (1.2) is applied to the network's output nodes, the XOR minima (both local and global) occur at infinity, i.e. one or more network weights must take on the value $\pm\infty$. In practice, therefore, MLPs are often trained using a modified training set with target values of 0.1 (instead of zero) and 0.9 (instead of one) to prevent network saturation. This option is ignored in the current chapter, but is related to the ERA global optimisation strategy discussed in Section 6.2. The characteristics of the MLP error surface for higher N-parity are broadly similar to those of the XOR error surface, although the number of local minima and the 'hardness' of the problem generally increases with N.

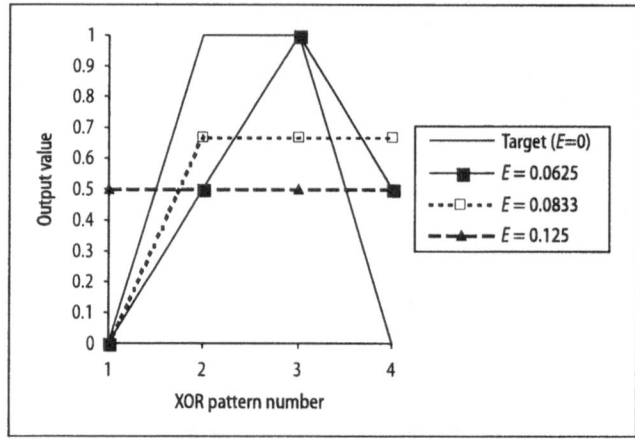

Fig. 5.1 Sample locations of the XOR stationary points in terms of the classification and misclassification of patterns in the XOR training set. (Note that permutations in the output values are possible with the E=0.0625 and E≈0.0833 local minima.)

N-parity is justly criticised as a benchmark training test for having little in common with real-life pattern classification applications; *N*-parity lacks redundancy and does not test a network's ability to generalise from the input data. However, *N*-parity has several positive characteristics:

- It is sufficiently small-scale (for small *N*) to allow a large number of training runs to be performed, but sufficiently 'hard' to afford a genuine test of a training algorithm's abilities.
- When tackled using a minimal *N*–*N*–1 architecture, the corresponding MLP error surface is known to be 'riddled with local minima' (Lisboa, 1992, p. 252), providing a convenient test of a training algorithm's 'global reliability'.
- It provides an easy way to assess how the performance of a training algorithm scales with the dimensionality of a problem (i.e. with different *N*).
- As the most widely used benchmark task, an extensive range of published results are available for comparison in the neural network literature.

The 2-, 3-, 4- and 5-parity problems were tested for this book using, in each case, a minimal 'standard' *N*–*N*–1 architecture.

5.1.2 The sin(*x*) Problem

The sin(*x*) problem is the first of three small, non-trivial function-learning tasks used in this book. The sine training set adopted here – following McInerney *et al.* (1989) – requires the network to approximate the sine function for a sample of 64 input points chosen uniformly in the interval [0,3π/2]. The sin(*x*) training set is illustrated in Fig. 5.2.

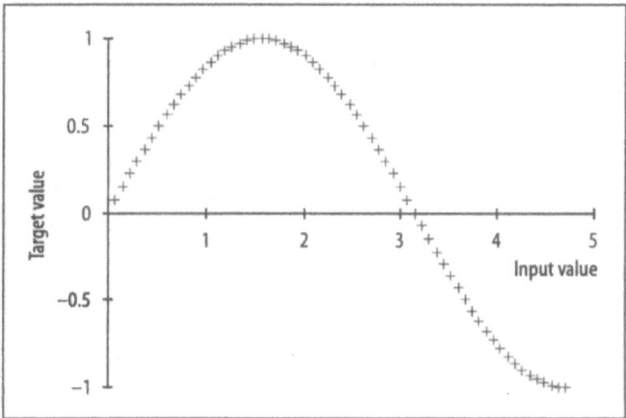

Fig. 5.2 The sin(x) training set with 64 samples.

The minimal 'standard' architecture capable of learning the sin(x) training set given in Fig. 5.2 is 1–2–1. An investigation of the corresponding MLP error surface undertaken by McInerney *et al.* (1989) – combining a smart raster scan of the error surface with numerical analyses of candidate minima – found local minima 'like pinholes in a large flat board' (McInerney *et al.*, 1989, p. 9). It appears that under 'normal' training conditions, an MLP is much less likely to become trapped in the sine local minima than it is to encounter local minima with the N-parity problem (using, in both cases, the appropriate minimal architecture). Using the mean-squared error function of equation (1.6), the sin(x) local minima identified by McInerney *et al.* occur at an error level of $E \approx 0.023$. McInerney *et al.*'s analysis also indicated that the sine global minima are at $E > 0$, i.e. there are residuals at the solution. The lowest error level attained for the sine problem with any of the training methods used here was $E \approx 3.2 \times 10^{-6}$.

In the tests conducted for this book and for Shepherd (1995), it has been found that MLPs occasionally converge to stationary points at other error levels; whether these are local minima or saddle points is not known. The locations of the sine stationary points in terms of the classification and misclassification of patterns in the training set are shown in Fig. 5.3.

5.1.3 The sin(x)cos(2x) Problem

The second function-learning benchmark is the sin(x)cos($2x$) problem. The training set used here – following van der Smagt (1994) – requires the network to approximate the sin(x)cos($2x$) function for a sample of 20 input points chosen uniformly in the interval $[0, 2\pi]$. The sin(x)cos($2x$) training set is shown in Fig. 5.4.

The main reason for choosing both the sin(x)cos($2x$) problem and the tan(x) problem (described in Section 5.1.4) is that it affords the opportunity to compare

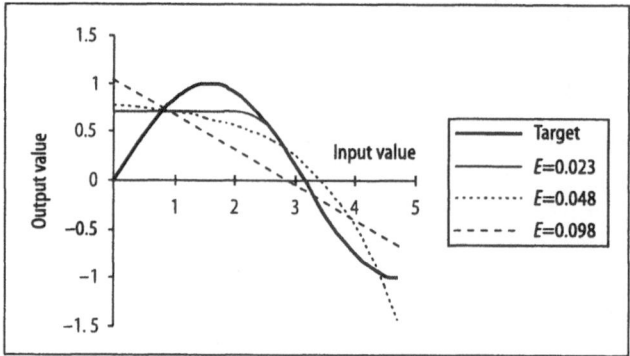

Fig. 5.3 Location of the sin(x) stationary points in terms of the classification and misclassification of patterns in the sin(x) training set.

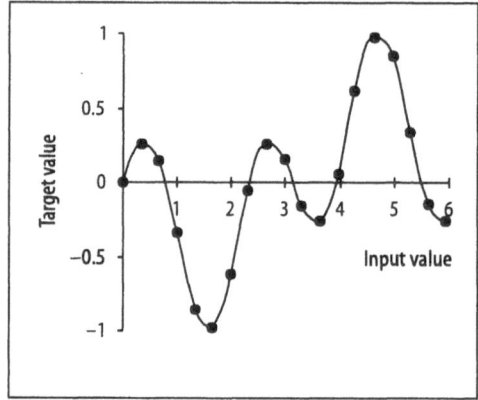

Fig. 5.4 The sin(x)cos($2x$) training set with 20 samples.

the results presented in this chapter with the first- and second-order training results in van der Smagt (1994)[1]. Following van der Smagt's example, a 'standard' 1–10–1 MLP architecture was used in tests for this book.

Unlike the XOR and sin(x) error surfaces, the sin(x)cos($2x$) error surface has not been subject to extensive analysis. In the tests conducted for this book using the mean-squared error function of equation (1.6), a small number of training runs converged to a stationary point at a comparatively high error level of $E\approx0.026$. The lowest error level attained for the sin(x)cos($2x$) problem with any of the training

---

1   Van der Smagt's results are for the following training algorithms: the DFP quasi-Newton method, the Fletcher–Reeves conjugate gradient method, the Polak–Ribiere conjugate gradient method with Powell restarts and steepest descent – all implemented with Brent's line search. 'Traditional' batch backpropagation with fixed training rate and momentum was the chosen backpropagation benchmark.

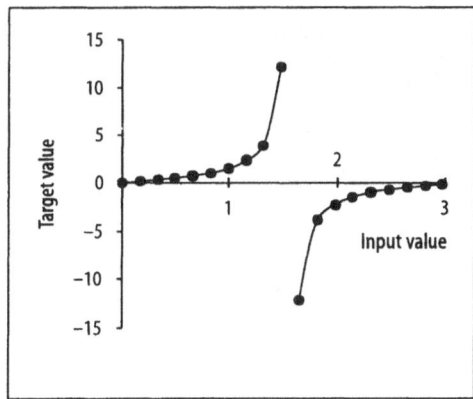

Fig. 5.5 The tan(x) training set with 20 samples.

methods used here was $E \approx 1.0 \times 10^{-21}$, i.e. it appears that the $\sin(x)\cos(2x)$ task has small residuals at the solution.

5.1.4 The tan(x) Problem

The third function-learning problem is the $\tan(x)$ function. The training set used here requires the network to approximate the $\tan(x)$ function for a sample of 20 input points chosen uniformly in the interval $[0,\pi]$. Unlike the $\sin(x)$ and $\sin(x)\cos(2x)$ problems, the $\tan(x)$ problem is discontinuous in the chosen interval – see Fig. 5.5. In this book, the $\tan(x)$ training set was tackled using the same 1–5–1 'standard' MLP architecture used in van der Smagt (1994).

The error surface for the $\tan(x)$ training tasks appears to contain numerous local minima at both high and low error levels. The lowest error level attained for the $\tan(x)$ problem with any of the training methods used here was $E \approx 3.1 \times 10^{-8}$, i.e. it appears that the $\tan(x)$ task has residuals at the solution.

5.2 Initial Training Conditions

It is well-recognised that MLP training is sensitive to initial conditions (see, for example, Kolen and Pollack (1990)). The performance of an MLP training algorithm may be sensitive to a range of factors, including the choice of error function, weight initialisation range, floating-point precision and termination criteria, as well as the value of any user-defined parameters. As a consequence, the usefulness of published training results is diminished when this type of information is omitted from the written account.

The aim of this section is to specify in detail the architectures (Section 5.2.1), training algorithms and parameter settings (Section 5.2.2) and termination conditions (Section 5.2.3) used in the benchmark tests conducted for this book. The abbreviations used in the presentation of training data later in this chapter are defined in Section 5.2.2.

5.2.1 MLP Architectures

The defining characteristics of the MLP architectures used in the benchmark tests are as follows:

- The tests were performed using the following 'standard' architectures: N–N–1 for the N-parity problem; 1–2–1 for the $\sin(x)$ problem; 1–10–1 for the $\sin(x)\cos(2x)$ problem; and 1–5–1 for the $\tan(x)$ problem. (These are the same architectures as the ones discussed in Section 5.1.)
- All training was in batch mode using the mean-squared error function of equation (1.6) and sigmoid squashing function of equation (1.2).
- Sigmoidal output nodes were used for the N-parity problem. However, since the function-learning problems have target values outside the range of the sigmoid squashing function (i.e. [0,1]), linear output nodes were used for these tasks.
- The network was initialised using 100 sets of starting weights – one for each training run – generated randomly in the range $[-r,r]$, where r was set according to the heuristic formula given by equation (1.3).
- All weights, derivatives and other variables were implemented with double (15-digit) precision arithmetic.

The scheme described in Section 4.2.2 for reducing the number of function and/or gradient calculations by storing the network's 'intermediate' output values ($y_{i,p}^{l}$) was *not* implemented for these tests.

5.2.2 Training Algorithms

The results in Section 5.3 are for the following multivariate algorithms:

BD   The bold driver method (Section 1.3.2). The bold driver user-defined parameters (equation (1.17)) were as follows for all training tasks: training rate growth constant $\rho=1.1$; training rate reduction constant $\sigma=0.5$; and initial training rate $\eta_0=0.5$.

SD   The classical steepest descent method (Section 2.1.1).

CG   The Polak–Ribiere conjugate gradient method (Section 3.3.4). The algorithm was implemented with the 'traditional' conjugate gradient restart scheme – that is, the search direction was reset to the steepest descent direction every W epochs (where W is the total number of network weights) and whenever the search direction generated by the multivariate algorithm was not a descent direction (i.e. failed to satisfy equation (2.4)).

NQN   The 'memoryless' BFGS quasi-Newton method (Section 3.3.3). The NQN algorithm was implemented with the same restart scheme as the CG algorithm.

IQN   The BFGS quasi-Newton method (Section 3.3.2) using the inverse Hessian representation. The IQN algorithm was implemented with the same restart scheme as the CG algorithm.

QN   The BFGS quasi-Newton method (Section 3.3.2) with the Hessian matrix represented by its modified Cholesky factors (Section 2.2.2). No resets were performed with the QN algorithm.

LM   The Levenberg–Marquardt nonlinear least-squares method (Section 3.4.2).

The preceding multivariate algorithms (excluding BD) were combined with one or more line-search and model-trust region strategies from the following list:

BR   Brent's line search with derivatives (Section 3.1.1). The line-search accuracy parameters were set to $\eta=0.5$ (equation (3.4)) and $\mu=0.25$ (equation (3.6)) for all training tasks. The BR algorithm was used with the following multivariate algorithms: SD, CG, NQN, IQN and QN.

BT   The Dennis–Schnabel backtracking line-search algorithm with derivatives (Section 3.1.3). The line-search accuracy parameters were set to $\eta=0.9$ (equation (3.4)) and $\mu=10^{-4}$ (equation (3.6)) for all training tasks. The BT algorithm was used with the following multivariate algorithms: QN and IQN.

MT(1) Fletcher's model-trust region strategy (Section 3.2.2). The user-defined parameters were set to the following values for all training tasks: model-trust region parameter $\mu_0=10^{-5}$ (equation (2.21)); ratio growth constant $\sigma=4$; ratio reduction constant $\rho=2$; upper ratio limit $r^U=0.75$; and lower ratio limit $r^L=0.25$. Fletcher's method was used with the following multivariate algorithms: QN and LM.

MT(2) Møller's 'scaled' model-trust region strategy (Section 3.2.4). The user-defined parameters were set to the following values for all training tasks: model-trust region parameter $\mu_0=10^{-6}$ (equation (3.34)); and finite-difference parameter $\omega=10^{-4}$ (equation (3.35)). For consistency, the ratio reduction constant and upper and lower ratio limits were set to the same values as for Fletcher's method. Møller's strategy was used with the following multivariate algorithms: CG, NQN and IQN.

A few comments are in order regarding the rationale behind this choice of training algorithms. In general, the aim has been to choose algorithms that are both effective and relatively simple to implement, as these are likely to be of greatest interest to the general reader. Thus, when choosing a suitable model-trust region strategy to use with the quasi-Newton and Levenberg–Marquardt methods, Fletcher's method was preferred to the simple model-trust region strategy of Section 3.2.1 (on grounds of efficiency) and to the double dogleg method of Section 3.2.3 (on grounds of ease of implementation). Newton's method and the finite-difference Newton's method have been neglected altogether because of their excessive computational costs at each training epoch. (The reason for implementing both the IQN and QN algorithms – i.e. the BFGS quasi-Newton method with and without resets – will become apparent in Section 5.3.)

Although generally less efficient than the other line-search and model-trust region strategies tested here, Brent's line search with derivatives has several positive characteristics when comparing the performance of different classical multivariate algorithms. First, it can be implemented with a wider range of multivariate classical algorithms than the other line search strategies and model-trust region strategies discussed in Chapter 3. Second, Brent's method is renowned for its robustness; although comparatively slow, it is exceedingly reliable. Reasonable progress is to be expected even under relatively unfavourable conditions. In other words, if the multivariate algorithm grinds to a halt, it is unlikely to be the 'fault' of Brent's method. So as not to penalise multivariate methods that are liable to suffer a degradation in performance when used with inaccurate line searches, Brent's line search was chosen to be 'fairly accurate' for all methods. A moderately accurate Brent's line search is probably the closest we can get to a 'level playing field' when comparing the performance of different types of multivariate classical algorithm. Note that both Brent's method and the Dennis–Schnabel backtracking algorithm were implemented with derivatives; this ensures that the accuracy of the line search can be regulated explicitly using parameter η in equation (3.4), and is more efficient with an inaccurate backtracking line search for the reasons given in Section 4.2.2.

Inevitably, the choice of a 'fair' backpropagation benchmark is difficult, given the diversity of possible implementations. The bold driver method was chosen here because, in preliminary tests on the benchmark tasks of Section 5.1, it outperformed fixed training-rate backpropagation – batch or on-line, with or without momentum – even with the training rate tuned to its near-optimal fixed value. It is worth stressing that no tuning of parameters was undertaken with any of the chosen algorithms; in the author's experience, none of these algorithms is particularly sensitive to the choice of parameter settings – in stark contrast to 'traditional' backpropagation – provided they are set within recommended bounds.

Finally, there are several ways in which it may be possible to enhance the performance of the chosen training algorithms:

- Møller's 'scaled' model-trust region strategy: calculate the term $\mathbf{Gp}$ exactly (using the algorithm discussed in Section 4.1.2) rather than by means of the finite-difference formula (3.35).

- Nonlinear least-squares methods: the quasi-Newton Hessian approximation of equation (3.70) is likely to be more effective than the standard Levenberg–Marquardt approximation (given by equation (3.69)) when the training problem has residuals at the solution.

- Model-trust region strategies: for multivariate algorithms that store a model of the Hessian matrix, the double dogleg algorithm (Section 3.2.3) is likely to be more efficient than Fletcher's method, although the extra cost in programming time should not be underestimated.

- First-order methods and, to a lesser extent, conjugate gradient methods, are likely to benefit from a suitable scaling or preconditioning scheme (see Section 2.2.3). The improvement with quasi-Newton methods is, however, likely to be marginal.

5.2.3 Termination Conditions

Three common-sense termination criteria are generally applied to unconstrained minimisation: "'Have we solved the problem?', 'Have we ground to a halt?' or 'Have we run out of money, time or patience?'" (Dennis and Schnabel, 1983, p. 159). All three criteria were used for the benchmark training runs, but the specific termination tests performed were somewhat different from those advocated in the optimisation literature (Dennis and Schnabel, 1983; Gill *et al.*, 1981). In order to accurately record the susceptibility of each training algorithm to becoming trapped in local minima, priority was given to the prevention of premature termination under all reasonable circumstances. A training run was deemed to have 'ground to a halt' only if the gradient fell to zero or the number of training epochs reached an upper limit of 50 000.

A training run was deemed to have been successful if the network successfully classified all patterns in the training set within a tolerance of 0.1 for each target element. Note that, in order to generate data for the figures in Section 5.3, successful training runs were allowed to 'run on' to lower error levels of $E=10^{-4}$ or $E=10^{-6}$ (depending on the training task), where E is the MSE for the full training set.

5.3 Experimental Results

This section presents a detailed analysis of the training results that were generated when the algorithms of Section 5.2.2 were applied to the benchmark tests of Section 5.1 using the architectures described in Section 5.2.1. Two aspects of training algorithm performance are assessed – 'global reliability' (i.e. how prone an algorithm is to getting trapped in local minima) and training speed.

To simplify the terminology, a training run that satisfies the fairly weak pattern-classification conditions defined in Section 5.2.3 will be deemed to have converged to a global minimum. (This may not be the case with the $\tan(x)$ training task, as the $\tan(x)$ error surface appears to contain numerous local minima at comparatively low error levels.) Similarly, the term 'local minima' will often be used where a more accurate description would be 'stationary points that are probably local minima'.

Note that the abbreviations used throughout this section are defined in Section 5.2.2 above.

5.3.1 'Global Reliability'

Figures 5.6 and 5.7 summarise the rates of successful convergence to global minima for the training algorithms listed in Section 5.2.2 when applied to the *N*-parity task of Section 5.1.1; Fig. 5.6 is for Brent's line-search implementations and Fig. 5.7 is for model-trust region implementations.

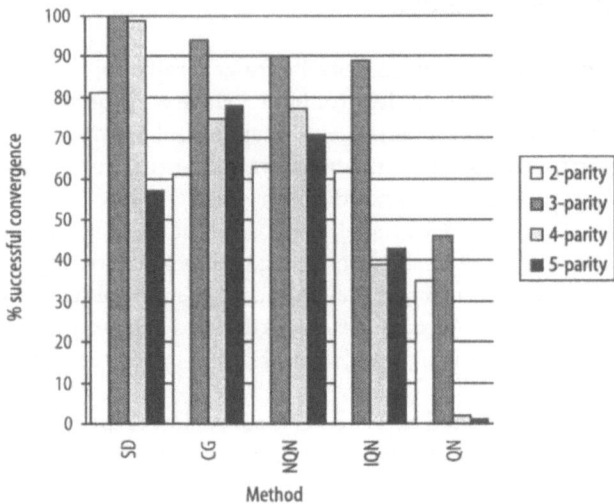

Fig. 5.6 The *N*-parity problem – rates of successful convergence for classical training methods implemented with Brent's line-search algorithm.

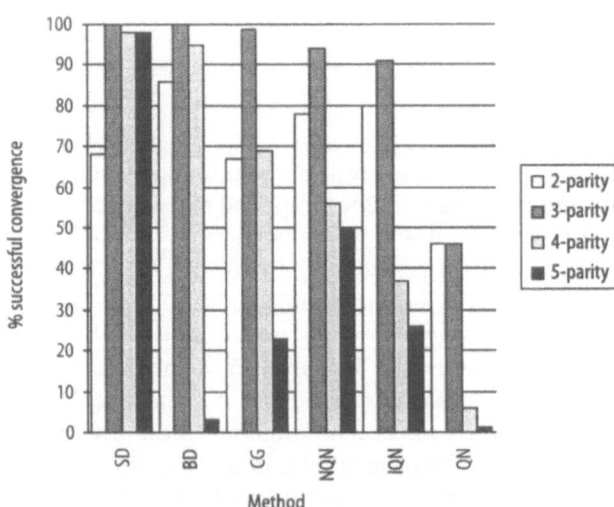

Fig. 5.7 The *N*-parity problem – rates of successful convergence for model-trust region strategies.

Commentary   Before considering the significance of these results, it is important to recognise that there is a fundamental distinction between the causes of training failure recorded in Figs. 5.6 and 5.7. Convergence to a stationary point (typically a local minimum) is the sole cause of training failure with second-order methods and is also the cause of failure for first-order methods (i.e. SD and BD) when applied to the XOR problem. However, the high failure rate for first-order methods when applied to the 5-parity problem is the result of a failure to converge to any stationary point within the allowed number of training epochs; experience suggests that, if allowed sufficient training time, the rate of successful convergence for first-order methods is considerably higher than that recorded in Figs. 5.6 and 5.7 for the 5-parity task.

In the light of these comments, a consistent pattern begins to emerge with respect to the 'global reliability' of different training algorithms. The LM, SD and BD algorithms are less likely to become trapped in local minima than the CG, NQN and IQN algorithms, which in turn are much more 'globally reliable' than the QN algorithm. Perhaps the most telling aspect of these results is the disparity between the performance of the IQN and QN algorithms. Effectively, the only difference between the IQN and QN algorithms is that the former resets to the steepest descent direction every W training epochs, whereas the latter never resets to the steepest descent direction. This disparity is underlined by results presented in Shepherd (1995), showing that the 'global reliability' of both the CG and NQN algorithms falls significantly if they are implemented without resetting (although less dramatically than with the BFGS quasi-Newton algorithm). The significance of these observations is discussed at the end of this section.

Another interesting feature of these results is the difference between the convergence characteristics for the Brent's line search implementation and the model-trust region implementation of the same multivariate algorithm. For example, it is particularly noticeable that the model-trust region implementation of an algorithm is typically much less successful than the Brent's line search implementation with the 4- and 5-parity problems. The reason for this disparity in performance is that a significant percentage of the training runs performed with model-trust region algorithms became trapped at the $E=0.125$ saddle point, whereas the robustness and accuracy of Brent's method was usually sufficient to make progress in the shallow neighbourhood of $E=0.125$. (Ultimately, this is a sign that the chosen weight initialisation range for 4- and 5-parity was too narrow.)

Commentary   As with the N-parity results, there is a clear distinction between the causes of training failure with first-order and second-order training methods in Figs. 5.8 and 5.9; the primary cause of failure with first-order methods appears to be slow convergence, rather than convergence to local minima, whereas for second-order methods the sole cause of training failure is convergence to local minima (or, possibly, saddle points). This observation is reinforced by the experience of van der Smagt (1994), who suggests that steepest descent (implemented with Brent's non-derivative line search) 'is not very sensitive to local minima' with the $\sin(x)\cos(2x)$ task, but requires 4×10^6 iterations 'on the average' to reach a global minimum (van der Smagt, 1994, p. 9). As with the N-parity results, the BFGS quasi-Newton algo-

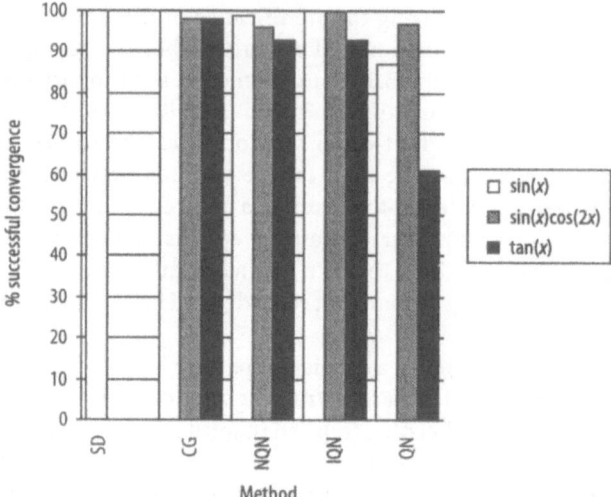

Fig. 5.8 Function-learning problems – rates of successful convergence for classical training methods implemented with Brent's line-search algorithm. Note that the steepest descent algorithm never succeeded in converging to an acceptable solution for either the sin(x)cos(2x) or tan(x) problems within 50 000 epochs.

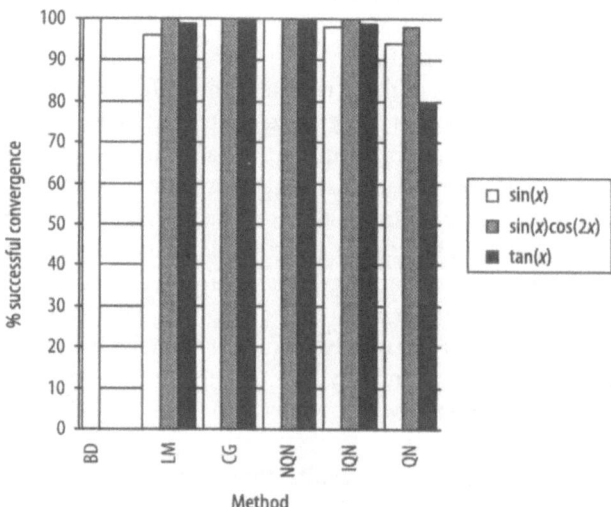

Fig. 5.9 Function-learning problems – rates of successful convergence for model-trust region strategies. Note that the bold driver method never succeeded in converging to an acceptable solution for either the sin(x)cos(2x) or tan(x) problems within 50 000 epochs.

rithm is by far the most likely to get trapped in local minima when no resets are performed (i.e. the QN algorithm), but is significantly more 'globally reliable' when resets are performed every W epochs (i.e. the IQN algorithm).

Summary   Drawing together the N-parity and function-learning results from Figs. 5.6–5.9, it is evident that there is a striking disparity between the global reliability of different training algorithms – a disparity that is not anticipated in classical optimisation theory, but is nevertheless confirmed by the empirical test results given in van der Smagt (1994). For example, a striking feature of van der Smagt's results for the XOR, $\sin(x)\cos(2x)$ and $\tan(x)$ tasks is that the DFP quasi-Newton method (without resets) converged to a global minimum much less frequently than the Polak–Ribiere conjugate gradient method with Powell restarts.

From the perspective of convergence to local minima the algorithms tested here can be grouped as follows, starting with the most 'globally reliable' algorithms:

- BD, SD and LM. (Note that the results in Shepherd (1995) show that the success rate for LM can be increased on both the XOR and sine problems by increasing the initial value of μ_0.)
- The 'resetting' algorithms: CG, NQN and IQN.
- The non-resetting QN algorithm. Tests conducted with the finite-difference Newton's method of Section 3.3.1 suggest that it is as likely as QN to get trapped in local minima.

Although there is no definitive explanation for this behaviour, it seems clear that periodically resetting conjugate gradient and quasi-Newton algorithms reduces the likelihood that they will 'dive into' a good local, but poor global, solution. The fact that CG is generally more 'globally reliable' than IQN may be ascribed to two factors – to the tendency of CG with the Polak–Ribiere update to reset automatically to the steepest descent direction (see Section 3.3.4), and/or to the greater speed and accuracy of IQN (so that fewer resets are performed during a typical training run).

These results have obvious implications for the design and selection of effective training algorithms:

- The choice of second-order training algorithm can have a significant impact on 'global reliability'. The Levenberg–Marquardt algorithm is the most 'globally reliable' second-order algorithm, followed by the Polak–Ribiere conjugate gradient algorithm with a restart scheme.
- It may be advisable to implement quasi-Newton algorithms with a suitable restart procedure, notwithstanding the loss of potentially useful derivative information.
- Global optimisation strategies appear to be of particular relevance when designing second-order training methods.

Global optimisation is the subject of Chapter 6.

5.3.2 Training Speed Metrics

Before proceeding with the analysis of the comparative speeds of different training algorithms, we need to adopt an appropriate measure of training speed. The main training speed metric adopted here is the number of *equivalent function evaluations* (EFEs), defined by

$$\text{EFEs} = \frac{\text{function evaluations} + \text{gradient evaluations}}{2} \tag{5.1}$$

This is the preferred training speed metric in the optimisation literature. In the context of MLP training, a single function evaluation consists of P forward passes (for a training set with P patterns), and a single gradient evaluation consists of P backward passes. The computational effort associated with an EFE is, therefore, roughly equivalent to that associated with a single epoch of batch backpropagation. (The number of training epochs is an inappropriate measure of training speed because the number of function and/or gradient evaluations varies from epoch to epoch with classical line-search algorithms.) The main drawback with the EFE as a training speed metric is that it takes no account of the computational complexity of the update rules for different methods; how significant this is in practice depends on factors such as the relative size of the training set and MLP architecture.

The tabulated results printed in the Appendix characterise the number of EFEs required to achieve a given error-tolerance using three statistics – the mean, the standard deviation and the median; in all three cases, runs that failed to achieve that error tolerance are ignored. The mean EFEs per run and the median EFEs per run represent different estimates of the 'typical' speed of a given training algorithm. Before embarking on an analysis of the comparative speeds of different algorithms, it is worth examining which of these two measures is superior. Figure 5.10 shows the distribution of the training speed data for a single combination of algorithm,

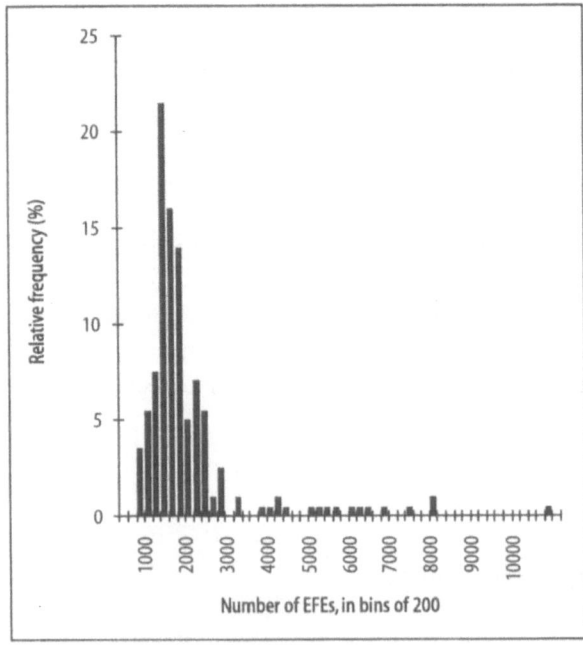

Fig. 5.10 Relative frequency histogram for the steepest descent method applied to the sin(x) training task, with an error tolerance of E=0.01. Note that the corresponding mean and median are 1680.3 EFEs and 1311.0 EFEs respectively. (This example was taken from Shepherd (1995).)

task and settings. A prominent feature of this distribution – and one that is common to most MLP training speed data – is the broad tail, caused by a small number of outlier points (corresponding to training runs that required a disproportionately large number of EFEs to reach a given error tolerance). Since the mean is sensitive to the breadth of the tail, whereas the median is not, the latter is the more robust estimate of the typical speed of an MLP training algorithm[2]. For this reason, the median EFE rate is the adopted measure of training speed in Section 5.3.3.

5.3.3 Training Speed Results

Before embarking on the analysis of training speed results, a few comments are in order concerning how the information is presented. Most of the figures in this section plot the mean-squared error on the x-axis and the median number of EFEs per training run on the y-axis. Note that the x-axis is plotted using a logarithmic scale; when the disparity between the performance of methods plotted on the same graph is sufficiently great, the y-axis is also plotted using a logarithmic scale. Only training runs that reached a given error level are plotted. As a consequence, there are circumstances where the 'true' speed of the first-order algorithms (i.e. SD and BD) will be slower than the value plotted, as the slowest runs will have been 'filtered out' by the upper epoch limit of 50 000. To complement the figures presented in this section, a parallel series of tables is given in the Appendix.

Before comparing the number of EFEs per training run expended by different training algorithms, it is useful to compare the cost of different line-search and model-trust region strategies at each training epoch. Using the parameter settings specified in Section 5.2.2, Brent's line search with derivatives (BR) typically cost 3.5–4.5 EFEs per epoch, compared with 1.0–1.75 EFEs per epoch for the backtracking line search with derivatives (BT). In the case of model-trust region strategies, Fletcher's method costs 1.0 EFEs per epoch and Møller's 'scaled' model-trust region strategy 2.0 EFEs per epoch. Full details are given in the Appendix tables.

Commentary (Figs. 5.11–5.13)   The rates of convergence for the XOR problem are substantially in line with expectations (see Section 3.5), as the following observations demonstrate:

- In Figs. 5.11 and 5.12 there is a distinction between the performance of the 'slow linear' methods (SD and BD), the 'fast linear' methods (CG and NQN), the 'super-linear' QN method and the 'quadratic (for zero-residual problems)' LM method. (This distinction becomes clearer with higher N.)

- The model-trust region implementation of a method (Fig. 5.12) is more efficient than a fairly accurate line-search implementation (Fig. 5.11), except at low error levels (where greater accuracy is likely to be advantageous).

---

2   There are several instances in the tabulated results of the Appendix where the mean EFE rate grossly overestimates the typical performance of an algorithm. A prime example is the 3-parity performance of the CG algorithm at $E=10^{-6}$ in Table A.5.

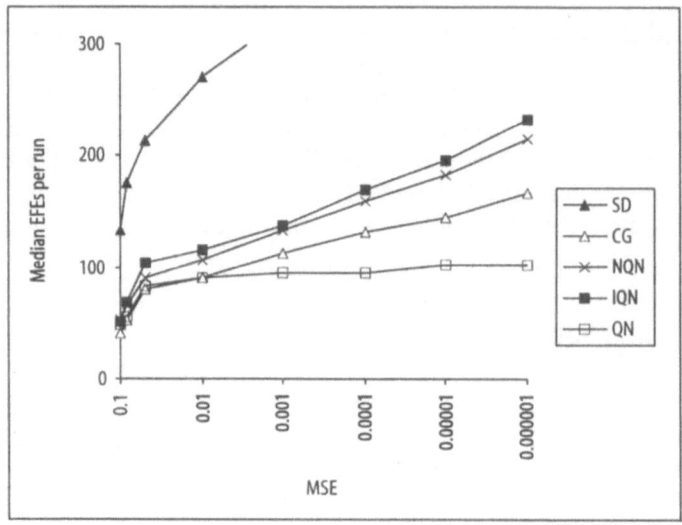

Fig. 5.11 The 2-parity (XOR) problem – Brent's line search (Table A.1).

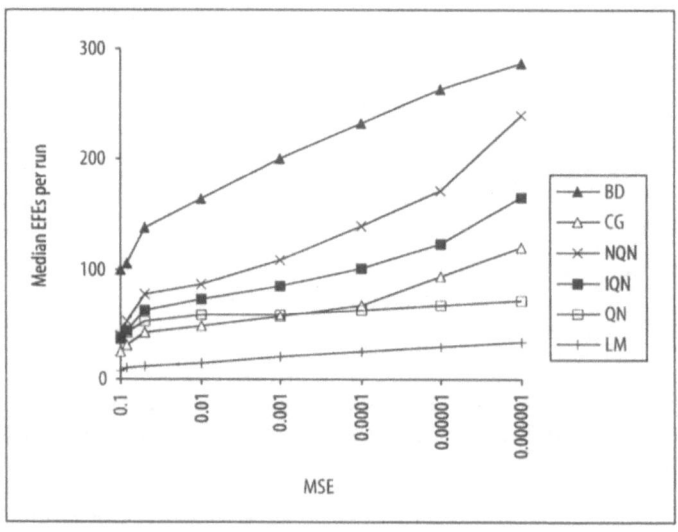

Fig. 5.12 The 2-parity (XOR) problem – model-trust region strategies (Table A.2).

- The BFGS quasi-Newton method is less efficient if useful derivative information is discarded every $W=9$ training epochs – i.e. QN is faster than IQN (Fig. 5.13).
- There is little to choose between a model-trust region (MT) implementation and an inaccurate backtracking line-search (BT) implementation of the non-resetting QN method (Fig. 5.13).

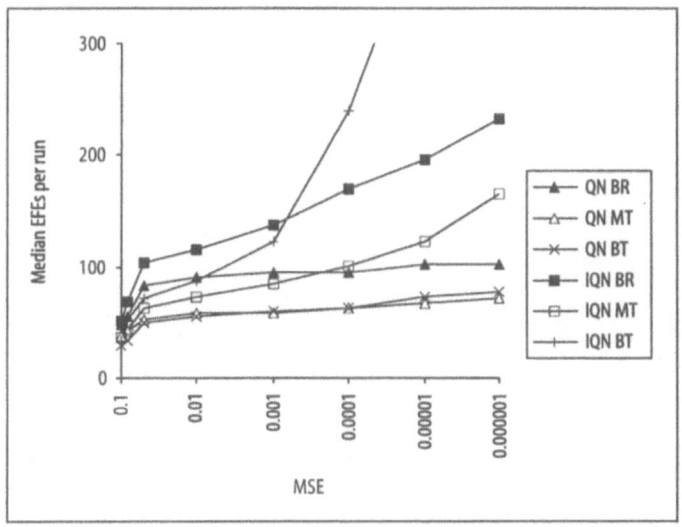

Fig. 5.13 The 2-parity (XOR) problem – BFGS quasi-Newton algorithms (Table A.3).

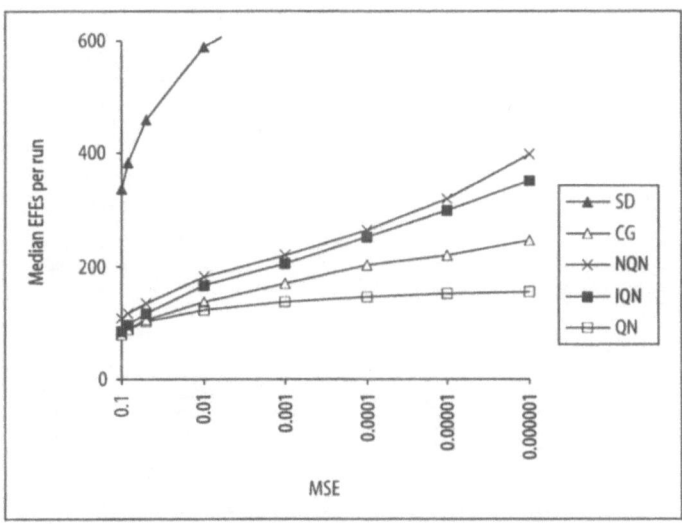

Fig. 5.14 The 3-parity problem – Brent's line search (Table A.4).

The performance of the IQN method is, however, noticeably poorer than anticipated relative to that of both the CG and NQN methods.

Commentary (Figs. 5.14–5.16)   The 3-parity results are broadly similar to those for 2-parity. The most noticeable difference is the increased disparity between the respective convergence rates of first- and second-order training methods (Figs. 5.14

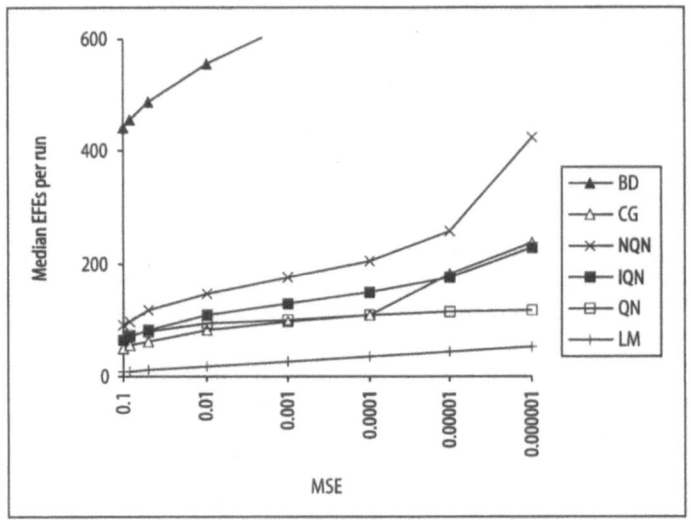

Fig. 5.15 The 3-parity problem – model-trust region strategies (Table A.5).

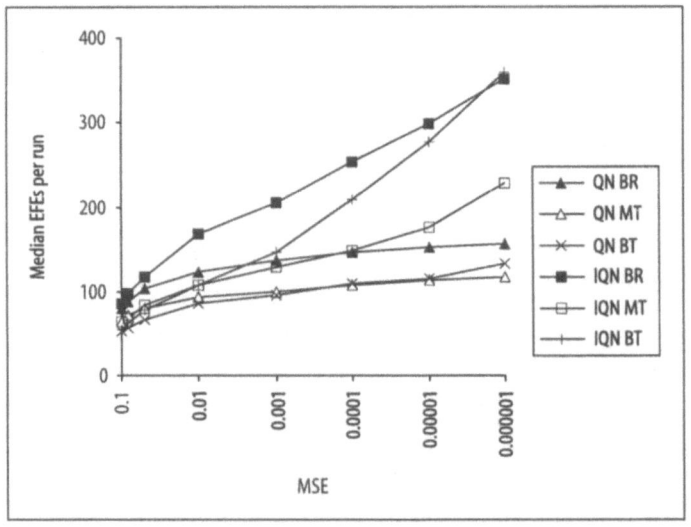

Fig. 5.16 The 3-parity problem – BFGS quasi-Newton algorithms (Table A.6).

and 5.15). This is the first indication of a consistent trend – namely that the superiority of second-order methods compared with first-order methods (with respect to convergence speed on the N-parity problem) increases consistently with N. As with the 2-parity problem,

- LM is the fastest second-order method, followed by QN.

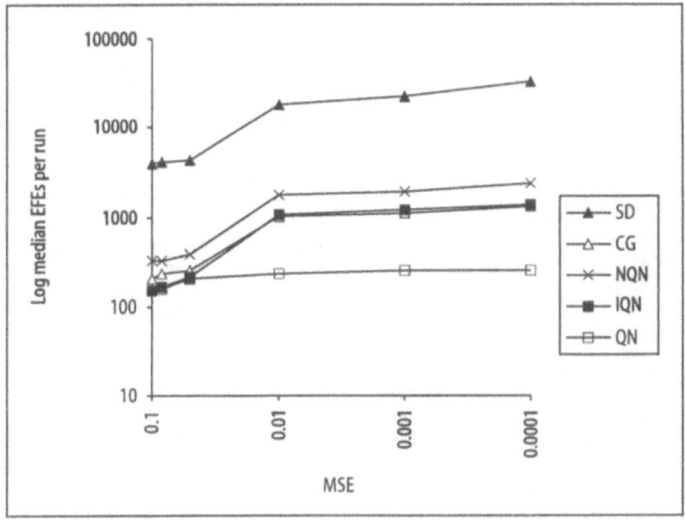

Fig. 5.17 The 4-parity problem – Brent's line search (Table A.7).

- The BFGS quasi-Newton algorithm is significantly faster without resets (QN) than with resets (IQN).
- The CG method is consistently faster than the (theoretically similar) NQN method and – more surprisingly – the IQN method.

Commentary (Figs. 5.17–5.19) With 4-parity, the disparity between the convergence rate of first- and second order methods is of sufficient magnitude to require a logarithmic scale on the y-axis of Figs. 5.17 and 5.18. Moreover, the results in Fig. 5.18 underline the superiority of the quadratically convergent LM algorithm over all the other methods.

With the 4-parity problem, the model-trust region implementations of the CG and NQN methods are relatively uncompetitive compared with Brent's line-search implementations. As with the 'global reliability' results of Section 5.3.1, this is attributable to the slower progress made by the model-trust region strategies in the flat region surrounding the $E=0.125$ saddle point. It is precisely in this kind of situation that the Polak–Ribiere conjugate gradient method (CG) has a tendency to reset automatically to the steepest descent direction (see Section 3.3.4); it is no great surprise, therefore, that the performance of the CG algorithm tends towards the performance of the BD method under these circumstances.

Commentary (Figs. 5.20 and 5.21) The 5-parity results are broadly similar to those for 4-parity. Unfortunately, the reliability of the 5-parity results is to some extent undermined by the high rate of convergence to local minima, particularly with the QN algorithm (hence the dashed lines for QN in Figs. 5.20 and 5.21).

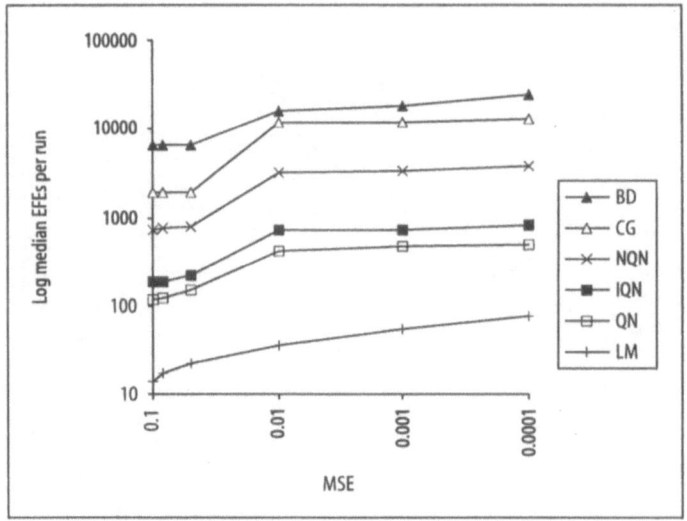

Fig. 5.18 The 4-parity problem – model-trust region strategies (Table A.8).

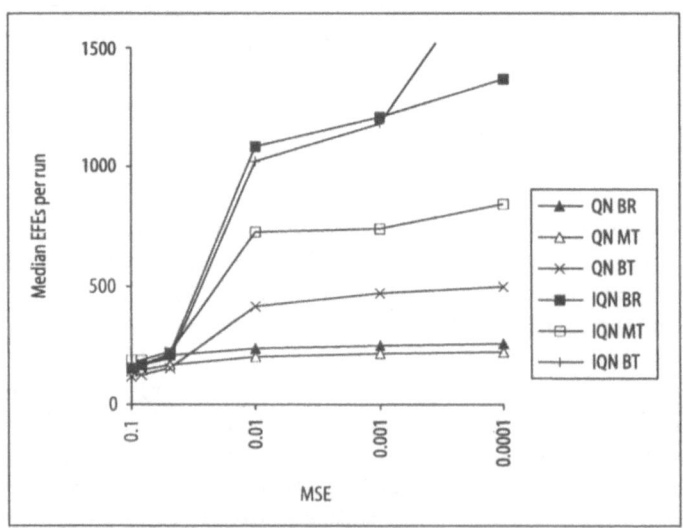

Fig. 5.19 The 4-parity problem – BFGS quasi-Newton algorithms (Table A.9).

At this point it is useful to assess how the convergence speed of different training methods scales with N for the N-parity problem (using minimal N–N–1 architectures). One way of doing this is to treat the 2-parity results for each method as a baseline performance, and measure the relative increase in training time for higher N. (For example, if the median number of EFEs for the 3-parity task is exactly twice that for 2-parity, the algorithm is given a 'score' of 2.0 for the 3-parity task.) This

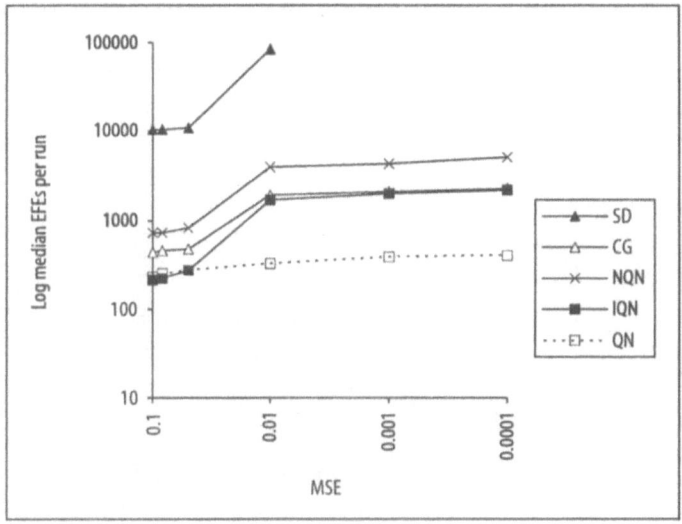

Fig. 5.20 The 5-parity problem – Brent's line search (Table A.10).

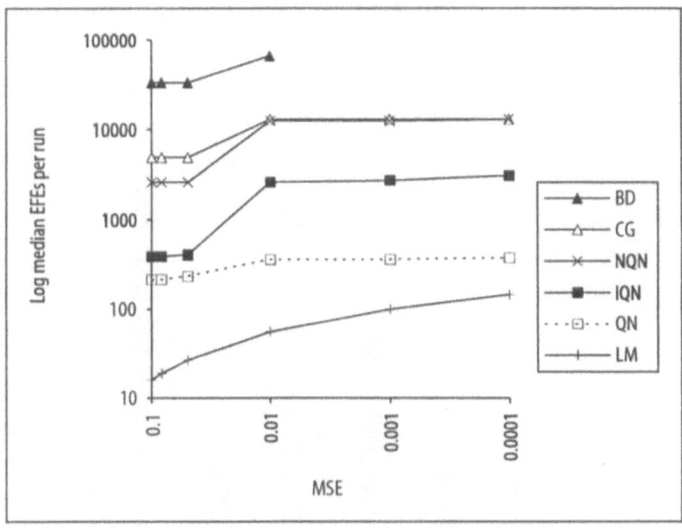

Fig. 5.21 The 5-parity problem – model-trust region strategies (Table A.11).

approach is illustrated in Figs. 5.22 and 5.23. Note that these figures are for a single error level of $E=0.01$. Since the first-order methods SD and BD typically failed to achieve $E=0.01$ within 50 000 epochs when applied to the 5-parity problem, some additional training runs (of longer duration) were performed with these methods in order to estimate their 5-parity performance.

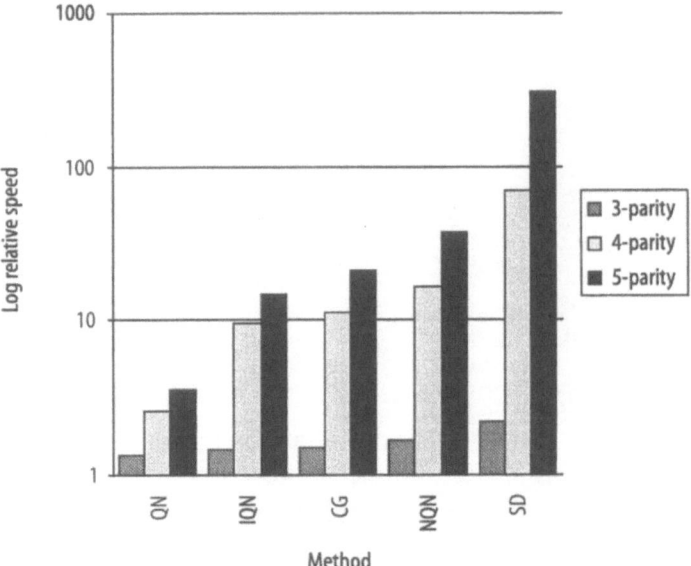

Fig. 5.22 Relative speed to $E=0.01$ – Brent's line search and the N-parity problem. The performance of an algorithm is measured relative to its performance on the 2-parity task. The 5-parity rating for the SD algorithm is an estimate.

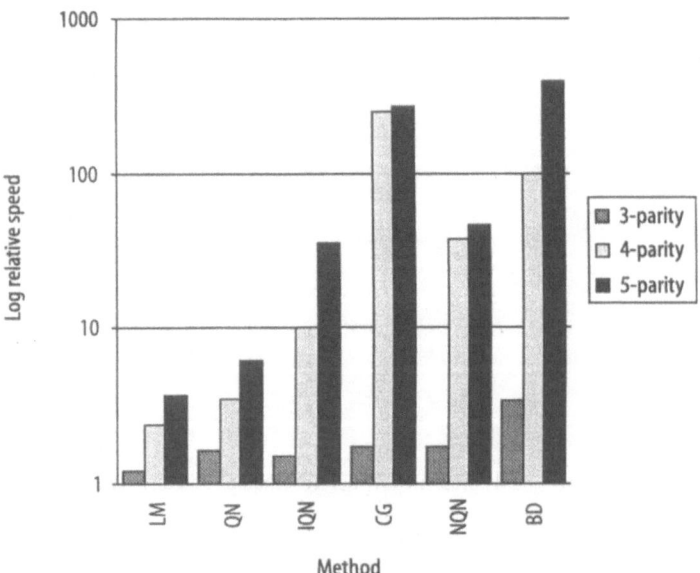

Fig. 5.23 Relative speed to $E=0.01$ – model-trust region strategies and the N-parity problem. The performance of an algorithm is measured relative to its performance on the 2-parity task. The 5-parity rating for the BD algorithm is an estimate.

Commentary   Figures 5.22 and 5.23 show that the benefit of using an algorithm with 'fast' convergence characteristics increases with N. To underline the point, let us compare the performance of the Levenberg–Marquardt (LM) algorithm – the fastest algorithm with the N-parity problem – with that of the bold driver (BD) algorithm – one of the slowest algorithms with the N-parity problem (Fig. 5.23). To achieve an error level of $E=0.01$ with the 5-parity problem, the LM algorithm required about four times the number of EFEs it required for the 2-parity problem, whereas the BD algorithm required an estimated 400 times the number of EFEs for 2-parity. These results strongly suggest that the benefit of using a second-order method increases with the scale of the problem. (For an explanation of the relatively poor performance of the CG method in Fig. 5.23, see the commentary on Figs. 5.17–5.19.)

Commentary (Figs. 5.24–5.26)   The rates of convergence for the sine problem are almost exactly in line with expectations (see Section 3.5), as the following observations demonstrate:

- All the second-order methods are substantially faster than the first-order methods (hence the logarithmically scaled y-axes of Figs. 5.24 and 5.25).
- The 'super-linear' BFGS quasi-Newton method is the fastest second-order method; IQN implementations are slower than QN implementations, owing to the loss of useful derivative information during restarts. The difference in performance between the 'fast linear' CG and NQN methods is negligible (Figs. 5.24 and 5.25).
- Although the LM method is the fastest method with the zero-residual N-parity problem, it is the slowest second-order method with the non-zero-residual sine problem (Fig. 5.25).

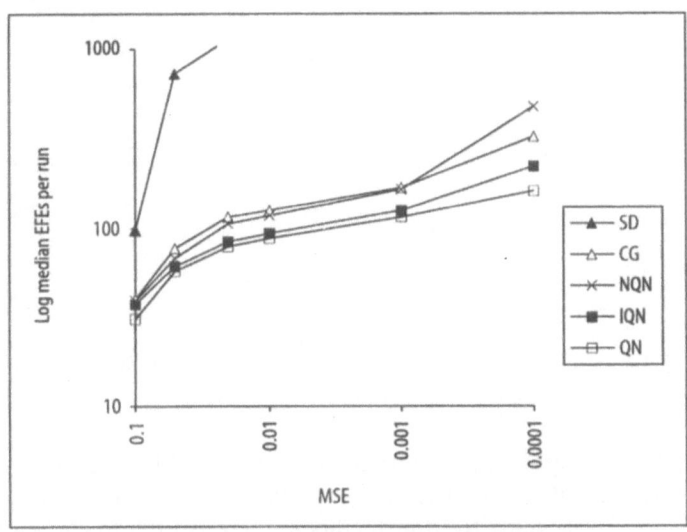

Fig. 5.24 The sin(x) problem – Brent's line search (Table A.13).

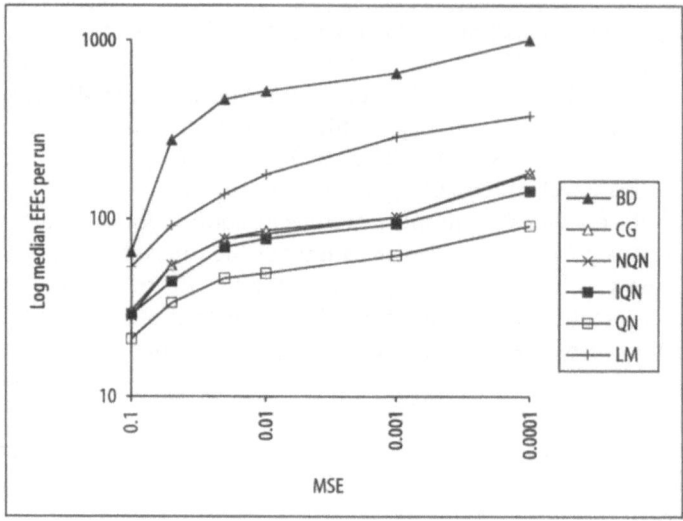

Fig. 5.25 The sin(*x*) problem – model-trust region strategies (Table A.14). Note that the performances of the CG and NQN methods are near-identical.

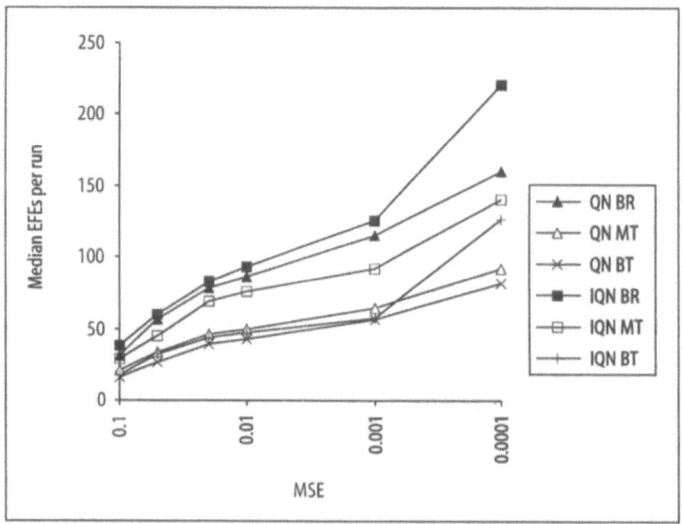

Fig. 5.26 The sin(*x*) problem – BFGS quasi-Newton algorithms (Table A.15).

- The model-trust region implementation of a method (Fig. 5.25) is more efficient than a fairly accurate line-search implementation (Fig. 5.24); BD is much faster than SD. For BFGS quasi-Newton methods, there is little to choose between a model-trust region strategy and a backtracking line-search; in this instance, the latter has the edge (Fig. 5.26).

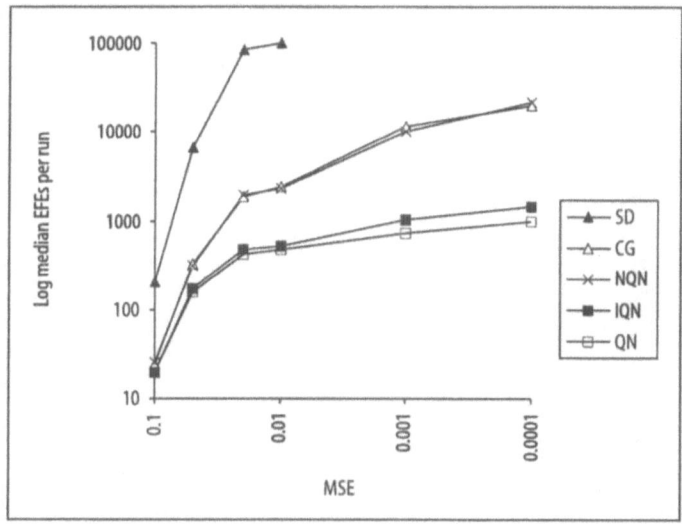

Fig. 5.27 The sin(*x*)cos(2*x*) problem – Brent's line search (Table A.16). Note that the performance of the CG and NQN methods is near-identical.

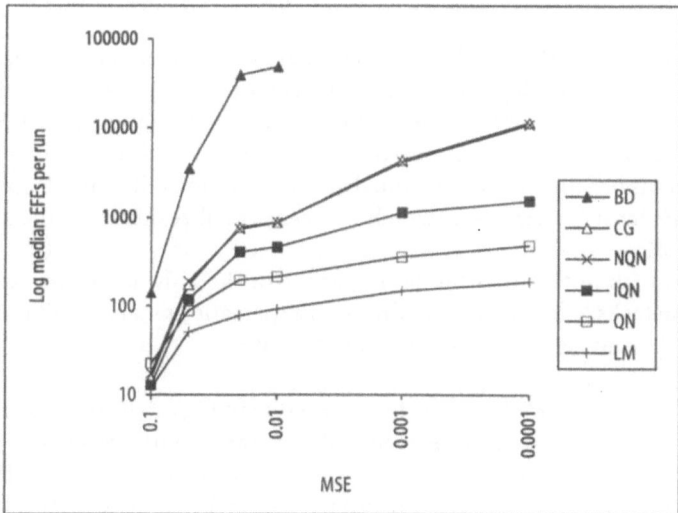

Fig. 5.28 The sin(*x*)cos(2*x*) problem – model-trust region strategies (Table A.17). Note that, as with Fig. 5.27, the performances of the CG and NQN methods are near-identical.

Commentary (Figs. 5.27–5.29)   Figures 5.27 and 5.28 (plotted with logarithmic *y*-axes) illustrate, almost perfectly, the different rates of convergence associated with different classes of classical optimisation method: the arbitrarily slow linear convergence of the first-order SD and BD methods; the 'fast' linear convergence of the

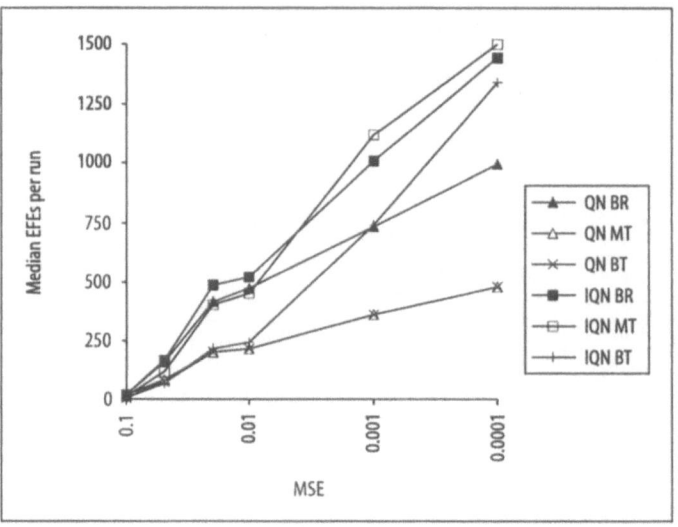

Fig. 5.29 The sin(x)cos($2x$) problem – BFGS quasi-Newton algorithms (Table A.18). Note that the performance of the QN MT and QN BT algorithms is near-identical.

$O(W)$ storage CG and NQN methods; and the super-linear convergence of the $O(W^2)$ QN method. The usual degradation in performance is experienced with the IQN method (with restarts) compared with the QN method (without restarts). Whereas the LM method was the slowest second-order method with the sin(x) problem (which has comparatively large residuals at the solution), it is the fastest method with the sin(x)cos($2x$) problem (which has very small residuals at the solution) – see Section 5.1.

It is also worth noting that the performance of the IQN algorithm on the function-learning tasks is much more in line with expectations – i.e. worse than QN, but better than CG and NQN – than it was for N-parity.

Commentary (Figs. 5.30–5.32)   The tan(x) results in Figs. 5.30 and 5.31 rival those for the sin(x)cos($2x$) problem in terms of the clarity with which they delineate the difference in convergence speed between 'slow linear' methods (SD and BD), 'fast linear' methods (CG and NQN); and the 'super-linear' QN method. As usual, the IQN algorithm with resets performs less well than the non-resetting QN algorithm.

The tan(x) problem (Fig. 5.32) has residuals at the solution that are larger than those of the sin(x)cos($2x$) problem, but smaller than those of the sin(x) problem. Given the sensitivity of the LM method to the presence of residuals, it comes as no surprise that the performance of LM with the tan(x) problem (relative to that of the other training algorithms) was better than it was for the sin(x) problem, but not as good as it was for sin(x)cos($2x$).

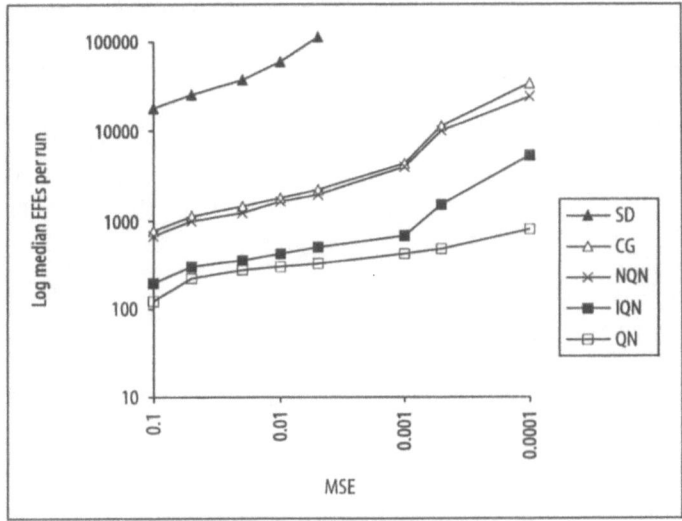

Fig. 5.30 The tan(x) problem – Brent's line search (Table A.19).

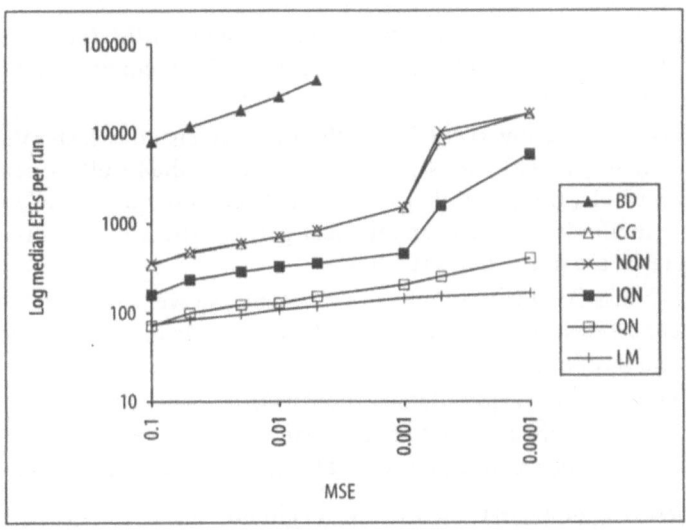

Fig. 5.31 The tan(x) problem – model-trust region strategies (Table A.20).

Summary   The comparative convergence speeds of the various first- and second-order MLP training algorithms tested for this book are very much in line with the predictions of Section 3.5, a point made clear by the following observations:

- The LM method – which is quadratically convergent for problems that have no residuals at the solution (see Section 3.4) – was by far the fastest training method

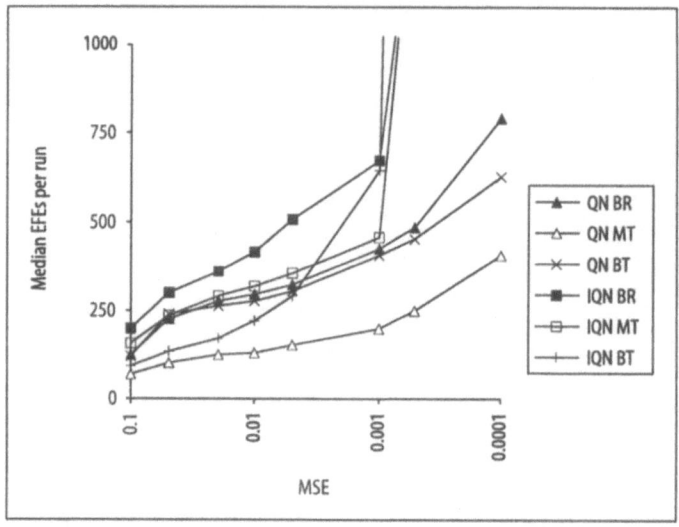

Fig. 5.32 The tan(x) problem – BFGS quasi-Newton algorithms (Table A.21).

with the zero-residual N-parity problem, and with the small-residual $\sin(x)\cos(2x)$ problem, but the slowest second-order method with the larger-residual $\sin(x)$ problem.

- The super-linearly-convergent QN method was consistently faster than the 'fast linearly-convergent' CG and NQN methods. Taking the results for convergence speed as a whole, there is little to choose between the theoretically similar CG and NQN methods. (Their near-identical performances on all three function-learning tasks are particularly striking.)

- The BFGS quasi-Newton method was consistently slower when reset periodically to the steepest descent direction (i.e. IQN was slower than QN), attributable to the loss of potentially useful derivative information.

- Although model-trust region strategies (and, with QN, the backtracking line search) generally proved more efficient than a moderately accurate Brent's line search, the latter was more effective in regions where the gradient was very shallow.

Above all, these results illustrate the orders of magnitude improvement in training speed that may be achieved by using a second-order training method instead of a conventional first-order training method, and justify the emphasis placed on second-order methods (as opposed to first-order methods) throughout the course of this book.

5.3.4 Conclusions

The 'global reliability' results of Section 5.3.1 and convergence speed results of Section 5.3.3 suggest the following simple guidelines when selecting an MLP training algorithm:

- To maximise training speed, use second-order methods. The LM method was the fastest method in the tests conducted here (with the exception of the $\sin(x)$ problem), but cannot be recommended unreservedly because of its sensitivity to the presence of residuals at the solution. The QN algorithm is consistently fast; if the $O(W^2)$ storage costs of the QN algorithm are prohibitive, both the CG and NQN algorithms are viable alternatives. Provided the chosen multivariate algorithm is sufficiently robust, the adoption of an inaccurate line-search strategy or a model-trust region strategy can further improve the training speed of an algorithm.

- To maximise the chance of avoiding local minima, use a first-order method or the LM method. Of the remaining second-order methods, the CG and NQN algorithms are more likely to avoid local minima than the QN algorithm; with all three of these algorithms, periodically resetting (to the steepest descent direction) appears to significantly improve the chances of avoiding local minima.

Taking these two points together, it is clear that the Levenberg–Marquardt (LM) algorithm performs best overall. There are, however, two key problems with the Levenberg–Marquardt algorithm – its $O(W^2)$ storage and $O(W^3)$ computational costs, and its sensitivity to the presence of residuals at the solution. On balance, the Polak–Ribiere conjugate gradient (CG) algorithm implemented with Møller's 'scaled' model-trust region strategy is the more natural choice for moderate- to large-scale training problems, as it combines better-than-average speed and reliability with only $O(W)$ storage costs. Moreover, the CG algorithm is relatively easy to implement. Consequently, it comes as no surprise to learn that conjugate gradient training algorithms are the most widely used second-order training algorithms among neural network researchers and practitioners.

6. *Global Optimisation*

6.1 Introduction to Global Methods

The purpose of this chapter is to consider various ways in which the fast second-order training algorithms discussed in Chapters 2 and 3 can be modified so that they are more likely to converge to global minima – rather than local minima – in the MLP error surface. Local minima are known to be a serious obstacle to successful training when MLPs are applied to many, if far from all, practical tasks (see the discussion in Section 1.2.2). In this respect, the significance of the benchmark test results presented in Chapter 5 is that they suggest that local minima are an even more serious obstacle for certain second-order training methods – notably the quasi-Newton methods of Section 3.3.2 and (to a lesser extent) the conjugate gradient methods of Section 3.3.4 – than they are for the conventional backpropagation-related training methods of Section 1.3.

The term 'global optimisation' covers a diverse range of strategies designed to improve the chances of converging to a global minimum. Global optimisation methods fall into two broad classes – stochastic (or probabilistic) methods and deterministic (or classical) methods. Typically, stochastic methods allow uphill motion with respect to the chosen error function, whereas deterministic methods do not. What constitutes the 'best' global optimisation strategy for a given MLP training task depends on a number of factors, including:

- The number, size and distribution of local minima in the MLP error surface.
- The choice of training algorithm. Certain combinations of global optimisation strategy and training method are more viable than others. (For example, we have already seen that 'noisy' on-line training strategies should not be used with second-order training methods that update the search direction using stored derivative information – see Section 4.3.1.)
- The priorities of the user (since there is, in general, a trade-off between training time and global reliability).

Rather than attempt a comprehensive survey of global optimisation methods, this chapter will concentrate on a relatively small number of global strategies that appear particularly well-suited to second-order MLP training. All of the global methods considered here involve modifications to the MLP training algorithm, or to the training set; readers interested in other types of global optimisation strategy relevant to MLPs – for example, weight initialisation schemes and schemes for dynamically changing the number of hidden nodes – are advised to consult the references cited in Section 1.2.2.

6.1.1 Stochastic Methods

The term *stochastic methods* covers a wide variety of techniques – of contrasting algorithmic complexity, performance and theoretical justification – for avoiding local minima (and other error-surface obstacles) through the addition of 'noise'. In contrast to the classical methods of Chapter 3, all these techniques allow uphill motion with respect to the chosen error function. Stochastic methods can be divided into two broad categories, depending on whether noise is added to the system from the outset of training, or only when the MLP has converged to a local minimum. The fundamental problem for schemes that fall into the latter category is that, once a network has become highly committed to a local solution, there is a strong possibility that the network will reconverge to the same local minimum, even if a large amount of noise is added to the system. Research by Gorse (1992) (using the Polak–Ribiere conjugate gradient algorithm described in Section 3.3.4) suggests that random perturbations of the search direction and 'various kinds of stochastic adjustment to the current set of weights' are largely ineffective at enabling MLPs to escape from local minima. In the light of this research, the following discussion will focus on stochastic methods that add noise throughout the training process.

The fundamental problem for all stochastic methods is how to determine the appropriate level of 'noise' for an arbitrary minimisation task. Too little 'noise', and the algorithm may become trapped in a local minimum; too much, and it may fail to converge to a global minimum within a reasonable number of iterations. What is needed is some scheme for adapting the level of noise during the minimisation process. For an arbitrary task with no special features, the intuitively sensible approach is to reduce the amount of noise as the minimisation proceeds. Two widely used strategies are to gradually reduce the level of noise as the number of iterations increases (known as *simulated annealing* (Kirkpatrick *et al.*, 1983)), or as the error level falls (known as *time-invariant noise algorithms* (TINA) (Burton and Mpitsos, 1992)).

In the context of multi-layer perceptron training, the most widely used stochastic method is on-line training (Sections 1.3.4 and 4.3). In its 'traditional' form (i.e. with the weights updated after the presentation of each randomly selected pattern), the amount of noise added to the system is an arbitrary function of the training set and architecture. This contrasts with simulated annealing and TINA, which regulate the amount of noise in a systematic way. Although, it is possible to regulate the amount of on-line noise with an appropriate scheme for adapting the size and composition of the subset of patterns presented to the network at each iteration, on-line training is essentially a heuristic approach to global optimisation. (Note that, in the case of the 'noise-free' on-line strategies discussed in Section 4.3.2, the subset of patterns is regulated with the aim of reducing or eliminating the amount of noise added to the system. Such strategies are therefore unlikely to improve the chances of the network avoiding local minima.)

From the perspective of second-order training, all of these stochastic methods present two serious difficulties. The first problem is that there is a fundamental mismatch between (on the one hand) the theoretically justified schedules for reducing the level of noise and adapting the training rate when using a stochastic method, and (on the other hand) the convergence properties of second-order training methods. (Contrast, for example, the STC on-line training rate schedule given by equation (1.22) with the anticipated rates of local convergence for second-order methods given in Chapters 2 and 3.) The second difficulty has already been identified in the context of on-line training (see Section 4.3.1), namely that second-order methods which rely on stored derivative information from previous training epochs (e.g. conjugate gradient methods, quasi-Newton methods and the 'memoryless' quasi-Newton method) are likely to be severely disrupted by the addition of noise in a way that methods which evaluate derivative information afresh at each epoch (e.g. steepest descent, Newton's method, the finite-difference Newton's method and the Levenberg–Marquardt method) are not.

These factors do not preclude the development of hybrid stochastic/second-order training methods. Indeed, we have already seen (in Section 4.3.1) that it is possible to combine a Newton-type method with a heuristic strategy for adapting the on-line training rate. However, rather than directly combine stochastic and second-order information, most researchers in this field have sought to isolate the second-order method from the effects of stochastic noise. One way of achieving this is to implement a hybrid algorithm with two distinct training phases – a stochastic phase followed by a classical second-order phase. Under favourable conditions, such an algorithm will successfully bypass any local minima during the stochastic phase and then converge rapidly towards the desired global solution during the second-order phase. An example of this type of algorithm is the hybrid on-line backpropagation/conjugate gradient algorithm proposed in Shepherd (1992), which switches from on-line backpropagation to a conjugate gradient method (implemented in batch mode) after a user-defined number of training epochs.

A second hybrid stochastic/second-order method that successfully isolates the second-order algorithm from the effects of stochastic noise is the 'sampling and search' method of Belew et al. (1991). This method uses a genetic algorithm to choose initial weights for a population of MLPs, each of which is trained (in the conventional manner) using a conjugate gradient algorithm.

6.1.2 Deterministic Methods

As noted in the introduction to this chapter, most *deterministic methods* for global optimisation – unlike stochastic global methods – share the property that an increase in network error is not required at any stage of the minimisation process. For this reason, deterministic strategies are intuitively more suitable than stochastic methods for use in combination with iterative descent methods (such as the second-order methods of Chapters 2 and 3). Unfortunately, most deterministic global optimisation methods are notoriously slow, or difficult to implement in the context of MLP training. This section focuses on two contrasting deterministic approaches to global optimisation – homotopic methods and tunnelling methods – both of which lie outside the mainstream of classical optimisation theory. Unlike the majority of global optimisation methods, homotopic methods and tunnelling methods appear particularly well-suited to being used in combination with second-order MLP training algorithms.

As their name suggests, *homotopic methods* for global optimisation derive from *homotopy theory*, the rudiments of which can be summarised as follows:

- Two functions $f(\mathbf{x})$ and $g(\mathbf{x})$ are said to be homotopic to each other if $f(\mathbf{x})$ can be continuously deformed into $g(\mathbf{x})$, or vice versa, i.e. there exists a *homotopy function* $h(\mathbf{x},\lambda)$, defined by

$$h(\mathbf{x},\lambda) = (1-\lambda)g(\mathbf{x}) + \lambda f(\mathbf{x}) \tag{6.1}$$

  which is continuous in both its variables.

- Parameter λ in equation (6.1) – the so-called *homotopy parameter* – is a non-negative scalar in the range [0,1]. With $\lambda=0$, the homotopy function h in (6.1) becomes $h(\mathbf{x},0) = g(\mathbf{x})$; with $\lambda=1$, h becomes $h(\mathbf{x},1) = f(\mathbf{x})$.

The fundamental idea behind homotopic methods for the solution of nonlinear systems – known as *homotopy continuation methods* – is to define a homotopy function in the form given by (6.1), with $g(\mathbf{x})$ a simple function that has a known solution, and $f(\mathbf{x})$ the nonlinear function to which a solution is desired; by monotonically increasing the homotopy parameter λ from zero to one, $h(\mathbf{x},\lambda)$ is progressively deformed from $g(\mathbf{x})$ to $f(\mathbf{x})$.

An essential requirement for the success of such a method is that the path traced by a given $\mathbf{x}$ as parameter λ varies from $\lambda=0$ to $\lambda=1$ – the so-called *homotopy path* of $\mathbf{x}$ – is continuously differentiable. This is guaranteed if the Jacobian matrix of $h(\mathbf{x},\lambda)$ is of full rank. In the case where g has a single global minimum $\mathbf{x}_*$ but f has multiple global minima, the homotopy path of $\mathbf{x}_*$ will have one or more *bifurcations*. For example, if f has two global minima, the homotopy path of $\mathbf{x}_*$ will split into two branches at some critical value of λ.

In practice, several variations to the basic homotopy formula of (6.1) are in general usage. One of the most popular is the *fixed point method*, given by

$$h(\mathbf{x},\lambda) = (1-\lambda)(\mathbf{x}_0 - \mathbf{x}_*) + \lambda f(\mathbf{x}) \tag{6.2}$$

where $\mathbf{x}_0$ is an arbitrary starting point (see, for example, Finhoff and Zimmerman (1992)). From a neural network perspective, the advantage of equation (6.2) is that, unlike equation (6.1), it does not require the generation of a function $g(\mathbf{x})$ with a known solution for a given combination of MLP architecture and training set, which is highly problematic in general. The ERA method, a homotopic strategy specifically designed for training MLPs, is the subject of Section 6.2.

Tunnelling methods, introduced by Levy and Montalvo (1985), are deterministic global optimisation strategies which differ fundamentally from homotopic methods (and most stochastic methods) in that no attempt is made to prevent the system getting trapped in a local minimum; rather, if the network converges to a local minimum, tunnelling methods aim to 'tunnel through' to the basin of attraction of a lower-level minimum. One advantage of this approach in the context of multi-layer perceptron training is that it has no effect whatsoever on either the minimisation algorithm, the training set or the MLP architecture, until such time as the network converges to a stationary point.

All tunnelling methods share the same iterative structure; they proceed in cycles, with each cycle comprising a minimisation phase followed by a tunnelling phase. In the minimisation phase, the MLP is trained in the normal manner, using a given minimisation algorithm, until a minimum $\mathbf{w}_*$ is located. The method then enters the tunnelling phase, during the course of which the algorithm 'tunnels through' regions of the error surface where $E(\mathbf{w})>E(\mathbf{w}_*)$ using a *tunnelling function* until a region is located where $E(\mathbf{w})<E(\mathbf{w}_*)$. The cycles are repeated iteratively until a global minimum is located. (For a useful summary of the development of effective tunnelling algorithms for global optimisation, see Cetin *et al.* (1993).) The TRUST method, a tunnelling method that can be readily adapted for training MLPs, is the subject of Section 6.3.

6.2 Expanded Range Approximation (ERA)

6.2.1 An Introduction to ERA

Expanded Range Approximation, or ERA for short, is an example of a deterministic global optimisation strategy, derived from homotopic theory, which was specifically designed for training MLPs. Where the ERA method differs from the 'standard' homotopic approach (introduced in Section 6.1.2) is that it does not attempt to formulate – for an arbitrary MLP architecture and training task – a simple function with a known solution (function $g(\mathbf{x})$ in equation (6.1)). Instead, ERA deforms the 'normal' MLP error surface E into a surface E' that is easier to solve; having minimised E', surface E' is progressively deformed back into the original surface E.

The fundamental idea behind the ERA strategy – developed by Gorse *et al.* (1993a,b; 1994a,b; 1995) – is to perform a homotopy on the target vectors $\mathbf{t}_p$ ($p=1,...,P$) of a given MLP training set, S. The homotopy is achieved by compressing the target vectors to their mean values – that is, the *mean target vector* <t> with elements $<t>_i$ ($i=1,...,N^L$) given by

$$<t>_i = \frac{1}{P}\sum_{p=1}^{P} t_{i,p} \tag{6.3}$$

– and then progressively expanding them back to their original values. The expansion of the compressed target vectors $t_p(\lambda)$ ($p=1,...,P$) is regulated by a *range parameter* λ ($0 \leq \lambda \leq 1$) according to the rule

$$t_p(\lambda) = <t> + \lambda(t_p - <t>)$$

(6.4)

With the range parameter set to $\lambda=0$, each $t_p(\lambda)$ is identical to the mean target vector $<t>$; with the range parameter set to $\lambda=1$, each $t_p(\lambda)$ is identical to the target vectors of the original training set.

In place of the error function E, the modified training set $S(\lambda)$ is evaluated using a corresponding modified error function $E(\lambda)$. For example, if the chosen error function is the mean-squared error function given by equation (1.6), $E(\lambda)$ is defined by

$$E(\lambda) = \frac{1}{2PN^L} \sum_{p=1}^{P} \sum_{i=1}^{N^L} \left[t_{i,p}(\lambda) - y_{i,p}^L(\lambda) \right]^2$$

(6.5)

With the range parameter set to $\lambda=1$, equation (6.5) is equivalent to the standard MSE function of equation (1.6). By monotonically increasing the range parameter from $\lambda=0$ to $\lambda=1$ in a series of steps, the error surface $E(0)$ is progressively deformed into the original error surface $E(1)$.

In order to prove that the ERA method works, it is necessary to show that

- the problem defined by $\lambda=0$ has only a single global minimum, and can be solved trivially
- having located the global minimum of $E(0)$, the range parameter λ may be increased by a small step η without displacing the system from the basin of attraction of the global minimum
- it is possible to progressively expand the range parameter up to $\lambda=1$ without displacing the system from the global minimum at any step

Gorse *et al.* have accumulated considerable evidence – both analytical and empirical – demonstrating that $E(0)$ has a unique global minimum at $E=0$. However, there is currently no general proof of this assertion. (A limited proof for a 2-layer MLP learning the XOR problem is given in the appendix to Gorse *et al.* (1995).) The empirical evidence comes from simulations performed with randomly generated architectures and training sets. The tests show not only that the problem $E(0)$ is easy to solve, but also that the MLP weights take on a special, predictable form – that is, the form necessary to ensure that the network output is the same whatever the input pattern. Let us consider the case of a 'standard' MLP architecture (i.e. one that is fully connected between adjacent layers, but which has no weights connecting non-adjacent layers) using the sigmoid squashing function of equation (1.2), with w_{10}^1 denoting the weight that connects node n_1^1 to the input layer bias unit (n_0^0). For a single-layer N-1 architecture with the scalar target value $<t>$ for each input pattern, the weight values

$$w_{10}^1 = \ln\left(\frac{<t>}{1-<t>}\right)$$

(6.6)

$$w_{1i}^1 = 0, \quad i = 1,...,N^0$$

are guaranteed to satisfy $E=0$. For a 2-layer MLP architecture with the target vector $<t>$ for each input pattern, the weight values

$$w_{i0}^2 = \ln\left(\frac{<t>_i}{1-<t>_i}\right) - \sum_{j=1}^{N^1} w_{ij}^2 f\left(w_{j0}\right), \quad i = 1,...,N^2$$

(6.7)

$$w_{jk}^1 = 0, \quad j = 1,...,N^1 \text{ and } k = 1,...,N^0$$

are guaranteed to satisfy $E=0$. (Function $f(x)$ in (6.7) is the sigmoid squashing function.)

The assertion that it is possible (having located the global minimum of $E(0)$) to increase the range parameter monotonically from $\lambda=0$ to $\lambda=1$ without displacing the system from the attractive basin of a global minimum derives from observations about the smoothness of the error surface. Having located the global minimum $w(\lambda)$ for the current step, we should expect a subsequent step of ε to keep the network within the attractive basin of the 'expanded' global minimum $w(\lambda + \varepsilon)$ – provided the network approximates $w(\lambda)$ with sufficient accuracy and ε is sufficiently small. This follows from the observation that the basin of attraction of $w(\lambda + \varepsilon)$ should contain location $w(\lambda)$ when $\varepsilon \to 0$, assuming that $w(\lambda + \varepsilon)$ is shifted from location $w(\lambda)$ by only $O(\varepsilon)$ as $\varepsilon \to 0$ – a reasonable assumption, provided the error surface is sufficiently smooth. (For a detailed analysis of the properties of the error surface at the first step $\lambda=\eta \ll 1$, see Gorse et al. (1995).)

Whereas the error surface $E(\lambda=0)$ has a unique global minimum, the error surface $E(\lambda>0)$ typically has many global minima (for the reasons given in Section 1.2.2), leading to bifurcations in the homotopy path of global minimum $w(\lambda=0)$. The possibility that one or more global minima in the error surface $E(\lambda_k)$ (for $0<\lambda_k<1$) may cease to be global minima in surface $E(\lambda_k +1)$ (for $\lambda_k<\lambda_{k+1} \leq 1$) is currently an obstacle to a general proof of the ERA method.

6.2.2 The ERA Method in Practice

Even if, in due course, it is shown that the ERA method is guaranteed to work in theory, there would be no guarantee that a practical implementation is possible. If, to successfully avoid local minima, it proved necessary to expand the range parameter from $\lambda=0$ to $\lambda=1$ in a very large number of steps and/or to approximate a global minimum of $E(\lambda)$ at each step to a high degree of accuracy, it is likely that ERA would be deemed excessively slow for most practical tasks. For this reason, the remainder of this section focuses on practical schemes for regulating the ERA parameters, and on empirical evidence for the method's effectiveness in practice.

The expansion of the ERA range parameter λ can be conveniently regulated using two user-defined parameters – the size of the first step ($\eta > 0$), and an expansion rate parameter ($\beta \geq 1$). Given initial values of $\lambda_0 = 0$ and $\lambda_1 = \eta$, subsequent values of parameter λ can be defined as follows:

$$\lambda_{k+1} = \min\left[1.0, \lambda_k + \beta(\lambda_k - \lambda_{k-1})\right], \quad k \geq 1 \tag{6.8}$$

An 'N-step ERA' method refers to the special case where $\beta = 1$ and η is chosen such that $1/\eta$ is a whole number – i.e. the range parameter λ is expanded in steps of a uniform size, so that the method requires the solution of the N problems $S(\lambda_n = n\eta)$ for $n = 1, \dots, N = 1/\eta$. (Note that, when using ERA with a conjugate gradient method or quasi-Newton method, it is advisable to reset the algorithm to the steepest descent direction at the start of each step, on the grounds that a descent direction for error surface $E(\lambda_k)$ is not guaranteed to be a descent direction for error surface $E(\lambda_{k+1})$.)

In addition to parameter λ, we need some scheme for regulating the accuracy with which a global minimum of $E(\lambda)$ is to be approximated at each ERA step (with $\lambda < 1$). One option is to terminate a step only when the gradient drops to zero. However, this approach is likely to entail an unacceptably large number of epochs per training run unless the number of ERA steps is small and the chosen training algorithm converges rapidly near a minimum. A more efficient strategy is to terminate intermediate ERA steps on the basis of the correct classification of patterns in the training set. This can be conveniently implemented using two user-defined parameters, so that an ERA step is terminated when $q \leq P$ patterns (for a P-pattern training set) are classified correctly; a given pattern p_s ($1 \leq s \leq P$) is deemed to be 'correctly classified' when the network outputs $y_{i,s}^L$ ($i = 1, \dots, N^L$) satisfy

$$\frac{y_{i,s}^L - <t>_i}{t_{i,s} - <t>_i} > r, \quad 0 < r \leq 1 \tag{6.9}$$

for each element (t_i, s) of target vector t_s. The value of parameter r in equation (6.9) determines the degree to which network output $y_{i,s}^L$ is required to match target output $t_{i,s}$ at each ERA step; with settings of $r = 1$ and $q = P$, an ERA step is terminated only when $E = 0$. Since equation (6.9) is not defined for $\lambda = 0$, the zeroth ERA step is terminated when the error level satisfies $E \leq \varepsilon$, where ε is a small tolerance. (In the extensive tests performed for Shepherd (1995), an error tolerance of $\varepsilon \leq 10^{-6}$ was found to give acceptable results.)

An examination of the network error at each ERA step suggests that the first step ($\lambda = \eta$) has a special role:

- Having solved the problem $S(\lambda_1 = \eta)$ at the first step, the network is predisposed to successfully solve the problem $S(\lambda_k)$ (for $k > 1$) at each subsequent step.
- If the network converges to a local minimum at a given step (with range parameter $0 < \lambda_k < 1$), it is apparently unable to converge to a global minimum at any subsequent step.
- The number of training epochs required to find a solution at the first step is typically greater than the number required at any subsequent step (of the same

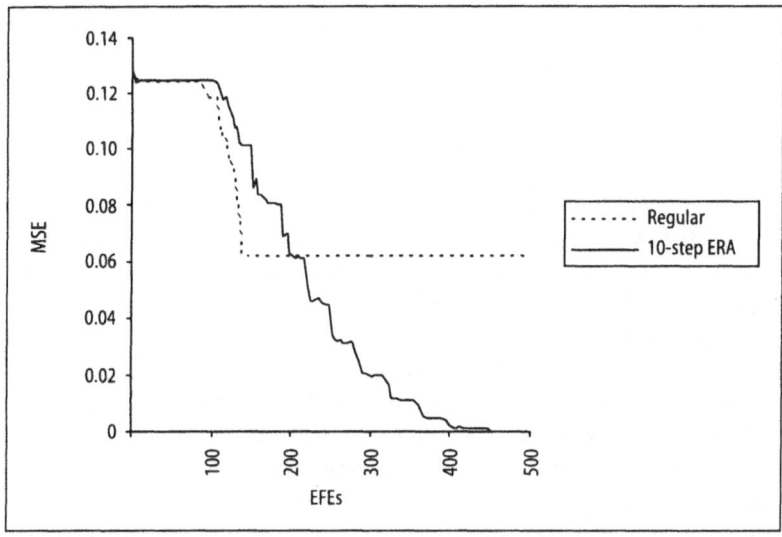

Fig. 6.1 An example of a 10-step ERA training curve for the BFGS quasi-Newton algorithm (without resets) applied to the XOR training task (Section 5.1.1). Without ERA, the BFGS algorithm converged to a local minimum at $E=0.0625$ using the same set of starting weights. Note that the 10-step ERA curve is plotted using the standard $E(\lambda=1)$ MSE function; although the error $E(\lambda_k)$ never increases at ERA step k, the error $E(\lambda=1)$ can (and in this instance does) show local increases for $\lambda<1$.

size). Taking as an example the 10-step ERA curve of Fig. 6.1, the number of EFEs taken at each step was as follows: 19 ($\lambda=0$); 129 ($\lambda=0.1$); 68 ($\lambda=0.2$); 30.5 ($\lambda=0.3$); 31.5 ($\lambda=0.4$); 36.5 ($\lambda=0.5$); 39.5 ($\lambda=0.6$); 35.5 ($\lambda=0.7$); 49.5 ($\lambda=0.8$); 5 ($\lambda=0.9$); 30 ($\lambda=1.0$).

Clearly, both the global reliability and convergence speed of the ERA method are substantially (but not exclusively) determined by the size of the first step. There is no 'natural' choice of first-step size. In practice, η should reflect the 'hardness' of the training task (if known) and the priorities of the user; broadly speaking, η should be set to a 'small' value for hard problems or when a high degree of global reliability is required, but to a 'large' value if convergence speed is a higher priority. One promising feature of ERA's performance in tests conducted by the author is that substantial benefits accrued even when η was set to a comparatively 'large' value. For example, when applying the (non-resetting) BFGS quasi-Newton method to the XOR training task, the rate of successful convergence to global minima rose from 36% without ERA to 54.5% with 1-step ERA (i.e. $\eta=1.0$), 66% with 2-step ERA (i.e. $\eta=0.5$), 72.5% with 5-step ERA (i.e. $\eta=0.2$), and 79.5% with 10-step ERA (i.e. $\eta=0.1$) (Shepherd, 1995). (For comparison, the success rate with the 100-step ERA method was 94.5%.)

The appropriate choice of range expansion parameter β and accuracy parameters q and r depends to some extent on the choice of initial step size η. A number of useful guidelines for setting the remaining ERA parameters emerged during a detailed empirical study (summarised in Shepherd (1995)), examining the effect of different parameter settings on the performance of the BFGS quasi-Newton algorithm when applied to the XOR and sine training tasks (with known local minima). This study suggests that:

- When the size of the first ERA step is comparatively large ($\eta \geq 0.1$), the range parameter can be expanded to $\lambda=1$ in a single step (with expansion rate parameter $\beta=1/\eta-1$) without reducing the global reliability of the algorithm. When the size of the first ERA step is small ($\eta \leq 0.05$), setting $\beta \leq 10$ has negligible (if any) impact on global reliability. However, with $\beta>10$ a significant deterioration in the rate of global convergence may occur.

- In terms of convergence speed, setting $\beta>1$ is most beneficial for small η. It is worth noting, however, that convergence speed does not increase consistently with the size of β; for example, with a first step of $\eta=0.01$, ERA is faster with $\beta=10$ than with $\beta=50$. This is attributable to the fact that increasing β from 10 to 50 does not reduce the number of ERA steps required (i.e. 3), but merely increases the size (and 'difficulty') of the intermediate step.

- When the size of the first ERA step is large ($\eta \geq 0.5$), reducing the accuracy required at each step produces only a modest improvement in convergence speed, but a substantial deterioration in the rate of global convergence. For smaller η, reducing the required accuracy brings about a greater improvement in convergence speed, and the impact on global reliability is somewhat reduced. (Note that, for the analysis presented in Shepherd (1995), a single error-tolerance parameter ε was used in place of the ERA 'accuracy' parameters q and r in equation (6.9); setting ε in the range $[10^{-8},10^{-6}]$ for all $\lambda<1$ gave good results with the XOR task, whereas $\varepsilon=10^{-5}$ was a better choice for the sine task.)

Finally, it may be possible to enhance the ERA method by devising a scheme which adapts the ERA parameters automatically as training proceeds. For example, if the network fails at a given step λ_k ($k>0$), one simple option would be to 'backtrack' to the location at the end of the previous (successful) step λ_{k-1} and try again with a reduced λ_k.

In contrast to the majority of global optimisation strategies, ERA is both easy to implement and fully compatible with second-order classical optimisation algorithms. Furthermore, the results of benchmark tests suggest that the ERA method represents a highly efficient compromise between global reliability and training speed; when applied to training tasks with known local minima, ERA (with appropriate parameter settings) proved highly effective at improving the global reliability of both first-and second-order MLP training algorithms without excessively increasing the number of training iterations required to find a solution.

6.3   The TRUST Method

Like all tunnelling methods, the *Terminal Repeller Unconstrained Subenergy Tunnelling (TRUST) method* – devised by Cetin *et al.* (1993) – proceeds in cycles, with each cycle comprising a minimisation phase and a tunnelling phase. Where the TRUST method differs from the original tunnelling method of Levy and Montalvo (1985) is in the choice of tunnelling function and the strategy used to propel the algorithm across the domain of interest during the tunnelling phase. The TRUST method is probably the most effective tunnelling strategy to date, and has been shown to be suitable for training MLPs (see Barhen *et al.* (1994)).

6.3.1 The Tunnelling Function

With any tunnelling method, the tunnelling function plays an essential role in enabling the algorithm to 'tunnel through' regions of the error surface $E(\mathbf{w})$ that are at a higher level than the current minimum $E(\mathbf{w}_*)$. The tunnelling function used by the TRUST method – known as a *sub-energy tunnelling function* – is given by

$$E_{SUB}(\mathbf{w},\mathbf{w}_*) = \log\left(\frac{1}{1+\exp[-(\hat{E}(\mathbf{w})+\alpha)]}\right) \qquad (6.10)$$

where α is a scalar constant and function $\hat{E}(\mathbf{w})$ is given by

$$\hat{E}(\mathbf{w}) = E(\mathbf{w}) - E(\mathbf{w}_*) \qquad (6.11)$$

The sub-energy function $E_{SUB}(\mathbf{w},\mathbf{w}_*)$ in equation (6.10) is a nonlinear but monotonic transformation of error function $E(\mathbf{w})$ with the following properties:

- All values of $E_{SUB}(\mathbf{w},\mathbf{w}_*)$ are less than or equal to zero (hence the term 'sub-energy').
- If $E(\mathbf{w})$ has any minima at lower levels than the current minimum $\mathbf{w}_*$, $E_{SUB}(\mathbf{w},\mathbf{w}_*)$ has minima at the same locations, and these minima are in the same relative order with respect to their error levels as the corresponding minima of $E(\mathbf{w})$.
- For all values of $\hat{E}(\mathbf{w}) \geq 0$ (i.e. for all $E(\mathbf{w}) \geq E(\mathbf{w}_*)$) within the domain of interest D, $E_{SUB}(\mathbf{w},\mathbf{w}_*)$ approaches zero asymptotically 'but quickly', at a rate determined by the value of α. Hence, if $\mathbf{w}_*$ is a global minimum, $E_{SUB}(\mathbf{w},\mathbf{w}_*)=0$ for all $\mathbf{w}$. Cetin *et al* (1993, p. 103) argue that $\alpha=2$ gives 'the most desirable asymptotic behaviour'.
- Any values of $\hat{E}(\mathbf{w})$ that are less than zero (i.e. any $E(\mathbf{w})<E(\mathbf{w}_*)$) are left 'nearly unmodified' (Barhen *et al.*, 1994, p. 371).
- The gradient of $E_{SUB}(\mathbf{w},\mathbf{w}_*)$ – known as the *sub-energy gradient* – given by

$$\frac{\partial E_{SUB}(\mathbf{w},\mathbf{w}_*)}{\partial \mathbf{w}} = \left(\frac{\partial E(\mathbf{w})}{\partial \mathbf{w}}\right)\left(\frac{1}{1+\exp[\hat{E}(\mathbf{w})+\alpha]}\right) \qquad (6.12)$$

is near-zero for all $E(\mathbf{w}) \geq E(\mathbf{w}_*)$, and the same as the gradient $g(\mathbf{w})$ (i.e. $\partial E(\mathbf{w})/\partial \mathbf{w}$, the gradient of $E(\mathbf{w})$) for any $E(\mathbf{w})<E(\mathbf{w}_*)$.

In terms of the sub-energy function $E_{SUB}(\mathbf{w},\mathbf{w}_*)$, the task at each tunnelling phase is to find a $\mathbf{w}$ such that the gradient of $E_{SUB}(\mathbf{w},\mathbf{w}_*)$ is non-zero, since such a $\mathbf{w}$ must lie within the basin of attraction of a minimum at a lower error level than $\mathbf{w}_*$. If such a $\mathbf{w}$ is found, the next minimisation phase is initiated; otherwise $\mathbf{w}_*$ is deemed the global minimum within domain D and the algorithm is terminated.

6.3.2 The Tunnelling Phase

The key to the success of the TRUST algorithm is the strategy used to locate a $\mathbf{w}$ during the tunnelling phase such that the gradient of $E_{SUB}(\mathbf{w},\mathbf{w}_*)$ is non-zero. This is achieved by adding an extra term to equation (6.10) so that the error function used during the tunnelling phase becomes

$$E(\mathbf{w},\mathbf{w}_*) = E_{SUB}(\mathbf{w},\mathbf{w}_*) - \rho E_{REP}(\mathbf{w},\mathbf{w}_*)H\left[\hat{E}(\mathbf{w})\right] \tag{6.13}$$

In equation (6.13), the repeller energy term $E_{REP}(\mathbf{w},\mathbf{w}_*)$ is given by

$$E_{REP}(\mathbf{w},\mathbf{w}_*) = (3/4)\sum_{i=1}^{W}(w_i - w_{*,i})^{4/3} \tag{6.14}$$

$H(\cdot)$ is the *Heaviside step function*

$$H(x) = \begin{Bmatrix} 1, & \text{if } x \geq 0 \\ 0, & \text{if } x < 0 \end{Bmatrix} \tag{6.15}$$

and ρ is a non-negative scalar known as the power of the repeller. The essential property of the error surface $E(\mathbf{w},\mathbf{w}_*)$ is that the repeller term dominates the gradient in those regions where $E_{SUB}(\mathbf{w},\mathbf{w}_*)$ is flat (i.e. where $E(\mathbf{w}) \geq E(\mathbf{w}_*)$), but is 'switched off' in regions where $E(\mathbf{w})<E(\mathbf{w}_*)$. Provided ρ is sufficiently large, the network will be repelled from $\mathbf{w}_*$ until either a lower-level valley or the edge of domain D is encountered. At the start of the first cycle, a point $\mathbf{w}_*$ is chosen as one corner of D, which is assumed to be a hyperparallelpiped. In the original formulation of the method (given in Cetin *et al.* (1993)), a *terminal repeller* is placed at $\mathbf{w}_*$ and the network is initialised to $\mathbf{w}_* + \varepsilon$, where ε is a small multi-dimensional perturbation that locates the network inside domain D. If $F(\mathbf{w}_* + \varepsilon)<F(\mathbf{w}_*)$, training begins with a minimisation phase; if $F(\mathbf{w}_* + \varepsilon) \geq F(\mathbf{w}_*)$, training begins with a tunnelling phase. The addition of an identical perturbation ε when each subsequent stationary point is encountered means that the network will tend to traverse domain D in its search for the global minimum.

In the one-dimensional case, the application of a small fixed perturbation ε (typically $\varepsilon=0.001$ or $\varepsilon=0.01$) whenever a stationary point is encountered is sufficient to ensure that the system is driven across the entire domain of interest; when the boundary of D is encountered (during the final tunnelling phase), the final $\mathbf{w}_*$ (located at the end of the preceding minimisation phase) is guaranteed to be the global minimum of D. (If the network encounters the boundary of D during a minimisation phase, the global minimum lies outside D, i.e. D is too small.) In the one-dimensional case, a suitable ρ is

$$\rho \cong \left(\frac{\varepsilon^{2/3}}{1 + \exp(\alpha)} \right) \left(\frac{\partial^2 F(w_*)}{\partial w^2} \right) \qquad (6.16)$$

Unfortunately, when this approach is generalised to the multi-dimensional case, global convergence is not guaranteed, since domain D may be traversed without encountering the basin of attraction of the global minimum. To guarantee global convergence in the multi-dimensional case, the TRUST method can be modified so that the error function is represented in terms of a single variable. One way of achieving this, outlined in Barhen *et al.* (1994), is to transform the error function using an Archimedes' spiral representation in a way that ensures a dense covering of weight space.

6.3.3 An Evaluation of the TRUST Method

The TRUST method has several desirable properties. It makes no modifications to the MLP architecture, training algorithm or training set unless the network encounters a local minimum, and convergence to a minimum is guaranteed within the domain of interest. Moreover, the method does not rely on a large number of user-defined parameters.

However, the TRUST method also has several potentially undesirable properties:

- There is no 'natural' choice of dimensions for the domain of interest D, which must be set heuristically by the user. D must not be too small, otherwise D may not contain a global minimum – or any minimum at all. On the other hand, since the network weights are initialised to a small perturbation from a corner of D, D must not be too large, otherwise there is a risk of node saturation (see Section 1.1.2). The published results in Barhen *et al.* (1994) for the TRUST method with gradient descent are based on comparatively small domains of interest, with weights restricted to the range $[-10, +10]$ or smaller. Such settings may be inappropriate when using the TRUST method with classical optimisation algorithms, owing to the tendency of such algorithms to generate weights of large magnitudes.

- The method requires that a given local minimum w_* is located with a high degree of accuracy at each minimisation phase. If the method switches to the tunnelling phase before convergence to w_* is near-complete, the network is liable to 'tunnel through' to a slightly lower location within the basin of attraction of w_*.

- The TRUST method is much more complicated to implement than the homotopic ERA method of Section 6.2.

Appendix

This appendix presents, in tabulated form, the results of extensive benchmark tests performed on a range of first- and second-order MLP training algorithms. It is hoped that these tables will provide the reader with a useful source of reference information about the comparative performance of different second-order training algorithms. A detailed analysis of these results is given in Section 5.3 of the main text.

The tables run in order of benchmark task, starting with 2-parity (XOR) and ending with the $\tan(x)$ problem. (For more information about the benchmark training sets, see Section 5.1; details of the conditions under which the tests were performed are given in Section 5.2.) There are three tables per benchmark task. The first table contains results for training algorithms implemented with Brent's derivative line search and the second contains results for algorithms implemented with an appropriate model-trust region strategy. (For convenience, the bold driver method is treated as an 'honorary' model-trust region method.) The third table contains results for different implementations of the BFGS quasi-Newton method (including the results from the other two tables).

A few comments are in order about the contents of the tables. Before consulting the tables, the reader is strongly advised to read the following information about the data presented in each column:

- *Success rate column* The percentage of training runs that successfully classified every pattern in the training set (within a tolerance of 0.1 for each target element). Training runs were terminated whenever the gradient fell to zero or the number of training epochs exceeded an upper limit of 50 000. A total of 100 training runs were performed with each combination of training algorithm and benchmark training set.

- *EFEs per k column* The mean number of EFEs performed per training epoch (k iteration) by $E=0.01$. In the case of model-trust region strategies, the figure is calculated according to the formula

$$\frac{\text{EFEs}}{(\text{EFEs} - \text{resets})}$$

where a reset is deemed to have occurred whenever the step s_k is rejected (with the network weights set to $w_{k+1}=w_k$).

- *Mean, S.D. and median columns* The median, standard deviation and median number of EFEs required to attain the stated error level (E). Training runs that failed to reach the error level in question (i.e. runs which ran out of training time or converged to a stationary point at a higher error level) are not included in the calculation of these numbers. Figures in brackets indicate that only a single training run attained the specified error level.

The abbreviations used in the tables are the same as those in Chapter 5, but are reproduced below for ease of reference:

BD   The bold driver method of Section 1.3.2

BR   Brent's method with derivatives (Section 3.1.1)

BT   The Dennis–Schnabel backtracking line-search with derivatives (Section 3.1.3)

CG   The Polak–Ribiere conjugate gradient method of Section 3.3.4, with restarts

EFE   Equivalent function evaluation (see equation (5.5))

IQN   The (inverse) BFGS quasi-Newton method of Section 3.3.2, with restarts

LM   The Levenberg–Marquardt nonlinear least-squares method of Section 3.4.2

MT   Fletcher's model-trust region strategy of Section 3.2.2 (with the QN method), or Møller's 'scaled' model-trust region strategy of Section 3.2.4 (with the IQN method)

NQN   The 'memoryless' (BFGS) quasi-Newton method of Section 3.3.3, with restarts

QN   The BFGS quasi-Newton method of Section 3.3.2, *without* restarts

SD   The (classical) steepest descent method of Section 2.1.1

S.D.   Standard deviation

Table A.1 The 2-parity (XOR) problem – Brent's method with derivatives.

Method	Success rate (%)	EFEs per k	$E=0.01$			$E=10^{-6}$		
			Mean	S.D.	Median	Mean	S.D.	Median
SD	81	3.60	314.7	226.9	270.5	469.4	232.2	436.0
CG	61	7.81	198.1	703.0	91.0	266.7	704.8	167.0
NQN	63	4.33	122.5	64.1	107.5	248.7	233.7	215.0
IQN	62	4.38	133.6	66.6	115.0	236.4	77.1	232.0
QN	34	4.34	103.8	38.7	90.8	118.2	48.0	102.0

Table A.2 The 2-parity (XOR) problem – model-trust region strategies.

Method	Success rate (%)	EFEs per k	$E=0.01$			$E=10^{-6}$		
			Mean	S.D.	Median	Mean	S.D.	Median
BD	86	1.10	188.8	131.2	164.0	306.6	137.8	287.0
CG	67	2.44	49.7	14.8	48.0	177.5	141.5	120.0
NQN	78	2.37	120.4	274.8	86.0	286.5	299.5	240.0
IQN	80	2.43	178.3	922.5	72.5	276.4	924.5	165.5
QN	35	1.44	63.5	24.3	58.0	79.4	26.8	72.0
LM	68	1.38	20.8	16.3	15.0	39.1	16.3	34.0

Table A.3 The 2-parity (XOR) problem – quasi-Newton methods. (The suffix '(r)' denotes the resetting IQN algorithm, as opposed to the non-resetting QN algorithm.)

Method	Success rate (%)	EFEs per k	$E=0.01$			$E=10^{-6}$		
			Mean	S.D.	Median	Mean	S.D.	Median
BR	34	4.34	103.8	38.7	90.8	118.2	48.0	102.0
MT	35	1.44	63.5	24.3	58.0	79.4	26.8	72.0
BT	43	1.05	98.8	165.7	55.0	118.5	167.8	77.0
BR (r)	62	4.38	133.6	66.6	115.0	236.4	77.1	232.0
MT (r)	80	2.43	178.3	922.5	72.5	276.4	924.5	165.5
BT (r)	80	1.85	650.5	1689.1	87.5	1091.4	1598.6	627.0

Table A.4 The 3-parity problem – Brent's method with derivatives.

Method	Success rate (%)	EFEs per k	$E=0.01$			$E=10^{-6}$		
			Mean	S.D.	Median	Mean	S.D.	Median
SD	100	3.54	787.0	682.7	589.8	1070.5	689.6	852.8
CG	94	4.45	206.7	221.4	136.8	357.0	343.4	247.0
NQN	90	4.70	259.6	504.1	181.3	486.1	630.9	396.8
IQN	89	4.16	268.5	262.6	168.0	570.3	600.1	352.0
QN	33	3.93	152.4	116.0	122.5	203.8	122.2	155.5

Table A.5 The 3-parity problem – model-trust region strategies.

Method	Success rate (%)	EFEs per k	$E=0.01$			$E=10^{-6}$		
			Mean	S.D.	Median	Mean	S.D.	Median
BD	100	1.13	668.6	351.1	557.0	863.3	352.0	760.5
CG	99	2.47	92.3	53.0	82.0	1434.8	8393.5	236.0
NQN	94	2.26	160.8	99.9	146.5	655.3	1890.9	425.0
IQN	91	2.71	160.7	202.1	108.0	304.3	416.6	229.0
QN	46	1.45	105.5	48.1	93.5	130.6	49.8	117.0
LM	100	1.25	19.7	11.8	18.0	56.4	11.9	54.0

Table A.6 The 3-parity problem – quasi-Newton methods. (The suffix '(r)' denotes the resetting IQN algorithm, as opposed to the non-resetting QN algorithm.)

Method	Success rate (%)	EFEs per k	$E=0.01$			$E=10^{-6}$		
			Mean	S.D.	Median	Mean	S.D.	Median
BR	33	3.93	152.4	116.0	122.5	203.8	122.2	155.5
MT	46	1.45	105.5	48.1	93.5	130.6	49.8	117.0
BT	59	1.05	126.5	215.0	85.0	169.0	218.1	132.0
BR (r)	89	4.16	268.5	262.6	168.0	570.3	600.1	352.0
MT (r)	91	2.71	160.7	202.1	108.0	304.3	416.6	229.0
BT (r)	93	1.73	652.5	2342.6	107.0	1165.5	3136.9	360.0

Table A.7 The 4-parity problem – Brent's method with derivatives.

Method	Success rate (%)	EFEs per k	$E=0.01$			$E=10^{-4}$		
			Mean	S.D.	Median	Mean	S.D.	Median
SD	99	3.58	27 678.7	27 496.7	18 654.0	38 722.6	33 558.7	32 931.5
CG	75	5.45	1 789.1	3 055.3	1 011.0	2 019.2	3 088.0	1 290.5
NQN	77	3.88	1 965.8	1 327.0	1 749.0	2 432.7	1 467.6	2 368.0
IQN	39	3.76	1 131.3	640.7	1 084.0	1 344.4	702.5	1 371.5
QN	1	4.03		–		(3 490.0)	–	(3 490.0)

Table A.8 The 4-parity problem – model-trust region strategies.

Method	Success rate (%)	EFEs per k	E=0.01			E=10⁻⁴		
			Mean	S.D.	Median	Mean	S.D.	Median
BD	93	1.14	18 006.0	10 677.6	16 134.0	23 508.3	12 410.9	24 613.0
CG	69	3.27	17 521.3	18 706.8	11 998.0	17 934.2	18 832.7	12 795.0
NQN	56	2.27	4 466.9	4 472.7	3 215.0	4 964.0	4 617.6	3 844.0
IQN	37	2.39	1 278.0	1 882.4	724.0	1 392.2	1 894.2	842.0
QN	6	1.45	227.5	90.6	202.5	253.3	100.0	218.5
LM	98	1.30	129.7	838.0	36.0	97.7	166.7	78.0

Table A.9 The 4-parity problem – quasi-Newton methods. (The suffix '(r)' denotes the resetting IQN algorithm, as opposed to the non-resetting QN algorithm.)

Method	Success rate (%)	EFEs per k	E=0.01			E=10⁻⁴		
			Mean	S.D.	Median	Mean	S.D.	Median
BR	2	4.03	232.8	120.6	232.8	252.8	199.9	252.8
MT	6	1.45	227.5	90.6	202.5	253.3	100.0	218.5
BT	8	1.04	1434.4	2766.1	415.5	1477.5	2779.9	495.0
BR (r)	39	3.76	1131.3	640.7	1084.0	1344.4	702.5	1371.5
MT (r)	37	2.39	1278.0	1882.4	724.0	1392.2	1894.2	842.0
BT (r)	80	1.27	1662.6	3489.6	1026.0	2336.5	3542.8	1923.5

Table A.10 The 5-parity problem – Brent's method with derivatives.

Method	Success rate (%)	EFEs per k	E=0.01			E=10⁻⁴		
			Mean	S.D.	Median	Mean	S.D.	Median
SD	64	3.71	> 50 000	–	> 50 000	> 50 000	–	> 50 000
CG	78	4.16	2 094.2	1211.8	1 897.0	2 618.0	1402.2	2 322.5
NQN	71	3.92	4 546.0	3909.2	4 017.8	5 407.8	4001.9	5 021.5
IQN	43	3.61	1 646.0	746.5	1 717.3	2 158.8	976.2	2 164.0
QN	1	3.42	(328.0)	–	(328.0)	(403.0)	–	(403.0)

Table A.11 The 5-parity problem – model-trust region strategies.

Method	Success rate (%)	EFEs per k	E=0.01			E=10⁻⁴		
			Mean	S.D.	Median	Mean	S.D.	Median
BD	6	1.14	> 50 000	–	> 50 000	> 50 000	–	> 50 000
CG	25	3.29	26 310.6	31 101.8	13 003.0	25 331.0	28 953.8	13 031.0
NQN	50	2.26	13 831.0	8 450.9	12 306.0	14 937.2	8 572.0	13 061.5
IQN	26	2.25	3 363.4	3 073.1	2 576.0	3 566.4	3 089.9	3 105.0
QN	1	1.47	(347.0)	–	(347.0)	(363.0)	–	(363.0)
LM	98	1.11	55.7	6.7	55.0	156.5	16.3	153.0

Table A.12 The 5-parity problem – quasi-Newton methods. (The suffix '(r)' denotes the resetting IQN algorithm, as opposed to the non-resetting QN algorithm.)

Method	Success rate (%)	EFEs per k	E=0.01			E=10⁻⁴		
			Mean	S.D.	Median	Mean	S.D.	Median
BR	1	3.42	(328.0)	–	(328.0)	(403.0)	–	(403.0)
MT	1	1.47	(347.0)	–	(347.0)	(363.0)	–	(363.0)
BT	1	1.08	1009.8	829.9	474.0	(487.0)	–	(487.0)
BR (r)	43	3.61	1646.0	746.5	1717.3	2158.8	976.2	2164.0
MT (r)	26	2.25	3363.4	3073.1	2576.0	3566.4	3089.9	3105.0
BT (r)	56	1.27	3226.5	5492.9	2300.0	3991.0	5582.1	3039.0

Table A.13 The sin(x) problem – Brent's method with derivatives.

Method	Success rate (%)	EFEs per k	$E=0.01$			$E=10^{-4}$		
			Mean	S.D.	Median	Mean	S.D.	Median
SD	100	3.23	2182.3	2788.6	1300.3	7629.5	9633.7	2643.3
CG	100	3.69	174.5	229.1	124.8	501.2	467.2	325.3
NQN	99	3.66	180.8	325.5	118.5	557.3	494.8	480.5
IQN	100	3.69	120.2	121.6	93.5	299.4	204.0	221.5
QN	87	3.40	90.7	26.6	86.5	196.1	155.4	160.5

Table A.14 The sin(x) problem – model-trust region strategies.

Method	Success rate (%)	EFEs per k	$E=0.01$			$E=10^{-4}$		
			Mean	S.D.	Median	Mean	S.D.	Median
BD	100	1.14	815.8	974.6	520.0	3044.9	4372.0	1007.5
CG	100	2.39	101.4	83.4	86.0	231.7	170.6	178.5
NQN	100	2.34	123.4	246.0	81.0	507.6	1606.5	176.0
IQN	98	2.41	94.8	150.8	76.0	190.1	194.1	140.5
QN	94	1.45	58.3	36.1	49.0	100.7	43.2	90.5
LM	96	1.21	175.0	44.1	184.0	409.3	90.5	455.5

Table A.15 The sin(x) problem – quasi-Newton methods. (The suffix '(r)' denotes the resetting IQN algorithm, as opposed to the non-resetting QN algorithm.)

Method	Success rate (%)	EFEs per k	$E=0.01$			$E=10^{-4}$		
			Mean	S.D.	Median	Mean	S.D.	Median
BR	87	3.40	90.7	26.6	86.5	196.1	155.4	160.5
MT	94	1.45	58.3	36.1	49.0	100.7	43.2	90.5
BT	90	1.14	62.9	66.3	43.0	118.9	96.8	81.5
BR (r)	100	3.69	120.2	121.6	93.5	299.4	204.0	221.5
MT (r)	98	2.41	94.8	150.8	76.0	190.1	194.1	140.5
BT (r)	100	1.23	83.7	215.8	47.5	331.4	452.2	126.5

Table A.16 The sin(x)cos($2x$) problem – Brent's method with derivatives.

Method	Success rate (%)	EFEs per k	$E=0.01$			$E=10^{-4}$		
			Mean	S.D.	Median	Mean	S.D.	Median
SD	0	4.37	> 50 000	–	> 50 000	–	–	–
CG	98	4.32	2 481.3	988.1	2 363.8	23 153.5	9 799.8	20 049.5
NQN	96	4.30	2 338.5	842.3	2 249.5	24 471.4	12 208.1	21 997.0
IQN	100	3.32	554.6	155.9	520.3	1 481.1	315.1	1 444.0
QN	97	3.26	496.4	198.2	471.5	1 068.7	386.3	992.5

Table A.17 The sin(x)cos($2x$) problem – model-trust region strategies.

Method	Success rate (%)	EFEs per k	$E=0.01$			$E=10^{-4}$		
			Mean	S.D.	Median	Mean	S.D.	Median
BD	0	1.14	47 267.6	2 258.5	48 277.5	–	–	–
CG	100	2.07	907.6	247.7	871.0	10 725.9	4 428.6	11 398.0
NQN	100	2.07	891.4	268.9	870.0	10 797.3	4 860.1	10 801.5
IQN	100	2.27	478.1	139.8	452.5	1 494.6	327.9	1 498.0
QN	98	1.37	256.1	134.1	213.0	549.7	327.5	477.0
LM	100	1.41	101.1	34.6	92.0	199.2	64.0	185.0

Table A.18 The sin(x)cos($2x$) problem – quasi-Newton methods. (The suffix '(r)' denotes the resetting IQN algorithm, as opposed to the non-resetting QN algorithm.)

Method	Success rate (%)	EFEs per k	$E=0.01$			$E=10^{-4}$		
			Mean	S.D.	Median	Mean	S.D.	Median
BR	97	3.26	496.4	198.2	471.5	1068.7	386.3	992.5
MT	98	1.37	256.1	134.1	213.0	549.7	327.5	477.0
BT	98	1.16	290.1	200.5	227.0	652.9	353.8	538.5
BR (r)	100	3.32	554.6	155.9	520.3	1481.1	315.1	1444.0
MT (r)	100	2.27	478.1	139.8	452.5	1494.6	327.9	1498.0
BT (r)	100	1.15	252.8	75.4	239.5	1460.2	633.6	1339.5

Table A.19 The tan(x) problem – Brent's method with derivatives.

Method	Success rate (%)	EFEs per k	$E=0.01$			$E=10^{-4}$		
			Mean	S.D.	Median	Mean	S.D.	Median
SD	0	4.63	> 50 000	–	> 50 000	–	–	–
CG	98	4.45	2 187.3	1614.6	1 796.3	34 769.4	14 776.1	34 082.0
NQN	93	4.40	1 922.2	1128.2	1 631.0	26 208.9	9 218.2	24 614.2
IQN	93	3.50	482.0	254.8	415.0	6 194.9	4 216.0	5 457.5
QN	61	3.42	365.1	258.3	295.0	1 435.8	1 880.1	790.5

Table A.20 The tan(x) problem – model-trust region strategies.

Method	Success rate (%)	EFEs per k	$E=0.01$			$E=10^{-4}$		
			Mean	S.D.	Median	Mean	S.D.	Median
BD	0	1.14	26 764.1	4343.1	25 695.0	–	–	–
CG	100	2.12	764.6	244.7	696.5	27 163.1	22 436.3	17 086.5
NQN	100	2.13	732.9	310.1	686.5	31 549.2	24 559.1	17 169.0
IQN	99	2.26	618.8	2739.9	319.0	8 790.4	8 014.8	5 716.0
QN	80	1.40	167.0	104.1	130.0	446.7	217.9	404.5
LM	99	1.27	108.0	12.8	107.0	173.3	24.5	168.0

Table A.21 The tan(x) problem – quasi-Newton methods. (The suffix '(r)' denotes the resetting IQN algorithm, as opposed to the non-resetting QN algorithm.)

Method	Success rate (%)	EFEs per k	$E=0.01$			$E=10^{-4}$		
			Mean	S.D.	Median	Mean	S.D.	Median
BR	61	3.42	365.1	258.3	295.0	1 435.8	1 880.1	790.5
MT	80	1.40	167.0	104.1	130.0	446.7	217.9	404.5
BT	65	1.10	387.0	455.5	278.0	895.3	999.1	626.0
BR (r)	93	3.50	482.0	254.8	415.0	6 194.9	4 216.0	5 457.5
MT (r)	99	2.26	618.8	2739.9	319.0	8 790.4	8 014.8	5 716.0
BT (r)	97	1.17	738.3	4092.8	219.0	18 223.1	16 677.3	10 558.0

Bibliography

Annema, A. J., Hoen, K. and Wallinga, H. (1994) Learning behaviour and temporary minima of two-layer neural networks, *Neural Networks*, 7(9), 1387–404.

Barhen, J., Fijany, A. and Toomarian, N. (1994) Globally optimal neural learning, *Proceedings of WCNN '94*, San Diego, June 1994, III-370–5.

Barnard, E. (1992) Optimization for training neural nets, *IEEE Transactions on Neural Networks*, 3(2), 232–40.

Battiti, R. (1989) Accelerated backpropagation learning: two optimization methods, *Complex Systems*, 3, 331–42.

Battiti, R. (1992) First- and second-order methods for learning: between steepest descent and Newton's method, *Neural Computation*, 4(2), 141–66.

Battiti, R. and Masulli, F. (1990) BFGS optimization for faster and automated supervised learning, *Proceedings of the International Neural Network Conference (INNC 90)*, Paris, France, 757–60.

Belew, R. K., McInerney, J. and Schraudolph, N. N. (1991) Evolving networks: using the genetic algorithm with connectionist learning, in *Artificial Life II* (eds. C. G. Langton, C. Taylor, J. D. Farmer and S. Rasmussen), SFI Studies in the Sciences of Complexity, vol. X, Addison-Wesley, Reading MA, 511–47.

Bishop, C. M. (1992) Exact calculation of the Hessian matrix for the multilayer perceptron, *Neural Computation*, 4, 494–501.

Bishop, C. M. (1995) *Neural Networks for Pattern Recognition*, Oxford University Press, Oxford.

Brent, R. P. (1973) *Algorithms for Minimization Without Derivatives*, Prentice-Hall, Englewood Cliffs NJ.

Burton, R. M. and Mpitsos, G. J. (1992) Event-dependent control of noise enhances learning in neural networks, *Neural Networks*, 5, 627–37.

Cetin, B. C., Barhen, J. and Burdick, J. W. (1993) Terminal repeller unconstrained subenergy tunneling (TRUST) for fast global optimization, *Journal of Optimization Theory and Applications*, 77(1), 97–126.

Darken, C., Chang, J. and Moody, J. (1992) Learning rate schedules for faster stochastic gradient search, in *Neural Networks for Signal Processing* Vol. 2 (eds. S. Y. Kung, F. Fallside, J. A. Sørensen and C. A. Kamm), IEEE Workshop, IEEE Press, 3–13.

Darken C. and Moody, J. (1990) Note on learning rate schedules for stochastic optimization, in *Advances in Neural Information Processing Systems* Vol. 3, Morgan Kaufmann, San Mateo CA, 832–8.

Dennis, J. E. and Mei, H. H. W. (1979) Two new unconstrained optimization algorithms which use function and gradient values, *Journal of Optimization Theory and Applications*, 28, 453–82.

Dennis, J. E. and Schnabel, R. B. (1983) *Numerical Methods for Unconstrained Optimization and Nonlinear Equations*, Prentice-Hall, Englewood Cliffs NJ.

Dixon, L. C. W. (1972) The choice of step length, a crucial factor in the performance of variable metric algorithms, in *Numerical Methods for Non-linear Optimization* (ed. F. A. Lootsma), Academic Press, New York, 149–70.

Fahlman, S. E. (1989) Faster-learning variations on back-propagation: an empirical study, in *Proceedings of the 1988 Connectionist Models Summer School* (eds. D. S. Touretzky, G. E. Hinton and T. J. Sejnowski), Morgan Kaufmann, San Mateo CA, 38–51.

Finhoff, W. and Zimmerman, H. G. (1992) Homotopy methods in circuit analysis, pre-print, Siemens, Munich.

Fletcher, R. (1987) *Practical Methods of Optimization* 2nd edn, John Wiley & Sons, New York.

Gill, P. E., Murray, W. and Wright, M. H. (1981) *Practical Optimization*, Academic Press, London.

Gori, M. and Tesi, A. (1992) On the problem of local minima in backpropagation, *IEEE Transactions on Pattern Analysis and Machine Learning*, 14(1), 76–86.

Gorse, D. (1992) Classical and stochastic search in conjugate gradient algorithms, *Proceedings of IJCNN '92*, Beijing, November, 435–40.

Gorse, D., Shepherd, A. and Taylor, J. (1993a) Avoiding local minima using a range expansion algorithm, *Neural Network World*, 5, 503–10.

Gorse, D., Shepherd, A. and Taylor, J. (1993b) Tracking global minima by progressive range expansion, *Proceedings of IJCNN '93*, Portland, Oregon, July, IV-350-3.

Gorse, D., Shepherd, A. and Taylor, J. (1994a) Avoiding local minima by a classical range expansion algorithm, *Proceedings of ICANN '94*, Sorrento, 1 May, 525–8.

Gorse, D., Shepherd, A. and Taylor, J. (1994b) A classical algorithm for avoiding local minima, *Proceedings of WCNN '94*, San Diego, June, III-364-9.

Gorse, D., Shepherd, A. and Taylor, J. (1995) The new ERA in supervised learning, *Neural Networks* (in press).

Guo, H. and Gelfand, S. B. (1991) Analysis of gradient descent learning algorithms for multilayer feedforward neural networks, *IEEE Transactions on Circuits and Systems*, 38, 883–94.

Hamey, L. G. (1995) Analysis of the error surface of the XOR network with two hidden nodes, *Computing Report 95/167C*, Department of Computing, Macquarie University, NSW 2109, Australia.

Hecht-Nielsen, R. (1990) *Neurocomputing*, Addison-Wesley, Reading MA.

Hestenes, M. R. and Stiefel, E. (1952) Methods of conjugate gradients for solving linear systems, *Journal of Research of the National Bureau of Standards*, 49(6), 409–36.

Hirose, Y., Yamashita, K. and Hijiya, S. (1991) Back-propagation algorithm which varies the number of hidden units, *Neural Networks*, 4, 61–6.

Huang, S. and Huang, Y. (1991) Bounds on the number of hidden neurons in multilayer perceptrons, *IEEE Transactions on Neural Networks*, 2(1), 47–55.

Jacobs, R. A. (1988) Increased rates of convergence through learning rate adaption, *Neural Networks*, 1, 295–307.

Kappen B. and Heskes, T. (1992) Learning rules, stochastic processes, and local minima, in *Artificial Neural Networks, 2: Proceedings of the 1992 International Conference on Artificial Neural Networks (ICANN-92)* (eds. I. Aleksander and J. G. Taylor), Brighton, 4–7 September, Elsevier Science Publishers, Amsterdam, I-71-7.

Kinsella, J. A. (1992) Comparison and evaluation of variants of the conjugate gradient method for efficient learning in feed-forward neural networks with backward error propagation, *Network*, 3, 27–36.

Kirkpatrick, S., Gelatt, C. D. and Vecchi, M. P. (1983) Optimization by simulated annealing, *Science*, 220, 671–80.

Kolen, J. F. and Pollack, J. B. (1990) Backpropagation is sensitive to initial conditions, *Complex Systems*, 4, 269–80.

Kollias, S. and Anastassiou, D. (1989) An adaptive least squares algorithm for the efficient training of artificial neural networks, *IEEE Transactions on Circuit and Systems*, 36(8), 1092–101.

Kramer, A. H. and Sangiovanni-Vincentelli, A. (1988) Efficient parallel learning algorithms for neural networks, in *Advances in Neural Information Processing Systems* Vol. 1 (ed. D. S. Touretzky), Morgan Kaufman, San Mateo CA, 75–89.

Le Cun, Y. (1989) Generalization and network design strategies, *Technical Report CRG-TR-89-4*, Department of Computer Science, University of Toronto, June.

Le Cun, Y., Denker, J. S. and Solla, S. A. (1990) Optimal brain damage, in *Advances in Neural Information Processing Systems* Vol. 2 (ed. D. S. Touretzky), Morgan Kaufmann, San Mateo CA, 598–605.

Levy, A. V. and Montalvo, A. (1985) The tunneling algorithm for the global minimization of functions, *SIAM Journal on Scientific and Statistical Computing*, 6, 15–29.

Lisboa, P. J. G. and Perantonis, S. J. (1991) Complete solution of the local minima in the XOR problem, *Network*, 2, 119–24.

Lisboa, P. J. G. (ed.) (1992) *Neural Networks: Current Applications*, Chapman & Hall, London.

Luenberger, D. G. (1984) *Linear and Nonlinear Programming*, 2nd edn, Addison-Wesley, Reading MA.

McInerney, J. M., Haines, K. G., Biafore, S. and Hecht-Nielsen, R. (1989) Error surfaces of multi-layer networks can have local minima, *Technical Report No. CS89-157*, Department of Computer Science and Engineering, University of California.

MacKay, D. J. C. (1992) Information-based objective functions for active data selection, *Neural Computation*, 4, 590–604.

Minsky, M. L. and Papert, S. A. (1969) *Perceptrons*, MIT Press, Cambridge MA.

Møller, M. (1993a) A scaled conjugate gradient algorithm for fast supervised learning, *Neural Networks*, 6(4), 525–33.

Møller, M. (1993b) Supervised learning on large redundant training sets, *International Journal of Neural Systems*, 4(1), 15–25.

Møller, M. (1993c) Exact calculation of the product of the Hessian matrix of feed-forward network error functions and a vector in $O(N)$ time, *Technical Report*, Daimi PB-432, Computer Science Department, Aarhus University.

Møller, M. (1993d) Adaptive preconditioning of the Hessian matrix, submitted to *Neural Computation* (reprinted in Møller (1993e, Appendix D)).

Møller, M. (1993e) Efficient training of feed-forward neural networks, *Ph.D. Thesis*, Daimi PB-464, Computer Science Department, Aarhus University.

Moré, J. J. (1983) Recent developments in algorithms and software for trust region methods, in *Mathematical Programming: the State of the Art, Bonn 1982* (eds. A. Bachem, M. Grotschel and B. Korte), Springer-Verlag, Berlin, 258–87.

Moré, J. J. and Sorensen, D. C. (1979) On the use of directions of negative curvature in a modified Newton method, *Mathematical Programming*, 16, 1–20.

Nash, J. C. (1990) *Compact Numerical Methods for Computers: Linear Algebra and Function Minimisation*, Adam Hilger, Bristol.

Osborne, M. R. (1976) Nonlinear least squares – the Levenberg algorithm revisited, *Journal of the Australian Mathematical Society*, 19 (Ser. B), 343–57.

Parker, D. B. (1987) Optimal algorithms for adaptive networks: second order back propagation, second order direct propagation, and second order Hebbian learning, *Proceedings of the First IEEE International Conference on Neural Networks*, June, IEEE Press, New York, II-593–600.

Pattichis, C. S., Charalambous, C., Schizas, C. N. and Middleton, L. T. (1991) EMG diagnosis using conjugate gradient backpropagation neural network learning algorithm, in *Artificial Neural Networks: Proceedings of the 1991 International Conference on Artificial Neural Networks (ICANN-91)* (eds. T. Kohonen, K. Makisara, O. Simula and J. Kangas), Espoo, Finland, 24–28 June, Elsevier Science Publishers, Amsterdam, 1621–4.

Poston, T., Lee, C. N., Choie, Y. and Kwon, Y. (1991) Local minima and back propagation, in *Proceedings of IJCNN '91, Seattle, WA*, July, II-173–6.

Powell, M. J. D. (1970) A hybrid method for nonlinear equations, in *Numerical Methods for Nonlinear Algebraic Equations* (ed. P. Rabinowitz), Gordon & Breach, London, 87–114.

Powell, M. J. D. (1977) Restart procedures for the conjugate gradient method, *Mathematical Programming*,12, 241–54.

Press, W. H., Flannery, B. P., Teukolsky, S. A. and Vetterling, W. T. (1992) *Numerical Recipes in C*, 2nd edn, Cambridge University Press, Cambridge.

Ricotti, L. P., Ragazzini, S. and Martinelli, G. (1988) Learning of word stress in a sub-optimal second order backpropagation neural network, in *Proceedings of the IEEE International Conference on Neural Networks* Vol. 1, IEEE Press, San Diego CA, 355–61.

Rigler, A. K., Irvine, J. M. and Vogl, T. P. (1991) Rescaling of variables in back propagation learning, *Neural Networks*, 4, 225–30.

Robbins, H. and Monro, S. (1951) A stochastic approximation method, *Annals of Mathematical Statistics*, 22, 400–7.

Rumelhart, D. E., Hinton, G. E. and Williams, R. J. (1986) Learning internal representations by error propagation, in *Parallel Distributed Processing: Explorations in the Microstructure of Cognition* Vol. 1 (eds. D. E. Rumelhart and J. L. McClelland), MIT Press, Cambridge MA, 318–62.

Santini, S. (1992) The bearable lightness of being: reducing the number of weights in backpropagation networks, in *Artificial Neural Networks, 2: Proceedings of the 1992 International Conference on Artificial Neural Networks (ICANN-92)* (eds. I. Alexander and J. G. Taylor), Brighton, 4–7 September, Elsevier Science Publishers, Amsterdam, I-139–42.

Shepherd, A. (1992) Towards a hybrid conjugate gradient/backpropagation algorithm for training feed-forward neural networks, *M.Sc. Thesis*, Department of Computer Science, University College London.

Shepherd, A. (1995) Novel second-order techniques and global optimisation methods for supervised training of multi-layer perceptrons, *Ph.D. Thesis*, Department of Computer Science, University College London.

van der Smagt, P. P. (1994) Minimisation methods for training feedforward neural networks, *Neural Networks*, 7(1), 1–11.

Solla, S. A., Levin, E. and Fleisher, M. (1988) Accelerated learning in layered neural networks, *Complex Systems*, 2, 625–40.

Vogl, T. P., Mangis, J. K., Rigler, A. K., Zink, W. T. and Alkon, D. L. (1988) Accelerating the convergence of the back-propagation method, *Biological Cybernetics*, 59, 257–63.

Watrous, R. L. (1987) Learning algorithms for connectionist networks: applied gradient methods of nonlinear optimization, *Proceedings of the International Conference on Neural Networks*, July, IEEE Press, New York, II-619–27.

Wessels, L. F. A. and Barnard, E. (1992) Avoiding false local minima by proper initialization of connections, *IEEE Transactions on Neural Networks*, 3(6), 899–905.

Wessels, L. F. A., Barnard, E. and van Rooyen, E. (1990) The physical correlates of local minima, in *Proceedings of the International Neural Network Conference*, Paris, p. 985.

Widrow, B. and Lehr, M. A. (1990) 30 years of adaptive neural networks: perceptron, madeline, and backpropagation, *Proceedings of the IEEE*, 78, 1415–42.

Wilkinson, J. H. (1963) *Rounding Errors in Algebraic Processes*, HMSO, London.

Wolfe, M. A. (1978) *Numerical Methods for Unconstrained Optimization: an introduction*, Van Nostrand Reinhold, New York.

Yu, X. (1992) Can backpropagation error surface not have local minima?, *IEEE Transactions on Neural Networks*, 3(6), November 1992, 1019–21.

Index